THE TREASURY OF
Family
Games

THE TREASURY OF
Family Games

JIM GLENN and
CAREY DENTON

The Reader's Digest Association, Inc.
Pleasantville, New York/Montreal

A READER'S DIGEST BOOK

This edition published by The Reader's Digest Association by arrangement with Amber Books Ltd.

Editorial and design by
Amber Books Ltd
Bradley's Close
74–77 White Lion Street
London N1 9PF
www.amberbooks.co.uk

FOR AMBER BOOKS
Project Editor: James Bennett
Copy Editor: Mary Devine
Additional material: Peter Delacorte, Jean Henderson, John Searcy, Katherine Slick
Design: Zoe Mellors
Picture Research: Natasha Jones

FOR READER'S DIGEST
U.S. Project Editor: Susan Byrne
Canadian Project Editor: Pamela Johnson
Project Designer: George McKeon
Creative Director: Michele Laseau
Executive Editor, Trade Publishing: Dolores York
Director, Trade Publishing: Christopher T. Reggio
Vice President & Publisher, Trade Publishing: Harold Clarke

Library of Congress Cataloging-in-Publication Data

Glenn, Jim, 1946-
     The treasury of family games : hundreds of fun games for all ages, complete with rules
   and strategies / Jim Glenn and Carey Denton.
        p. cm.
     Includes index.
     ISBN 0-7621-0431-7
     1. Games. 2. Family recreation. I. Denton, Carey. II. Title.

GV1201.G544 2003
793--dc21
                                                                    2003046602

Address any comments about *The Treasury of Family Games* to:
        The Reader's Digest Association, Inc.
        Adult Trade Publishing
        Reader's Digest Road
        Pleasantville, NY 10570-7000

For more Reader's Digest products and information, visit our website:
www.rd.com (in the United States)
www.readersdigest.ca (in Canada)
www.readersdigest.com.au (in Australia)
www.readersdigest.co.uk (in the United Kingdom)

Printed in Italy

1 3 5 7 9 10 8 6 4 2

A Note to the Reader
This publication is not authorized or endorsed by any of the game companies whose products appear in
this publication. Some of the game names and game-related terms that appear in this publication are
trademarks of their respective game companies. In creating this publication, Amber Books Limited has
indicated with an ® symbol various trademarks that it is aware have been registered in at least one country
in the territory in which this publication is published.

Contents

Introduction.................8   How to Use This Book.....11

PART 1 BOARD GAMES

Commercial Games.........13
Apples to Apples®.............14
Clue® (Cluedo®)................14
Monopoly®......................15
Risk®...........................16
Scrabble®......................17
Trivial Pursuit®................18

Dice Games...................19
Aces in the Pot.................20
Drop Dead......................20
Hearts Due.....................21
Help Your Neighbor..........21
Pig.............................21
Shut the Box..................22
Yacht..........................22

Domino Games...............24
Dominoes......................25
All Fives (Muggins)...........29
Bergen.........................30
Blind Hughie..................31
Five Up........................31
Mah-Jongg....................33

Race Games...................37
Backgammon..................38
Chutes and Ladders®
   (Snakes and Ladders)......40
Fox and Geese................40
Halma..........................42
Ludo...........................44

Strategy Games.............45
Checkers (Draughts)..........46
Chess..........................50
Shogi (Japanese Chess).....58
Xiangqi (Chinese Chess)....59

Territorial Games............61
Alquerque.....................62
Four Field Kono..............62
Go.............................62
Hex............................66
Horseshoe.....................67
Mill (Nine Men's Morris)....68
Othello® (Reversi)............69
Owari.........................70

PART 2 CARD GAMES

Card Games for Groups..73
Canasta.......................74
Casino........................76
Contract Bridge...............78
Crazy Eights..................84
Cribbage......................84
Euchre........................86
Five Hundred.................88
Gin Rummy...................90
Hearts........................92
Pinochle......................93
Scopa.........................97
Slobberhannes................98
Whist.........................98

Card Games for One.....100
Clock Patience...............101
The Four Corners...........102
Grandfather's Clock........103
Klondike......................104
Lovely Lucy..................106
Monte Carlo.................107
Ninety-One 108

Children's Card Games..109
Beggar My Neighbor......110
Cheat (I Doubt It) 110
Concentration (Pelmanism)111
Donkey.......................112
Go Boom 112

Go Fish......................113
My Ship Sails 114
Old Maid.....................114
Rolling Stone 114
Slapjack......................115
Snap 115
Snip Snap Snorem
   (Earl of Coventry).........116
Spit (Speed).................116
War...........................117

Games of Chance..........118
Blackjack (Twenty-One)....119
Michigan (Newmarket)....122
Poker.........................123

PART 3 · PARTY GAMES

Children's Party Games..131
Blindman's Bluff............. 132
Bobbing for Apples
   (Apple Ducking)........... 132
Dead Lions.................... 133
The Farmer in the Dell..... 133
Guess the Smell............. 134
Matchbox Race.............134
Musical Chairs.............134
Oranges and Lemons...... 135
Pass the Balloon............136
Pass the Package........... 136
Ring-Around-the-Rosy
   (Ring-a-Ring-a-Roses)......136
Simon Says................... 137
Squeak, Piggy, Squeak!... 137
Statues........................138
Telephone....................138
What's On the Tray?....... 138

Family Party Games 139
Beetle.......................... 140
Blow Ball......................140
Dumb Crambo...............140
The Game....................141
In the Manner of the
   Word........................ 142
Murder in the Dark........143
Pictionary®.................... 143
Sardines...................... 144
Twister®........................144
Winking........................145

**Old-Fashioned Parlor
Games 146**
Do You Love Your
   Neighbor?.................. 147
Feather........................147
Follow the Leader...........147
Hot and Cold 147
Lookabout 148

Mummies..................... 148
Pass the Slipper 148

Racing Games...............149
Back-to-Back Race 150
Balloon Race 150
Egg and Spoon Race 150
Piggyback Race.............151
Potato Race 151
Relay Races..................151
Sack Race 152
Three-Legged Race 152
Wheelbarrow Race 152

Super Party Games.......153
Buzz & Buzz-Fizz............154
Dinner Party Murder
   Mystery..................... 154
Good Morning, Madam ..155
I Have Never.................156
Likes and Dislikes...........156

PART 4 · GAMES TO PLAY ANYWHERE

Games on the Go..........158
Association....................159
Botticelli...................... 159
Definitions 160
Earth, Water, Air............160
Five of a Kind................161
How Many Words?........161
I Spy...........................161
License Plates.................161
Rubik's Cube®................162
Twenty Questions...........163

Ten-Minute Games 164
Fingers.........................165
Hangman......................165
Outlines....................... 165
Rock, Paper, Scissors
   (Scissors, Paper, Stone). 166
Spoof...........................166
Tic-Tac-Toe
   (Noughts and Crosses).. 166

PART 5 · INDOOR GAMES

Games of Skill 168
Carom Billiards...............169
Cat's Cradle...................170
Darts 171
Fivestones 172
Foosball® (Table Football).173
Jacks.............................175
Marbles 176
Nok Hockey®..................177
Pickup Sticks...................177
Table Tennis (Ping Pong®).178
Tiddlywinks 179

**Pencil and Paper
    Games 182**
Alphabet Race................183
Anagrams......................183
Battleship 184

Boxes............................185
Bridge the Word 185
Categories.....................186
Century Game................186
Consequences 187
Crossword......................188
Guggenheim
    (Scattergories®).............188
Headlines.......................189
Legs..............................189
Lotto 190
Pictures 190
Poetry Game 191
Quizzes.........................191
Short Stories...................191
Sprouts 192
Stairway 192
Transformation 192

**Word and Spoken
    Games 193**
Analogies.......................194
Coffee Pot 194
The Dictionary Game 194
Forbidden Words 195
Ghosts 195
I Love My Love...............196
I Packed My Bag 197
Spelling Round 197
Taboo...........................198
Who Am I?....................198

PART 6 · OUTDOOR GAMES

Active Games...............200
Cat and Mouse..............201
Clapping Games 201
Dodge Ball...................201
Exchange Tag................202
Follow the Leader...........203
Fox and Rabbit..............203
Hare and Hounds 203
Hide and Seek...............203
Hopscotch.....................204
Jump Rope (Skipping)......204

Juggling........................206
Leapfrog 207
Sevens..........................207
Treasure Hunt 208
Tug of War....................208

Sports Games 209
Badminton......................210
Baseball.........................211
Cricket...........................217
Croquet 223

Football (American).........226
Frisbee®....................... 232
Horseshoe Pitching.........233
Lawn Bowls 235
Rounders........................236
Skittles 238
Soccer (Football)............239
Softball 243
Volleyball 245

Index.........................248

Introduction

For thousands of years, games have been passed down from generation to generation, kept alive by the people who play them. Despite the advent of television, video games, and computers, the tradition continues. Older children often share the rules of playground and yard games with younger ones, and card games and board games can be explained by parents.

However, as much as we enjoy the culture of game playing, sometimes there are gaps in our knowledge. *The Treasury of Family Games* is the ideal resource for filling this gap. It features an encyclopedic range of games, from old favourites like dominoes, gin rummy, and Monopoly® to more obscure games from around the world, such as Shogi, which is Japanese chess, and Owari, the board game from West Africa.

The book describes all those childhood challenges, from hopscotch to rope jumping or skipping, Tiddlywinks to jacks, along with myriad game ideas for hosting a successful children's party. It also offers plenty of group games and sports ideas for playing with family or friends.

History of Games

Game playing is an activity that dates back well beyond recorded history and probably arrived soon after people themselves. Ball games, for instance, were probably first played with a stone thrown by youngsters as a way of preparing for the hunt—or for defending the tribe or attacking enemies. Then people started to polish and shape these stones to make them round and good for throwing. Archaeologists have found stones like these that date back at least 5,000 years.

Over the centuries balls have been made from stone, papyrus, marble, wood, and terra cotta, or sewn together from animal hides and stuffed with hay, kapok, sawdust, or seeds.

It was not until the early 19th century that the solid, bouncing rubber ball was first introduced.

Race and tag games had similar origins. Participants built up agility and strength for the hunt—and no equipment was needed, except for a pair of sturdy legs. Other games may have evolved out of ancient rituals. Apple Ducking has been a traditional Halloween game since medieval times but may have its roots even earlier in Celtic Britain and the festival of Samhain. This was when the worlds of the living and the dead were believed to move closer together and past, present, and future were said to merge.

When the Romans conquered Britain, they brought with them the apple tree and its fruit, which represented the goddess Pomona, who was associated with fertility. The Celts believed the apple had special powers to predict the future. During their celebrations their young people had to bite into apples that were floating in water—and the first successful couple would be the next to marry. There is a world of difference between the supposed origins of this game and the extravagant manner in which the young King Edward VII of England is said to have played Apple Ducking in the mid-19th century, with the apples bobbing in a wine bucket filled with champagne!

It is, however, hugely difficult to pinpoint the exact origins of many games. Most have been around for a very long time, and although early records such as an ancient tomb painting may be evidence of a game's existence, it does not help to determine whether the game originated in that culture or was simply adapted from somewhere else. Centuries of migration, trade, war, and travel have carried games all around the world.

What Makes a Good Game?

No one can say with certainty what makes a game endure and spread in popularity, or why arcane, forgotten games hang on and thrive in one region and not others. Sometimes fashion plays an unexpected trump, as when backgammon rose from near obscurity to become fashionable during the 1960s and 1970s. The poker world of today is dominated by Texas Hold 'Em, which for the first century of its existence was perhaps known only in Montana saloons.

Several elements do appear to influence survival in the game world. A sense of competition is obviously important, and so is portability. Many children's games endure because they require little or no equipment. Often, race and tag games simply involve energy, while word games need only pencil and paper. A mix of luck and skill is eternally present in successful games. Children enjoy the surprises of chance more than grown-ups do. For older players it's more a matter of personal taste—though we still love a lucky break, we hope to have the skill to cope with whatever is dealt.

Why Play Games?

Today, playing games is largely seen as a leisure-time activity—something we do for pleasure, and perhaps to stretch ourselves physically or mentally. Physical games promote flexibility and agility, strength and stamina. Word and number games build up literacy and numeracy skills in a fun but challenging way. Games may be relaxing or challenging, and both types can be beneficial in releasing the tensions of a busy life. Game playing can also help to build social skills.

Children can learn leadership skills, the importance of rules, as well as develop their ability to participate as a team player.

They can experience success and failure and learn how to accept both with grace. Taking part in games of all sorts builds confidence and self-expression regardless of the skills of the player.

Games of Strategy

Games of strategy are played—and have been for many thousands of years—in nearly all cultures in the world. These games mirror the skills we hope to develop in life: To work with foresight, to plan ahead, and to take into account the

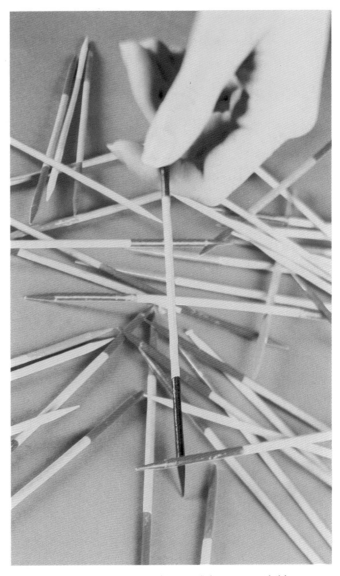

Above: *Pickup sticks help build manual dexterity in children.*

Right: Team games such as volleyball help us learn to work together.

decisions and moves of other people. Examples are chess, checkers, and the ancient Chinese game of Go. In these games clear rules and restricted moves mean it is possible—although not always easy—to plan ahead. In games where accurate probabilities of all move results are known, as in most card games, strategy also plays a key role.

Perhaps because the human mind ceaselessly tries to detect patterns and base future decisions on an otherwise chaotic progression of events, people will often search for a winning key when Lady Luck is the only one available. Thus the most carefully contrived, openly advertised randomness will not dissuade players from seeking strategic advantage. For example, devotees of roulette are apt to keep long tallies of numbers and sieve months' worth of results in order to establish a winning 'system.' However, their efforts are unlikely to produce a winning streak. In the case of a completely random game, all strategies are equally good.

Technology and Game Playing

As we have seen, there are many benefits to recommend the playing of games. And when you are overwhelmed by passion for a game, it is worth remembering that the technology of the 21st century can contribute to the art of game playing as well. Computer programs can hone skills for games such as chess—we can pit our wits against the computer and, with practice, scale the levels of difficulty available. Over the Internet we can engage opponents half a world away and see the results of our moves instantly. At any hour of the day, games are open—chess, contract bridge, gin rummy, word puzzles, quizzes, and virtual sports—the list has no limit.

How To Use This Book

In this book we offer something for everyone's taste: games of skill and luck, indoor and outdoor activities, pastimes for all ages, games requiring physical exercise, and those that only exercise the brain.

With the help of *The Treasury of Family Games,* there should be no excuse for that well-worn childhood phrase: 'I'm bored! What can I do?' There are suggestions for passing the time on tedious journeys and ideas to make every type of social occasion more fun.

The games in this book are divided into six broad categories: Board Games, Card Games, Party Games, Games to Play Anywhere, Indoor Games, and Outdoor Games. The games within each of these chapters are organized under a subheading. In the chapter on Card Games, for example, there are sections on Card Games for Groups, Games for One Player, Children's Card Games, and Games of Chance. The games in each section are then arranged alphabetically.

There are special sections for children's card games and party games, but there are many other games that are suitable for children throughout the book. Many board games, race games, word and number games, as well as outdoor activities and sports are particularly popular with children. If you know the game you are looking for, you can find it through the extensive index included at the end of the book. If you're looking for a word game but don't know its name, look first in the Word and Spoken Games section in Indoor Games, then consider that it could be listed under the Ten-Minute Games or Games on the Go sections in the Games to Play Anywhere chapter. If you are just looking for an idea, a flick through *The Treasury of Family Games* is bound to bring you just that!

Each game starts with an at-a-glance guide to the number of players and equipment needed, a rating on how difficult it

is to play, and a time guide that indicates how long the game lasts. It is easy to learn new games or settle disputes during seemingly familiar games as the rules are presented under three simple headings: Setup, Playing the Game, and Winning the Game. In addition there are sections on strategy that provide hints and tips on how to be a winner, plus unusual variations for some of the well-known classics.

Plus, throughout the book there are brief histories and anecdotes detailing the backgrounds of some of the games.

The Treasury of Family Games is designed as a source of inspiration as well as a reference guide to rules and the necessary equipment for playing a rich cross-section of games. If you don't become an expert in every game listed here, may you at least enjoy each one you choose to play!

***Above:** Checkers (Draughts) is popular all over the world.*

BOARD GAMES

Commercial Games 13

Dice Games 19

Domino Games 24

Race Games 37

Strategy Games 45

Territorial Games 61

Commercial Games

Commercial board games such as Monopoly®, Trivial Pursuit®, and Scrabble® can accommodate all levels of skill and are enjoyed by millions worldwide.

APPLES TO APPLES®

NUMBER OF PLAYERS: Four to ten

EQUIPMENT: Set of game cards

DIFFICULTY: More suitable for adults than children

DURATION: About 20 to 30 minutes

In this rather eccentric commercial card game—with no particular object other than fun—outcomes are determined by quirks of the imagination.

Setup

The full deck consists of 321 red apple cards and 107 green apple cards. Red apple cards are essentially nouns—people, places, things, or events—but a very unusual selection, with amusing usage, quotes, or commentary supplied. Green apple cards are adjectival in nature, being arch descriptions in search of something to modify.

Playing the Game

One player, nominated to be the judge for a round, deals seven red apple cards to each player. The judge places one green apple card from the stack faceup in the middle. All players select a 'best' match from their hands for the middle card, and place that red apple card facedown on the table. The judge gathers up the red apple cards, shuffles them, and turns them faceup, reading each aloud. The judge then pronounces which one is the best match; the player of that red apple card is the round's winner and is awarded the green apple card. In the next round the player to the judge's left becomes the new judge.

Winning the Game

A game continues until one player is first to amass a certain number of green apple cards, in a range from eight (in a four-player game) to four (up to ten players).

Variations

It is possible, of course, to play the cards in reverse order, dealing out green adjectives and matching them to a single red apple card—a variation called Apple Turnovers. Or time pressure may be dispensed with, so that every played card, however tardy, is judged—Baked Apples. In the Crab Apple version, a judge is instructed to search out the worst matchup. With expanded card sets, available from the game publisher, the rules may be twisted in still more ways.

CLUE® (CLUEDO®)

NUMBER OF PLAYERS: Three to six

EQUIPMENT: Board, two dice, cards, pieces

DIFFICULTY: Easy to master and play

DURATION: About 30 minutes; longer if there are six players

The game of Clue, which has spawned both a book series and a Hollywood movie, takes the form of a murder mystery. Your host, Mr. Boddy, has been killed in his own mansion by one of his guests. Players race to solve the case by deducing the identity of the killer, the murder weapon, and the scene of the crime.

Setup

Included with the game are 21 cards representing the six suspects (Colonel Mustard, Professor Plum, Mr. Green, Mrs. Peacock, Miss Scarlett, and Mrs. White), the six murder weapons (dagger, lead pipe, candlestick, rope, wrench, and revolver) and the nine rooms of the mansion (kitchen, hall, lounge, ballroom, billiard room, dining room, study, library, and conservatory).

Playing the Game

At the start of the game, one card from each category is slipped into an envelope without being seen by anyone—these represent the true 'facts' of the crime. The remaining cards are regrouped and reshuffled, then dealt out to the players, who meanwhile have each taken on the identity of one of the suspects.

Moving

Players then take turns rolling dice and moving their game pieces around the board, which is laid out as a floor plan of the mansion. Each time a player arrives in a new room, he must make a suggestion as to the details of the murder. For example, he might suggest, 'Mrs. Peacock killed him in the conservatory with the revolver.' At this point, the game pieces representing the suspect and weapon are whisked into the appropriate room, even if this means changing the location of another player's marker.

Players take turns examining their cards to see if they can disprove the suggestion. If a player holds a card for the revolver, for example, then that card is obviously not in the envelope. That player would then show the revolver card to the poser of the suggestion, who would make the appropriate marking in his Detective Notebook—a slip of paper given to all the players. Other players would also make markings in their notebooks, but without the benefit of knowing exactly which card had been shown.

Winning the Game

Play progresses until a player is ready to make a formal accusation, which involves announcing what he believes to be the details of the crime and checking the envelope to see if his theory is correct. If he is right, he wins the game. Otherwise, he must put the cards back into the envelope and sit on the sidelines until one of his competitors is successful.

MONOPOLY®

NUMBER OF PLAYERS: Two to six

EQUIPMENT: Board, cards and pieces for play, two dice

DIFFICULTY: Concentration and planning are necessary in this fun family game

DURATION: Between 1 and 2 hours, depending on the pace of the game

A much-loved board game of luck and some skill in which players move around a board buying up properties and trying to bankrupt their opponents.

One of Fidel Castro's first moves upon seizing power in Cuba was to ban the game of Monopoly and confiscate all existing sets. Although these actions may seem extreme, they highlight the uncanny grip this board game holds over the imagination of the world. Indeed, since the game's invention in 1933 by an unemployed heating engineer named Charles Darrow, American capitalism has had few more enduring symbols than Monopoly and its tuxedo-wearing mascot, Mr. Moneybags.

The game itself is basically an exercise in imaginary landlording—in fact, Darrow 'borrowed' the basic idea for his invention from The Landlord's Game, created by Elizabeth Magie in the 1800s. The American and British versions differ in that each uses street names and places that are familiar in their own country.

Setup

Its key feature is an outside track of squares representing specific properties—mostly named after actual streets in Atlantic City in the U.S. version and the city of London in the British version—which can be bought or sold by the players as they move their game pieces around the board. Players each choose a token that represents them as they move around the board, and they are each allowed a specified amount of money at the start of the game.

Playing the Game

In turn, players throw the dice and the numbers shown indicate the number of squares along which they must move. Depending entirely on chance, a player may land on a square that orders him to go to jail, or to pick another card from the Community Chest, which may award him more money or order him to pay a forfeit, or he might land on the most expensive property on the board, which he may or may not have the funds to buy.

The chance factor

Many games have attracted, at one time or another, the serious attentions of mathematicians. Chess, checkers, and Go lend themselves to computer simulations; cards and dice dissolve into theorems of probability. (Indeed, a very practical question about winning expectations in a dice game led directly to famous mathematician Blaise Pascal's analysis of the rules of probability in the 17th century.) There is even a branch of mathematics, game theory, which can be used to find best-possible strategies in any kind of game, or at least for proving that such strategies exist.

Monopoly, too, has a mathematical side to it. The question in Monopoly is whether all the squares have about the same likelihood of being landed on. It may or may not be the case that, using two dice and everyone starting from the same place, all the possible leaps will visit and revisit all squares equally.

To find out, the mathematician Ian Stewart used a mathematical tool called a Markov chain. He found that, although likelihoods ebb and flow with successive throws, they eventually smooth out, like a disturbed pool of water, into evenly attractive real estate. Of course, in the important early stages some properties will be hit more frequently, and this may also happen toward an average game's end.

Moving

Anyone landing on a property already owned by another player is obliged to pay rent to the owner, with rents increasing dramatically as houses and hotels are built. Other factors complicating game play are jail sentences, mortgages, and Chance and Community Chest cards, which confer financial blessings and calamities in equal measure and are drawn randomly from stacks in the middle of the board.

Winning the Game

The object of Monopoly is to amass enough wealth to force all of one's opponents into bankruptcy. Thus, the last player left in the game is the winner.

Variations

Shorter version

Since achieving this goal can often take several hours, there is also a shorter version of the game which ends after two players have been driven out of the game. At this point, assets are added up and the victory goes to the richest player.

RISK®

NUMBER OF PLAYERS: Two to six

EQUIPMENT: Board, cards, pieces, five dice

DIFFICULTY: Clever tactics needed

DURATION: About 1 to 1½ hours

While the object of Monopoly is to take over city blocks, the object of Risk is to take over the entire world.

Setup

The board is a map of Earth, divided into 42 territories on six continents. At the start of the game, players are each given a certain number of pieces representing armies. They take turns placing their armies in the different territories until all armies are on the board. The rest of the game basically consists of war, with players going head to head in attempts to conquer each other's territories.

Playing the Game

On each turn, players can choose to deploy armies, attack the opposition, or fortify their positions. When an attack is launched, victory is determined through a series of competitive dice rolls. As the game progresses, players can also earn Risk cards, which can be traded in for additional armies.

Winning the Game

In the traditional version of Risk, game play continues until one player has completely eliminated all opponents from the board. This player obviously is the winner.

Variations

Secret Mission Risk

To shorten playing time, players can also choose to play Secret Mission Risk, in which cards are dealt out at the beginning of the game assigning each player a mission—generally involving the acquisition of a certain collection of territories. In this version, the winner is the first player to complete his secret mission, regardless of his overall status on the global front. This adds a new element of deception and intrigue to the game, since it is to the players' advantage to keep the actual goals of their missions unclear.

SCRABBLE®

NUMBER OF PLAYERS: Two to four

EQUIPMENT: Board, four letter racks, 100 letter tiles, letter tiles bag

DIFFICULTY: Suitable for older children and adults

DURATION: About 1 hour

The world's most popular word game, Scrabble has been produced in 31 languages and sold in 120 countries. It can be played by children but is challenging enough to form the basis of international tournaments.

Setup

In theory, game play is exceedingly simple. A Scrabble set consists of 100 wooden tiles marked with letters, four wooden tile racks, and a board partitioned into a grid. At the start of the game, players each draw seven tiles at random from a bag and place them onto their respective racks, keeping them hidden from view. To determine who will go first, they each draw an additional letter from the bag and show it to their opponents—whoever draws the letter closest to the start of the alphabet begins the game. Play then proceeds clockwise.

Playing the Game

Players then take turns forming words on the board with their letters, drawing new tiles from the bag to replace the ones that are used. The first player can form any word he chooses, but he must place at least one tile on the central square of the board, which is marked with a star. Subsequent players can then only form words by branching off from existing words, in the manner of a crossword puzzle.

Words can be horizontal or vertical. A tile cannot be placed adjacent to another unless a valid word is thus created. The validity of words is an issue unto itself, but proper names and abbreviations are generally disallowed, and it is best if a specific edition of the dictionary is agreed upon beforehand as the final authority.

Scoring

Scores are based on both the tiles played and the squares they are placed on. Each letter is worth a certain number of points, and the score for a word is determined by adding up the letters. However, certain squares on the board, with names such as triple word score, may double or triple the value of a letter or word. The game also includes two blank tiles, which can be used in place of any letter. If the tile is used afterward to form another word by a different player it must remain the same letter chosen by the player who placed it on the board.

Strategy

The rest is pure strategy. The difference between a novice Scrabble player and a world champion lies first in a broad vocabulary but also in a keen sense of which letters to play early and which to keep in reserve. A would-be champ also needs to assess whether it is in his best interest to aim for an open board, in which there are plentiful scoring opportunities, or a blocked board, in which it is difficult for anyone to form words.

Winning the Game

Once all tiles have been drawn from the pool, the game progresses until either one player uses all his tiles or no one can form any additional words. Players' scores are then added up and decreased by the number of tiles left on their racks. If one player has an empty rack, his score is increased by the sum of these same remaining tiles. The player with the highest score is the winner.

TRIVIAL PURSUIT®

NUMBER OF PLAYERS: Two to six

EQUIPMENT: Board, one die, question cards, tokens, scoring wedges

DIFFICULTY: Good general knowledge is essential

DURATION: About 1 hour

Players try to answer questions and gain the most points. This game, which soared to international prominence during the 1980s, is a simple trivia game at heart, but notable for the elegance of its game play and the depth and variety of its questions.

Setup

Questions in Trivial Pursuit are divided into six categories, each represented by a colour:

- **Blue:** Geography
- **Pink:** Entertainment
- **Yellow:** History
  - **Brown:** Art and Literature
  - **Green:** Science and Nature
  - **Orange:** Sports and Leisure.

Each player is given a game token partitioned into six symmetrical wedge-shaped holes. The object of the game is to fill up the token with wedges of the six different colours, which can only be achieved by answering trivia questions correctly while one's token is at the appropriately coloured category headquarters section of the board.

Playing the Game

Game play involves rolling dice and moving the tokens around the board in an attempt to obtain all six wedges. Each move is generally followed by a trivia question which, if answered correctly, entitles the player to another roll of the die. However, only questions answered at the aforementioned category headquarters entitle the player to a coloured wedge.

Winning the Game

Once a player collects all six wedges, he must make his way to the hub in the middle of the board and answer a trivia question in a category chosen by his opponents. If he answers correctly, he has won the game. Otherwise, he must leave the hub on his next turn and attempt to re-enter it at a later time.

Dice Games

Games using dice have been played for thousands of years, despite—or perhaps because of—the fact that very little skill is required; the outcome of the game is left entirely to chance.

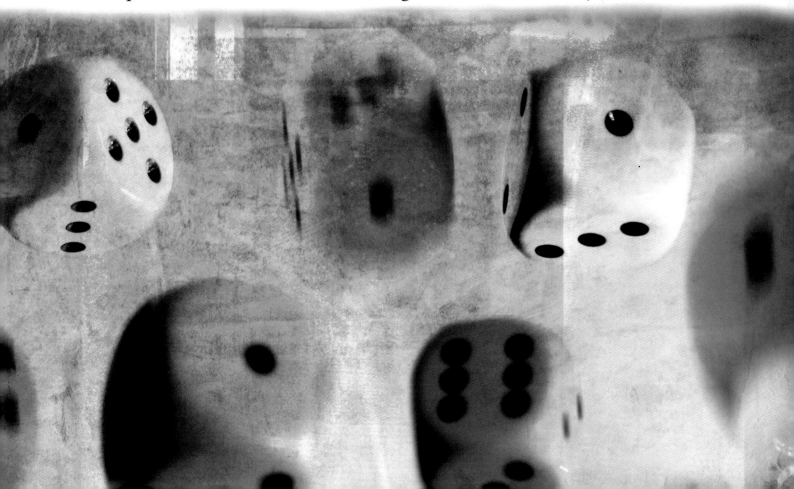

ACES IN THE POT

NUMBER OF PLAYERS: Two or more

EQUIPMENT: Two dice, counters (chips), dice cup

DIFFICULTY: No skill required, just luck

DURATION: About 20 to 30 minutes

A simple counters-and-dice family game that requires a certain amount of luck.

Playing the Game

In this game, players roll a pair of dice and attempt to be the last holding one of the two counters with which each player begins. Before starting, players throw a single die, and the one with the highest number goes first.

Each player in turn rolls both dice thereafter. Unless an ace (1) or a 6 is thrown—appearing on the uppermost face of either die—a player keeps the counters and passes the dice to the next player. If the rolls turn up an ace, the player puts a counter into the pot, the *kitty*, in the middle of the table; for two aces, 'snake eyes,' both counters are lost. For each 6 that comes up, a counter is forfeited to the player on the left.

The throw moves clockwise around the table. Any player who runs out of counters is out of the game. The last player still having a counter must make three throws without rolling a 6 in order to win the pot. If a 6 comes up, the counter is passed to the player on the left, regardless of whether he has any counters, who in turn attempts to roll three times without a 6. The first player to accomplish this feat wins.

Roman dice

■ ■

Playing and betting on dice games was popular in ancient Rome. Their design has barely changed since: Romans used six-sided cubes called *tesserae*, very much like modern dice, except that opposite faces added up to 7, instead of 6 as with modern cubes. A four-sided variety, called *tali*, was also in use. Dice were rolled from a cup just as they are today.

Of the plentiful Roman dice recovered by archaeologists, some had clearly been 'loaded' with small pieces of lead. Inserted near-invisibly on one side, the extra weight tended to pop the opposite face upright as the die rolled, making the die's owner an uncommonly lucky player. A pertinent inscription on a Roman dice game advises players: 'LEVATE DALOCU LUDERE NESCIS IDIOTA RECEDE' ('Push off, you idiot, you'll never figure this game out'.)

DROP DEAD

NUMBER OF PLAYERS: Any number can play

EQUIPMENT: Five dice, dice cup

DIFFICULTY: Only luck is needed

DURATION: It depends on how many rounds are played

Playing the Game

In this game, players roll five dice, attempting to score points without rolling the faces 2 or 5. First, players roll one die, and the player with the lowest number wins. Then each player in turn throws five dice, scoring the total number on the faces, unless a 2 or 5 is thrown, in which case there is no score, and any die with the lethal number on it is taken out of play.

For example, if a player throws 6-4-3-1-1, he scores 15 and continues his turn with five dice. If he then throws 5-4-3-2-1, he does not score, and the dice with the 5 and 2 are taken out of play. A player continues throwing the remaining dice and scoring as appropriate until all five are out of play. It is then the next player's turn to roll the five dice. The player with the highest score wins.

HEARTS DUE

NUMBER OF PLAYERS: Two or more

EQUIPMENT: Six dice, paper and pencil

DIFFICULTY: It is all down to luck

DURATION: About 30 minutes

Once played with six special dice, each with the letters H-E-A-R-T-S on their six faces, this game can be played with regular dice: 1=H, 2=E, 3=A, 4=R, 5=T, 6=S. Play requires no more effort than rolling dice and adding up the scores.

Playing the Game

Players roll one die to see who will start, with the lowest number going first. They take turns rolling all six dice at a time and score as follows:

H (1): 5 points

H-E (1-2): 10 points

H-E-A (1-2-3): 15 points

H-E-A-R (1-2-3-4): 20 points

H-E-A-R-T (1-2-3-4-5): 25 points

H-E-A-R-T-S (1-2-3-4-5-6): 30 points.

Winning the Game

Only one copy of each number can be used. If, for example, a player throws 1-1-2-2-3-6, he scores 12. There is one special penalty rule: A player who rolls three 1's in a turn loses all points and must start over. One hundred fifty points wins the game.

HELP YOUR NEIGHBOR

NUMBER OF PLAYERS: Two to six

EQUIPMENT: Three dice, ten counters (chips) per player, dice cup

DIFFICULTY: A game of luck

DURATION: About 1 hour

Players roll the dice and try to get rid of all their counters.

Setup

In this counters and dice game, each player chooses a number corresponding to one face of a die. When five players participate, the 6 is out of play, and when four participate, both the 5 and 6 are out of play. If there are three players, each takes two numbers apiece; two players take three numbers apiece.

Playing the Game

Each player starts with ten counters. Three dice are used. Beginning with the player whose number is 1, players take turns throwing all three dice one time per turn, with play moving clockwise. Whenever a player's number comes up, he must put a counter in the pot. If it comes up more than once in a throw, a counter must be put in for each occurrence.

Winning the Game

The first player to run out of counters wins the pot. The player with number 2 starts the next round.

PIG

NUMBER OF PLAYERS: Two or more

EQUIPMENT: Pencil and paper, one die

DIFFICULTY: Easy for all ages

DURATION: About 30 minutes

In Pig, players repeatedly throw a single die and try to score 100 or more points.

Playing the Game

First, the order of play is decided by having each player throw the die. The lowest number goes first, the next lowest will throw second, and so on. The first player rolls the die, notes the score, rolls again, and continues to add to his total until he chooses to stop, or throws a low ace (1). The ace cancels the entire score for the round. In either case, the die then passes to the next player.

Winning the Game

The first player to reach 100 (or more) wins. To reduce the advantage to the first player, a rule can be adopted that

permits any player who has not yet rolled in the round—after 100 has been reached—to take a turn. The person with the highest score at the end of this full last round is the victor. Advantage shifts to the last player, since only he knows when it is safe to stop.

SHUT THE BOX

NUMBER OF PLAYERS: Two or more

EQUIPMENT: Two dice, paper, pencil, 12 counters (chips) per player

DIFFICULTY: An ideal family game

DURATION: About 1 hour

Also known as Canoga, or Round Dozen, this game involves rolling dice and 'shutting' 12 boxes numbered 1 to 12.

Setup

Each player has a paper with 12 boxes and 12 counters. The object is to shut as many boxes as possible by covering them with counters.

Playing the Game

The first player rolls a pair of dice and then 'shuts boxes' corresponding to the total thrown. For example, if a total of 8

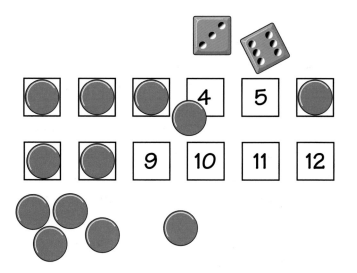

Diagram 1: Shut the Box

is rolled, boxes 7 and 1; 6 and 2; 5, 2 and 1; or any group with the right total could be shut, regardless of how the dice actually rolled. A player continues to throw and shut more boxes by covering them with a counter but throwing only a single die in the event boxes 7–12 are shut. A turn ends when a total is thrown for which it is impossible to find a set of open boxes.

Winning the Game

When all players have had a turn, the player with the fewest open boxes wins the round.

YACHT

NUMBER OF PLAYERS: Two to ten, or can be played as a solo game

EQUIPMENT: Five dice, pen and paper, dice cup

DIFFICULTY: For adults and older children

DURATION: About 30 minutes

In this game, points are scored by matching as closely as possible certain set patterns in successive throws of five dice, over 12 rounds. A commercial version is sold as Yahtzee®.

Playing the Game

To begin, players roll a single die to determine the order of play (highest goes first). A game of Yacht consists of 12 rounds. In each round, a player begins by rolling five dice from the cup. He may decide to keep some of the dice and roll others again in a second throw. Again he may keep some and roll others in a third throw. Three throws are the limit. A player decides in which of the 12 categories to enter a score when the throw is finished. A different category must be attempted on each subsequent round, so that scores have been marked for each at the end of the 12 rounds.

Scoring

The categories are:

- **Yacht:** Five of a kind (50 points)
- **Big Straight:** 2-3-4-5-6 (30 points)
- **Little Straight:** 1-2-3-4-5 (30 points)
- **Four of a Kind:** 29 points maximum (that is, 4 times *x*, plus the fifth die)
- **Full House:** 3 of one number and 2 of another (28 points maximum)
- **Choice:** Highest score one can make in three throws (30 points maximum)
- **Sixes:** 30 points maximum
- **Fives:** 25 points maximum
- **Fours:** 20 points maximum
- **Threes:** 15 points maximum

- **Twos:** 20 points maximum
- **Ones:** 5 points maximum.

At the end of each turn, a player records on the score sheet the sum of all the dice thrown that fit into the chosen category. For example, a 4-4-4-3-2 would count 12 in the Fours. If a player gets four of a kind, the fifth die is also included in the sum. A Yacht, Big Straight, or Little Straight always score their full values.

Winning the Game

When the 12 rounds are over, scores are added and the highest total wins.

Variations

General

General resembles Yacht, except that there are ten categories (one, instead of two, Straights, no Choice category), and the scoring includes bonuses for making certain categories in one throw.

Specifically:

- **General:** Five of a kind wins the game on the first throw (Big General), otherwise it scores 60 points (Little General)
- **Four of a Kind:** 45 on first throw; otherwise 30
- **Full House:** 35 on first throw; otherwise 30
- **Straight:** 25 on first throw; otherwise 20
- **Ones to Sixes:** Always score sum of matching dice.

Domino Games

In all domino games, the playing pieces (known as dominoes, tiles, or bones) are turned facedown and shuffled before play. A large flat area such as a kitchen table is best for domino games.

DOMINOES

NUMBER OF PLAYERS: Two to five

EQUIPMENT: One set of double 6's (28 bones/tiles)

DIFFICULTY: Children can play a fun game, while adults can play a more vigorously strategic game

DURATION: Around 30 minutes, but less for a children's game

The basic game is played using a standard set of 28 dominoes (also known as tiles or bones). Each half tile is called an end and has from zero to six spots. An end with no spots is a blank. A doublet is a tile with the same number of spots on each end. Players take turns matching one of the tiles in their hands to a tile already on the table, with the object of getting rid of all their tiles.

Setup

All the dominoes are turned facedown on a table and shuffled—that is, randomly rearranged. Players then draw hands of five tiles (in four- and five-player games) or seven tiles (in two- and three-player games). Each player places his tiles on their sides facing toward him, so that they are not visible to other players. The remaining tiles comprise the *tileyard*, from which players draw when they cannot play.

Playing the Game

The game is started by the player with the highest doublet, who sets the game by laying the doublet faceup on the table. The next player to the left then plays a tile with an end that matches the doublet, placing it at a right angle with the matching end touching the doublet. Play then passes to the left, with each player placing the matching end of a tile next to an open end on the table. All the tiles are placed next to each other horizontally; only doublets are placed vertically.

In the example shown in diagram 1, the double 5 was the first tile played. The second player had to play a tile with a 5 on one end, and played the 5-1. The third could have played either a 5 or a 1. He played the 5-3, leaving open a 3 and 1 as options for the fourth player.

Scoring

Only tiles that match one end of the layout are playable. If a player does not have a playable tile, he draws from the tileyard until a match comes up, and adds all non-matching draws to his hand. If all the tiles in the tileyard are drawn and the player still cannot play, he must pass.

The first player to get rid of all his tiles wins the hand, yelling, 'Domino!' to signal the end of play. If no player dominoes, the hand continues until none of the players can play—a situation called a blocked game. In this case, the player with the lowest number of spots on his remaining tiles is the winner.

To determine the winner's score, each player adds up the total number of spots on his unplayed tiles. If the winner has dominoed, his score is the total number of spots remaining in the hands of all the other players. The winner of a blocked game scores only the difference between his own remaining spot total and the spot totals of each of the other players. For example, if the winner has 9 spots and the other two players 11 and 12 spots respectively, the winner scores 2 (11 minus 9)

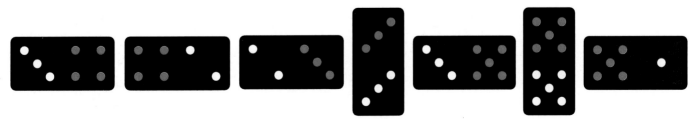

Diagram 1: Playing Dominoes

from one player and 3 (12 minus 9) from the other, for a total of 5 points. A game of dominoes is usually played to 100 points, but may also be played to 50.

Strategy

Because players sometimes have options in selecting a domino, strategy is part of the game. These are the basic considerations:

If a player has four or more ends with the same number of spots, he can try to play so as to leave open ends with that number on the table. This makes it easier for him to play and may also force the other players, who are less likely to have ends with that number, to draw or pass.

A player who concludes that he does not have much chance of winning a hand can focus on playing dominoes with the highest numbers of spots, in order to be left with as few spots as possible to contribute to the score of the eventual winner.

A player should try to cover both ends of a doublet played by another player as soon as possible, in case the opponent chose to play the doublet because he has other matching tiles in his hand.

VARIATIONS

Block Dominoes

This simplified children's version begins in the same way as basic dominoes. The tiles are shuffled, each player draws a hand, and the highest doublet is set on the table. Instead of proceeding with play, however, all the dominoes are then rearranged and divided among the players. For two players, each gets 13; if there are three, each gets eight; and if there are four, each gets six. There is no tileyard; the extra dominoes are simply set aside. Eliminating the tileyard increases the role of chance; the outcome of the game depends largely on which tiles are out of play.

Cross Dominoes

This variation of dominoes requires that four matching tiles be played on the first doublet, in the form of a cross, before any other tiles can be played. In diagram 2, for example, the first play was the double 4, on which the next four players laid a 4-3, 4-6, 4-1, and 4-5. After the formation of the cross, there are four open ends, instead of two, on which to play but otherwise the game proceeds like basic dominoes.

Cyprus

This game, suitable for four or more players, uses a set of double 9s, in which dominoes with 0 through 9 spots are used, making 55 pieces in all. Instead of a cross, an eight-pointed star using 9's must be formed before the ends of the 9's already played can be matched. The number of tiles drawn is scaled to the number of players in the game. With four players, each gets 13; if there are five, each gets 11; for six, 9; for seven, 7; with eight or nine, each takes 6; and if there are ten, each gets 5.

The player with the double 9 begins. (If no one has it, the dominoes are reshuffled and redrawn.) The next four plays must form a cross as in Cross Dominoes, and the subsequent four tiles, which must also match the double 9, are played diagonally to create a star as shown in diagram 3. After the star is finished, eight open ends are available, and play continues as in basic dominoes.

Diagram 2: Cross Dominoes

Diagram 3: Cyprus

Diagram 4:
Double Cross Dominoes

Double Cross Dominoes

Play begins as in Cross Dominoes, but this variation of the game requires that a second doublet be played on one end of the cross before play can continue. Diagram 4 shows how a double cross is formed. In the example, the double 3 was played first, followed by the 3-5, 3-1, 3-2, and 3-6. The only dominoes that could be played next are the double 5, double 1, double 2, or the double 6. Since the double 2 has been laid down, the rest of the game can now be played according to the usual rules.

Double Nine Cross Dominoes

This game, for two to ten players, employs a set of double 9's. If there are fewer than four players, each draws seven; otherwise each draws five.

The game starts with the formation of a cross, as in Cross Dominoes. Thereafter, play continues as in regular dominoes, except that when a doublet is laid down, subsequent players can play not only against the open side, but also against the ends. Thus, each doublet permits the layout to branch in two additional directions. Diagram 5 shows a game in which the double 9 has been played and two of its three open ends have been used.

Maltese Cross Dominoes

Play proceeds as in basic dominoes until the first doublet is played. In this game a doublet must be played on each arm of a plain cross before other plays can be made. Diagram 6 shows a Maltese Cross with its doublets in place. In this case, as the Maltese Cross is completed, regular play has proceeded, with the 1–5 laid on a matching open end.

The game continues using the four open ends as in Cross Dominoes.

Diagram 5: Double Nine Cross Dominoes

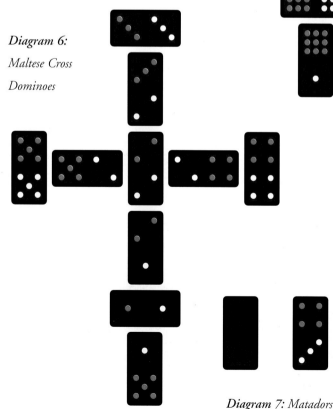

Diagram 6:
Maltese Cross
Dominoes

Matador

This game, also known as All Sevens or Russian Dominoes, differs slightly from conventional domino games in that it employs 'wild tiles' (or wild bones). Players arrange sets of dominoes according to the number of spots on each piece, matching the end of one piece with the end of another on the table. The player who gets rid of all his pieces first or with the lowest score wins.

From the shuffled tiles seven are drawn for a two-player game, or five for a three- or four-player game. The remaining tiles go into the tileyard. In Matador, players can draw from the tileyard even if they have a playable tile, but must draw if they do not have one. Two tiles must be left in the tileyard.

The player with the highest doublet begins the game, and play continues clockwise. Doublets are not played crosswise as in other domino games; they are simply part of the straight line layout. The aim in Matador is not to match like ends but to make each pair of adjacent ends add up to seven. Thus, an open 4 requires a 3 to be played against it, an open 5 requires a 2, and so on. For example, if the first tile played is the 4-4, a 3-5 might be played against one end, and a 3-4 against the other. The next play would have to be a tile with a 2 (against the 5 end), or a tile with a 3 (against the 4 end).

There are four special Matadors that operate like wild cards. These are the three tiles whose two ends add up to seven (the 3-4, 5-2, and 6-1), plus the double blank. A Matador can be played against any end, and any end can be played against a Matador. When in the course of play a blank appears on an open end, only a Matador can continue the game on that end (since there are no domino ends that can combine with 0 to total 7).

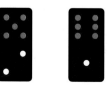

Diagram 7: Matadors

A player can win a hand by getting rid of all tiles and calling 'Domino!' or, if the game is blocked, by having the fewest total spots remaining in hand.

A winner who dominoes gets 1 point for each spot remaining in the hands of all the opponents. The winner of a blocked game gets the difference between the number of spots in hand and the number in each opponent's hand. For example, if the winner has 7 spots and an opponent has 10 spots, the winner gets 3 points from that opponent. Additional hands are played until a player reaches the point total needed to win the game, either 50 or 100.

ALL FIVES (MUGGINS)

NUMBER OF PLAYERS: Two to four

EQUIPMENT: One set of double 6's (28 tiles/bones)

DIFFICULTY: Concentration and alertness required

DURATION: About 20 to 30 minutes

This form of dominoes is the one most often played in the United States. All Fives permits a player to score points during a hand by making the open ends of the layout add up to multiples of five. Each player draws five tiles from the shuffled set, the remainder forming the tileyard/boneyard. The player with the highest doublet starts the game, and the game continues as in basic dominoes, except that players attempt to score points during a hand as well as to win it.

Setup

The layout and play is the same as in basic dominoes, with doublets being played at right angles to the other bones. In All Fives, however, a player's primary aim is to make the spots on the open ends of the layout add up to five or a multiple of five. Any such multiple scores points equal to the number of spots.

Scoring

Diagram 8 illustrates a two-player game in which the first player scored 10 points by setting the double 5 (which has a total of 10 spots). The second player played the 5-blank and also scored 10 points because the open blank counts as 0, and the double 5 was still open on the other end. None of the next three plays, the 5-3 (open ends 3 + 0 = 3), the blank 3 (open ends 3 + 3 = 6), or the double 3 (open ends 3 + 6 = 9) scored any points. On the next play, Player One laid down the 3-4, and scored 10 points (open ends 4 + 6 =10). Player two also scored 10 points by playing the 3-6 (open ends 4 + 6 = 10).

A player who scores must declare his points aloud. Otherwise, after the next play, any player may call 'Muggins!' and thus win the points.

The tileyard is used as in basic dominoes, with one exception: The last two tiles cannot be drawn.

Winning the Game

The first player to get rid of all his tiles calls 'Domino!' and wins the hand. If no one dominoes, but no one can make any additional plays, the hand stops, and the hand with the fewest spots is the winner.

Points scored for winning are also in multiples of five. Each player adds up his total spots and rounds this number to the

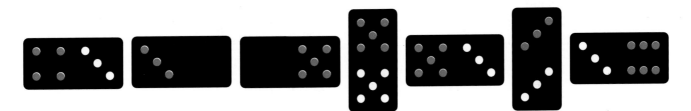

Diagram 8: All Fives

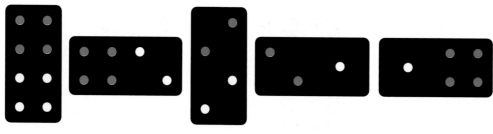

Diagram 9: Bergen

nearest such multiple—upward or downward. A player with 7 remaining spots would round to 5, and a player with 8 remaining spots would round to 10. A winner who has dominoed scores the total of the adjusted points from all players. The winner of a blocked game scores only the difference between her own adjusted spot total and the adjusted totals of each of the other players.

For example, if the winner had 4 points (rounded to 5) and another player had 7 points (rounded to 5), the winner would get 5 minus 5, or 0 points from that player. From a player with 8 points (rounded to 10), the winner would get 10 minus 5, or 5 points. Games are generally played to 100 points.

BERGEN

NUMBER OF PLAYERS: Two to four

EQUIPMENT: One set of double 6's (28 tiles/bones)

DIFFICULTY: Fairly easy

DURATION: About 30 minutes

This employs a standard set of dominoes. Unlike most point-scoring domino games, scores in Bergen are not related precisely to spot numbers. Instead, players make points by laying down doublets or by matching the open ends of a domino layout.

Setup

The dominoes are shuffled and players draw hands: six bones each for two players; five bones each for three or four players. The remaining tiles make up the tileyard. The player with the lowest doublet sets it to start the game. Play proceeds as in basic dominoes, except that only one tile per turn can be drawn from the tileyard, and the last two tiles cannot be drawn at all.

Scoring

The aim of the game is to earn points in any of the following ways:

- **Doublet:** Playing any doublet (2 points)
- **Double header:** Making each of the two open ends match (2 points)
- **Triple header:** Matching a doublet on one end to the other open end (3 points)
- **Domino:** Being first to go out (1 point)
- **Blocked game point:** If one or more players has no remaining doublets, the game point goes to the player in the no-doublet group with the lowest spot total; if all players have doublets, it goes to the player with the lowest remaining doublet (1 point).

For example, in diagram 9, Player One scores 2 points for the initial doublet. Player Two's 2-1 does not score, nor does Player One's 4-2. Player Two then plays the 4-1 for a double header and scores 2 points. Finally, Player One lays down the 4-4 and gets 2 points for the doublet plus 3 points for a triple header. The game is normally played to 15 points. Strategically, it is important to try to play doublets so as to score triple headers. Also, one should keep track of the number of times each type of end has been played, in order to know the potential for future matches.

Variations

Since Bergen is a matching game, it can be played using children's picture dominoes. A change in the awarding of the game point in a blocked game would be needed; it might, for example, be given to the player with the fewest remaining dominoes.

BLIND HUGHIE

NUMBER OF PLAYERS: Two to five

EQUIPMENT: One set of double 6's (28 tiles/bones)

DIFFICULTY: A game of pure luck

DURATION: Around 30 minutes

Diagram 10:

Blind Hughie

In this game hands are revealed one tile at a time. No one gets to see his hand before play starts.

Setup

Players draw for the right to go first, with the highest domino winning. The tiles are replaced and the set mixed up and rearranged; they are then divided equally among players, with leftovers (one in a three-player game and three in a five-player game) set aside. Keeping the tiles facedown, players arrange their hands in a vertical row, as shown in diagram 10. In three- and five-player games, one of the leftover tiles is played to start the layout, while in two- and four-player games, the first player turns up and lays out a tile to start.

Playing the Game

After an initial tile has been set—by either method—the first player turns up the top tile in her row. If it matches an open end, she plays it; if not, she turns it facedown again and moves it to the bottom of her row. If the unplayable tile is a doublet, it is moved to the bottom of the row, but remains faceup.

Winning the Game

Play continues clockwise until a player gets rid of all his tiles, or until the game is blocked.

Scoring

Scoring is the same as for basic dominoes, and games are usually played to 50 or 100 points.

FIVE UP

NUMBER OF PLAYERS: Four; two pairs of partners

EQUIPMENT: One set of double 6's (28 tiles/bones)

DIFFICULTY: Scoring is too complicated for young children

DURATION: About 20 to 30 minutes

Although the rules are simple, playing well is challenging.

Setup

Partners are determined by drawing dominoes. The two who draw tiles with the highest number of spots play together, and the individual who draws the very highest tile starts the game. After the draw, the dominoes are rearranged and players draw five-tile hands. The remaining dominoes comprise the tileyard, from which players draw when they cannot play. The last tile in the tileyard cannot be drawn, and a player without a play must pass. (In the two-player game, the last two tiles must remain in the tileyard.)

Playing the Game

The starting player may set any tile to begin. Play then continues clockwise, with players matching ends while trying to make the ends add up to multiples of five as often as possible. As in All Fives, a player must call out a score before the next person's turn begins, or an opponent can claim it. The hand ends when one player has no more tiles in hand and calls 'Domino!' or when the game is blocked. In a blocked game, the team (or individual, in the two-player game) whose remaining tiles contain the fewest total spots wins.

A special feature of Five Up concerns doublets. After a doublet is laid down, crosswise—as in most domino

History

Dominoes are probably a Chinese invention, thought to have been based on dice, which came into China from India in ancient times. Each domino displays a pattern of spots that corresponds to one of the possible outcomes of rolling a pair of dice (with the exception, of course, of the blanks, which might correspond to the throw of a single die—but there is no analog in dice for the double blank).

There is some debate about the relationship between the Chinese dominoes game and the European version. Some historians believe that the game of dominoes, if not the concept of the tiles, was invented in the West. The first record of dominoes games comes from Italy in the early 18th century. The term domino is likely associated with hooded cloaks, called dominoes, worn by cathedral canons in France and Italy. They were black on the outside and white on the inside.

Diagram 11: Five Up

games—and another tile is played against the open side, the doublet becomes a *spinner*. Subsequent tiles may be played against the two crosswise ends of the doublet, creating two additional open ends. Any doublet played may become a spinner, adding more and more ends. When determining whether or not the ends add up to a multiple of five, all of the ends must be counted, although the crosswise end of a spinner against which no tile has yet been played is not considered for scoring purposes.

Scoring

Multiples of five made during play earn points based on the multiplier, so that a total of five scores 1 point (5 x 1), a ten scores 2 points (5 x 2), a 15 scores 3 points (5 x 3), and so on. At the close of a hand, the winner(s) earn points based on the spots remaining in the hand(s) of the opponent(s). Points are again based on the number of multiples of five, so the first step in scoring is to round the raw number of spots up or down to the nearest such multiple. For example, a raw total of 12 is rounded to 10, as is a raw total of 8. Since 10 contains two fives, either raw score would end up being worth 2 points to the winner(s). The partners' game is played to a score of 61, and the two-player game to a score of 21.

For example, in diagram 11, the first player lays the 3-1, and the second player lays 1-1. scoring 1 (3+1+1). The third player lays 1-2 and also scores 1 (3+2). Note that the ends of the spinner, 1-1, are only considered for scoring once a tile has been played to them.

Strategy

Doing well at Five Up requires close attention, strategic knowledge, and the astute use of *kickers,* tiles which automatically score after an opponent scores in certain circumstances. These include:

- After an opponent scores, the double blank, double 5, and 5-blank played anywhere will score.
- After an opponent scores, the 1-2 played on the double 1, the 2-4 played on the double 2, and 3-6 played on the double 3 will make the same score as them on the next play.
- After an opponent scores, the following will also score, although at a lower level: 3-1 on a double 3, 4-3 on a double 4, 6-2 on a double 6.

Always be aware of the total of the open ends in order to avoid missing a scoring opportunity.

Playing a doublet matching a tile in hand insures that a player will be able to play in the next round.

MAH-JONGG

NUMBER OF PLAYERS: Four is best, but three or two can also play

EQUIPMENT: 144 tiles, two dice, counters, wind discs, racks to support the tiles

DIFFICULTY: Mah-Jongg takes about an hour to learn

DURATION: From 5 minutes to an hour for a hand. The game can also be played for an entire evening

This enthralling game, invented in China, has an elaborate scoring method and requires a lot of equipment. There are similarities in aim to gin rummy (see page 90), but with many twists and restrictions. Players try to collect sets of three different kinds of tiles. The game works best with four players, though two or three can play. Players collect sets of tiles, some of which earn higher scores than others, and try to be first to complete a hand, a Mah-Jongg.

Tiles

There are two basic kinds of tiles (see diagram 12; there are 136 tiles in all):

- **Honor tiles:** These are Dragons—four each of Green, Red, and White; and Winds—four each of North, South, East, and West.
- **Suit tiles:** There are three suits: Bamboos (also called Bams or Sticks), Circles (also called Dots or Balls), and Characters (also called Cracks). Within each suit are tiles numbered 1 to 9—four of each number. The 1's and 9's of each suit are called *head tiles,* while the rest are called *middle tiles.*

Sets

Three different kinds of sets can be collected. These are:

- **Chow:** A sequence of three, and only three, tiles in the same suit, such as the 4-5-6 Circles
- **Pung:** Three identical honor or suit tiles
- **Kong:** Four identical honor or suit tiles

Four sets plus one pair form a complete hand.

Setup

Players' positions at the table correspond to compass points, and are named North, South, East, and West Wind. Each position has a matching wind disc (labeled N, S, E, and W) that is placed beside the appropriate player. Since East Wind goes first and has the chance of earning extra bonuses, the player rolling the highest score with a pair of dice becomes East Wind; other players assume Wind names corresponding to their relative positions around the table.

Next, each player takes 2,000 points' worth of counters: two 500-point counters, nine 100-point counters, eight 10-point counters, and ten 2-point counters. These will be used to pay other players at the end of the game. Finally, the 136 Mah-Jongg tiles are turned facedown and shuffled. Each player draws 34 tiles and, leaving them facedown, stacks them into a straight wall two tiles deep and 17 tiles long. Using tile racks, players push their walls toward the middle

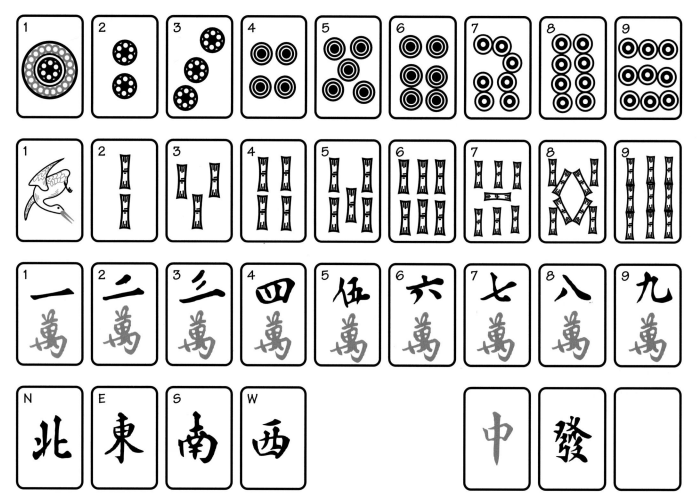

Diagram 12: Mah-Jongg tiles

Preparing to play

Drawing tiles is preceded by the opening of the wall (see diagram 12), a two-step procedure. First, East Wind throws the dice and counts counterclockwise around the four sides of the wall, beginning with her own side, until the sum on the dice is reached. The side she stops on is the one that will be opened.

Then the player on this side rolls the dice, adds the sum of this second throw to that of the previous throw, and counts tiles from right to left along the top row of her wall (turning the corner to the next side if the total is more than 17), stopping when the total is reached. The tile she stops

of the table until they come together, forming a square, called the *wall*.

on, and the one beneath it, are removed, creating a gap, and are placed facedown on top of the wall to the right of the opening. These top tiles are called *loose tiles*. (When the loose tiles have been drawn, they are replaced by the two tiles in the stack to the right of the opening.)

Drawing hands

The actual process of drawing hands is begun by East Wind, who takes the two stacks of tiles immediately to the left of the opening. South Wind takes the next two stacks to the left, and players continue to take turns drawing four tiles at a time until each has 12. Then each player takes a 13th tile, continuing to move left, and finally East Wind takes a 14th. At this point, players examine and arrange their tiles, placing them so they cannot be seen by others.

Playing the Game

Players try to create the required sets and pair by drawing and discarding tiles. During the game, hands remain one tile short of complete. The last step is to match a 14th tile with the rest, thus completing the hand. East Wind begins by discarding one tile faceup in the middle of the table, calling its name aloud. Play moves counterclockwise. Players in turn draw a tile from the wall, starting from the opening and moving left or, if appropriate, picking up a discarded tile instead. After a tile is taken in by either means, another must be discarded into the middle and called aloud, as long as the hand is incomplete.

Game rules

Only the tile just discarded may be picked up, and then only if it is one that completes a set, or an entire hand. The player retrieving a tile

Diagram 13: Opening the wall

must announce what it will be used for (for example, Pung, Kong, Chow, or Mah-Jongg), and must lay the completed set faceup on the table. A player may Pung, Kong, or Mah-Jongg a tile out of turn, but may only Chow a tile if it is discarded by the player to her immediate left. If more than one player wants a discarded tile, Mah-Jongg has precedence over all others, and a Pung or Kong has precedence over a Chow.

Sets that are laid on the table constitute a player's *exposed hand*. The remainder of the hand is the *concealed hand*. Sets in the concealed hand generally score double.

Strategy

Special considerations apply when a player declares a Kong. First, it cannot be declared in the same turn as a Chow or Pung. Secondly, since a Kong requires one more tile than the other sets, for every Kong laid down an extra tile must be added to the hand to keep it one tile short of complete. The extra tile is drawn from the loose tiles on top of the wall. When holding a concealed Kong—it need not be declared—a player may wish to save it, playing one of its tiles instead in a Chow. The extra tile requirement also means that a player cannot complete a hand by completing a Kong, because a loose tile must be drawn. As a  routine matter, if a wall tile is drawn that converts an exposed Pung to a Kong, it is played and a loose tile taken before discarding.

Winning the Game

A player who completes her hand immediately declares Mah-Jongg and lays down her concealed hand. In addition to the usual methods, a hand may be completed by 'stealing' the fourth tile in the exposed Kong of a player who made the Kong from a previously exposed Pung. Stealing the fourth scores bonus points.

If no one declares Mah-Jongg before the wall is down to its last 14 tiles, the game is a draw. No one scores any points, tiles are reshuffled, and the hand begins again with the same player as East Wind.

Traditionally, Mah-Jongg games are played in rounds corresponding to the number of players at the table. After each round, the wind discs are passed to the right, so that each player is East Wind one time.

Scoring

The total value of a hand includes basic scores for exposed and concealed combinations, and doubling scores based on the honor tiles. The value of the winning hand is enhanced by bonus scores as well. In addition, there are optional bonus discs and special limit hands that can increase total scores dramatically.

Each player pays the winner the value of the winning hand in counters. (Counters are like chips in poker, but they are not essential; a scorepad can be used instead.) If the winner is East Wind, the value is doubled. The loser with the highest score receives from the other losers counters equal to the difference between her score and theirs. The loser with the second highest score also receives counters from the lowest-scoring loser.

SCORES FOR COMBINATIONS	Exposed Points	Concealed Points
Three of a kind (middle tiles of a suit)	2	4
Three of a kind (head tiles of a suit)	4	8
Three of a kind any Winds	4	8
Three of a kind any Dragons	4	8
Four of a kind (middle tiles of a suit)	8	16
Four of a kind (head tiles of a suit)	16	32
Four of a kind any Winds	16	32
Four of a kind any Dragons	16	32
Pair of any Dragons or player's own Wind	2	2

BONUS SCORES FOR WINNER	Points
Mah-Jongg (winning the hand)	20
Drawing last tile (rather than a discard) (not used with next bonus)	2
Last tile was a loose tile	10
No score other than Mah-Jongg	10
No Chows	10
Stealing fourth to win	10
Winning with last drawable tile from the wall	10

DOUBLES OF TOTAL SCORES	
Three or four of own Wind	Double once
Three or four Dragons	Double once
Only one suit, plus Winds and Dragons	Double once
Hand all one suit	Double three times
Hand entirely honor tiles (no suits)	Double three times

Flowers and Seasons

There are eight optional Flower and/or Season tiles numbered to correspond to the four wind discs. They do not participate in sets. When a Flower or Season is drawn it is laid faceup. The player then draws a replacement tile from the last 14 tiles of the wall (which are otherwise not used). A Flower or Season that corresponds to the wind disc of another player counts 4 points (for the player with the tile). Drawing one's own Flower or Season doubles the total score; drawing a second of one's own calls for another doubling. If a player collects all four of her own Flower or Season tiles, the total score is doubled three times.

Limit hands

Certain hands score the maximum number of points, the limit (300 or 500 points). These include:

- **Hand from heaven:** East Wind draws a Mah-Jongg in her first 14 tiles.
- **Snake:** A player draws 1 through 9 of a suit plus one of each of the Winds and any pair, during the initial draw.
- **13 hidden orphans:** Each of the four Winds, the three Dragons, and one head tile from each suit in the concealed hand. Any matching tile completes the hand.
- **Three great scholars:** A Pung or Kong of one of the Dragons, plus any Chow or Pung and a pair.
- **Hand from earth:** A player other than East Pungs East's first discard for Mah-Jongg (scores half the limit).
- **Seven twins:** Any seven pairs (scores half the limit).
- **Lucky 13:** A player who draws a set hand but cannot complete it with the first discard may declare the hand before the first draw, then wait to get the last necessary tile (scores one-third the limit).

MUGGINS (see ALL FIVES)

Race Games

In all race games the object is to be first past the post—there is nothing to kill or capture and no territory to be gained. Classic race games include Backgammon and Ludo.

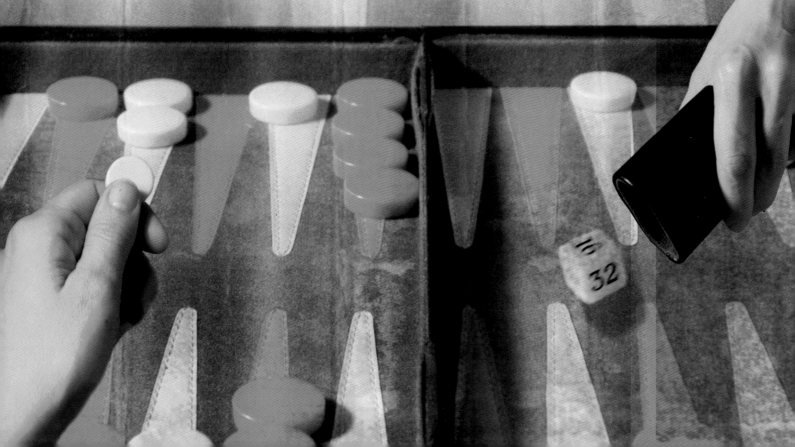

BACKGAMMON

NUMBER OF PLAYERS: Two

EQUIPMENT: Board, 15 black pieces and 15 white pieces, four dice, a doubling cube

DIFFICULTY: Although the basic moves are easy, the game can become highly complex

DURATION: A friendly game takes about 10 minutes, but the game can continue for much longer

Backgammon is essentially a simple race to move the pieces around the board toward the inner table and end up with no remaining pieces. This ancient game dates back some 5,000 years and waxes and wanes in popularity—not so long ago it was the preferred pastime of the 'jet set.' The game originated in the Middle East but was disapproved of by the church in the West for its associations with gambling. It is fast and can be strategically complex. Despite the chance factor of rolling dice, the best player wins most of the time.

Setup

Players start with 15 pieces each, arranged as in diagram 1. Positions of black and white mirror each other, occupying several of the board's *points*—the sawtooth pattern. White is assumed to be sitting opposite points 1–12; Black is on the board's other side, opposite points 13–24. The object is to move all pieces around and off the board—the phrase in backgammon is *bear them off.*

Moving

White's pieces travel counterclockwise, ultimately leaving the board at point 1. Black's move in the other direction, bearing off at point 24. Points 1-6 make up White's *inner table;* 7-12 are the *outer table.* (Correspondingly, points 19-24 are Black's inner table; 13-18 the outer.) Though all pieces start on the board, some may be knocked off in the course of play: Whites can only re-enter at point 24; Blacks at point 1.

Playing the Game

Both players roll a single die. The higher die goes first, but using the combined result of the starting throw. (Clearly, the game cannot begin if together they roll a double; they must try again.) On subsequent turns players roll two dice. Pieces move a number of points as determined by each die taken separately or both together: Having rolled a 6-2, White could move one piece 8 points, or one of them 6 points and another

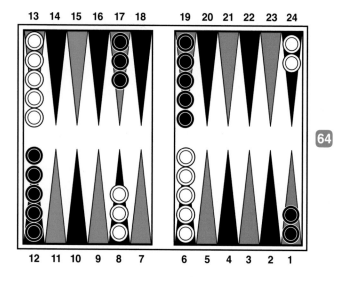

Diagram 1: Backgammon starting position

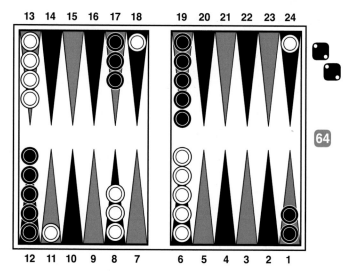

Diagram 2: The board after White's first move

2, as in diagram 2. Note, however, that the longer move is really two moves added together, one after the other, both of which must be allowable moves of 2 and 6.

Pieces may not land on a point already occupied by two or more opposing pieces; that point is, temporarily at least, *closed*. Neither can a closed point be an intermediate landing place for any leg of a multiple move: in the 6-2 roll discussed above, a piece must have a valid landing at 6 or 2 before using the remainder for a total of 8.

Dice doubles, called *doublets* in backgammon, are bonus throws, worth twice their face value. A doublet 5, for example, counts as four 5's; the throw can be allotted to different pieces as four moves of 5 points each, or a 10-point move and two 5's, or two 10's, or one long 20-point reach.

Should a piece land on a point occupied by a single opponent, the opponent is sent to the *bar*—the open strip running across the middle of the board. (Unprotected, lone pieces are referred to as *blots*.) Remember that 'landing' includes any intermediate points touched in the course of a long, multiple move. It is conceivable, rolling a doublet, that one piece could hit four blots in a single move, sending them all to the bar. A blot must re-enter the game, on any usable throw, before any other move is allowed to that player. (An unusable throw is one that lands a re-entering piece only on closed points; if no move is possible, the turn passes without any advance.)

Naturally, players would prefer to close all their points and avoid leaving blots in an opponent's path. This is a chief consideration in deciding how to distribute moves among the various pieces, given choices imposed by the dice. There is, by the way, no limit to how many 'friendly' pieces (that is, pieces of the same colour) can accumulate on a closed point.

Bearing off

Once all the pieces are stationed somewhere within a player's inner table, they can be taken off. Pieces can exit either by an exact throw or by a larger number, but only if the dice decree

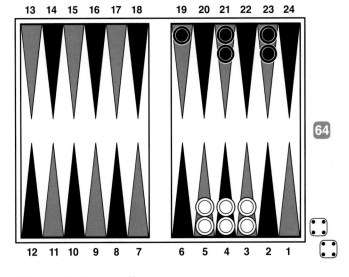

Diagram 3: Bearing off

a move that is bigger than any piece can utilize. The conditions are clarified in diagram 3: If White rolls 4-4, he will bear off the pieces at point 4, an exact exit, but must move the two pieces at point 5 up to point 1. Pieces at point 3 cannot bear off because legal moves are available to those at point 5. Another doublet, of 3 or more, would allow White to finish the job. Black, rolling 6-3, has a choice. The piece at 19 could bear off and one of those at 21 advance to 24; or the hindmost, at 19, can move 3, making a piece at 21 eligible to bear off on the 6. (It is always the rearmost that are first to bear off when allocating parts of an oversized throw.)

If, as often happens, a blot is sent to the bar while a player is bearing off, the process halts until all pieces have once again reached the inner table.

Scoring

The first to finish bearing off wins the game, usually scored as 1 point. If an opponent has not yet borne off a piece when the game ends, called a *gammon*, the winning score is doubled. In the much rarer event that the loser still has a piece in the winner's inner table, a *backgammon*, the score is tripled.

The potential to score is spiced up in backgammon with a *doubling die*. Its six faces display successive doublings—the powers of 2, up to 64. It is placed on the bar at the game's beginning, with '64' showing. Either player, perceiving an advantage in the way the game is going, may pick it up in the course of a turn and offer it, with '2' upturned, to the other. If accepted, all points at stake in the game are doubled. To refuse is to forfeit, but at an undoubled loss of points. In accepting the challenge, a player takes the die; if the game later seems to trend in his direction, he may in turn offer it up, this time with '4' exposed, quadrupling the stakes. Among experienced players doublings and redoublings seldom reach '8' and almost never '16.'

CHUTES AND LADDERS® (SNAKES AND LADDERS)

NUMBER OF PLAYERS: Two or more

EQUIPMENT: Board, a die, four counters in different colours

DIFFICULTY: Easy for children

DURATION: About 15 to 20 minutes

A children's game for two or more players, Chutes and Ladders, known as Snakes and Ladders in the United Kingdom, takes place on a 10 x 10 checkerboard, with squares numbered 1 to 100. Scattered among these are approximately ten chutes and ten ladders—of varying lengths—connecting distant squares to each other.

Moving

Each player attempts to move his own coloured counter from square 1 to square 100 by rolling the die, though a piece cannot enter the board until its owner rolls a 6. If a piece lands at the base of a ladder, it has the privilege of ascending to the square at the top of the ladder. If a piece lands at the top of a chute, however, it suffers the misfortune of sliding down it. Additionally, if a piece lands on a square occupied by an opponent, the opponent is sent back to square 1.

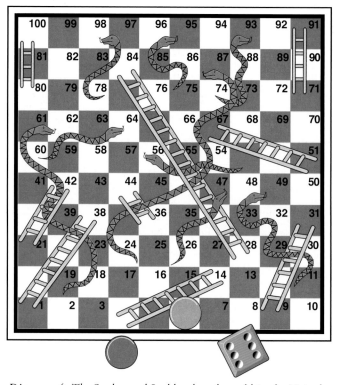

Diagram 4: The Snakes and Ladders board as sold in the United Kingdom; in the United States children play Chutes and Ladders.

Winning the Game

The object of the game is to land exactly on square 100. If you throw too high a number, you must complete the move by going backward. For example, if you throw a 5 from square 97, you will have to move to square 100 and then back to 98. The first player to land exactly on square 100 is the winner.

FOX AND GEESE

NUMBER OF PLAYERS: Two

EQUIPMENT: Board and 14 or 18 pieces

DIFFICULTY: Requires cunning strategy

DURATION: About 20 to 30 minutes

Moving in turn around the board, the 'fox' tries to capture the 'geese,' while at the same time the geese try to surround the fox.

Setup

In this game, 14 pegs or counters are laid out on a board, as shown in diagram 5—one fox (marked in black) and 13 geese (marked in red). One player is the fox and the other represents the geese.

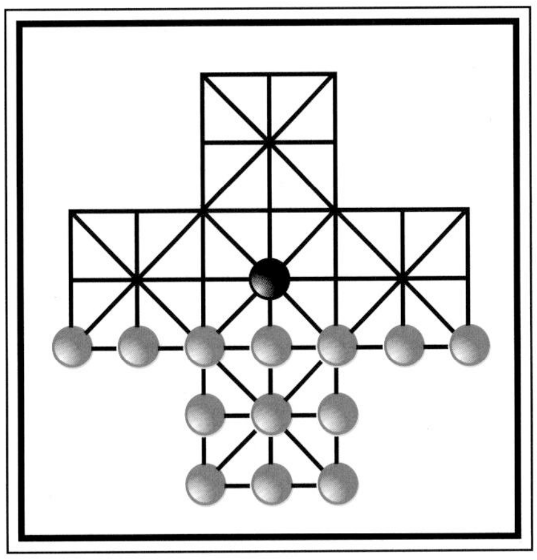

Moving

Both fox and geese can move one square at a time along any of the lines on the board: forward, backward, horizontally, vertically, or diagonally.

Playing the Game

The fox can capture an adjacent goose by leaping over it and landing on a vacant square. Also, as in checkers, it is possible for the fox to capture several geese in one turn through a series of such leaps. The geese, on the other hand, cannot leap over themselves or the fox, but must attempt to crowd the fox into a corner until he finds it impossible to move.

Winning the Game

If the geese manage to crowd the fox into a corner, they win the game, whereas the fox wins either by making it to the geese's end of the board or by capturing so many geese that there are not enough left to trap it.

Variations

Seventeen Geese

Another version of this game, shown in diagram 6, uses 17 geese, whose superior quantity is balanced by the fact that they are not allowed to move either backward or diagonally. In some variations, the fox is not allowed to move diagonally either, but this is usually seen as giving an undue advantage to the geese.

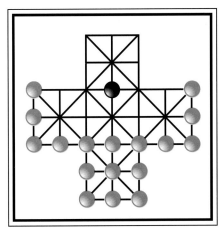

Diagram 5: Fox and Geese starting position (14 pieces)

Diagram 6: Fox and Geese starting position (18 pieces)

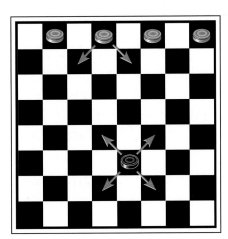

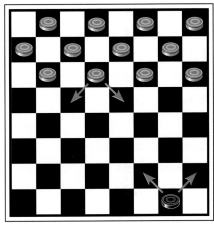

Diagram 7: Cows and Leopards starting position

Diagram 8: Wolf and Goats starting position

Cows and Leopards

This version of Fox and Geese originated in Sri Lanka and is played on the black squares of an 8 x 8 checkerboard (draughtboard).

To start with, the four cows (white checkers) are placed on the back row and the leopard (a black checker) on any black square on the board (see diagram 7).

The cows can move one diagonal square forward on any turn, much like uncrowned pieces in checkers (draughts). The leopard, on the other hand, can move two diagonal squares either forward or backward. Neither piece can leap or capture.

The cows win if they are able to hem in the leopard, leaving him without a legal move. The leopard wins if he breaks through the line of cows and reaches their end of the board.

Wolf and Goats

This game is nearly identical to Cows and Leopards, with a few important exceptions.

First, there are 12 goats rather than four cows, and they are placed on the back three rows of the checkerboard as in diagram 8. The wolf, like the leopard, can be placed on any available black square.

The goats move in exactly the same way as the cows—one diagonal square forward. The wolf can move one diagonal square backward or forward, and it can also capture goats by leaping over them. Just as with the cows, goats try to hem in the wolf, leaving him without a legal move, while the wolf tries to make it to the goats' end of the board.

Fox and Geese Solitaire

This is an enjoyable game for a single player that uses the standard Fox and Geese board. At the beginning, all the holes are filled with pegs except for the one in the middle, as

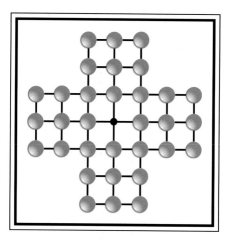

Diagram 9: Fox and Geese Solitaire starting position

shown in diagram 9. Unlike the other variations only one type of move is allowed: a leap over an adjacent piece into a vacant spot, removing that piece from the board. Leaps can be horizontal or vertical, but not diagonal.

The object of the game is to remove all the pieces from the board except one—a frustratingly difficult task to achieve.

HALMA

NUMBER OF PLAYERS: Two to four

EQUIPMENT: Board and 64 pieces

DIFFICULTY: A game of skill

DURATION: About 1 hour

Setup

Players try to be the first to cross the board to the opposite camp in a series of moves, jumps, and leaps. The game's unusual name is from the Greek word for leap, and it dates back to the 1880s.

Halma is played on a 16 x 16 checkerboard with camps marked in each corner. Two, three, or four players can compete.

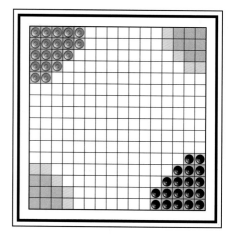

Diagram 10: Halma starting position (two players)

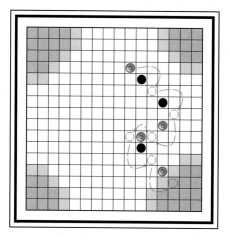

Diagram 11: The ladder technique in Halma

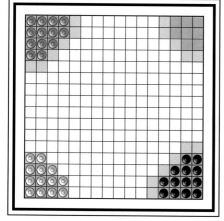

Diagram 12: Halma starting position (three players)

In the two-player version, each side has 19 pieces, which are initially arranged as shown in diagram 10. The three- or four-person version is described below.

Moving

A piece in Halma (chips or counters can be used) can move in one of two ways: a step or a jump. In a step, the piece moves one square in any direction—vertically, horizontally, diagonally, backward, or forward—and stops there. In a jump, the piece jumps over an adjacent piece to land on a vacant square beyond it. As in checkers, one jump can be immediately followed by an unlimited number of successive jumps in a single turn, as long as the moves are legal. However, in Halma, the pieces that are jumped over suffer no ill consequences and, indeed, can be pieces belonging to either side—it makes no difference. In neither case is any piece removed from the board.

Playing the Game

The object of Halma is to move all of your pieces into the squares of your opponent's camp. The first player to do so is the winner.

Strategy

The easiest way to do this is to construct 'ladders,' as shown in diagram 11, by which a piece can quickly traverse the board in a single move. Be warned, however, that your own ladders can also be used by your opponent, so the game is trickier than it looks.

Variations

Three or four players

In a three- or four-player game, each player is given 13 pieces, as shown in diagram 12. Game play moves in a clockwise direction, and the object is exactly the same: to occupy the camp in the opposite corner of the board. In a three-player game, the player moving toward the empty

Diagram 13: *Chinese Checkers starting position (two players)*

corner has a slight disadvantage, so players should switch positions on each round.

Chinese Checkers

Despite its exotic title, the variation known as Chinese Checkers was invented in the United States by J. Pressman & Co. around 1880. At first the game was called Hop Ching Checkers, but over the years the name became more informal. It is basically a version of Halma, but it is played on a board in the shape of a six-pointed star, as shown in diagram 13.

Chinese Checkers can be played by two to six people. In a two-player game, each player has 15 pieces, which start off at opposite points of the star. In a three-player game, opponents have only ten pieces, which are arranged so that each is headed for an empty point. In a four-to-six player game, also played with ten pieces each, the arrangements and target points are agreed and chosen at the start—the middle becomes a confused mob, with progress uncertain.

Otherwise, game play is identical to Halma. Pieces can move in either steps or jumps, and the winner is the first player to complete a cross-board migration and occupy the intended destination point of the star.

LUDO

NUMBER OF PLAYERS: Two to four

EQUIPMENT: Board, 16 counters (chips), one die

DIFFICULTY: Great fun for children; easy for all

DURATION: About 20 to 30 minutes

Players compete to move their counters around the board and be the first to reach the center. Ludo is a modified form of the Indian game of Pachisi, and has been sold commercially as Parcheesi®, Patchesi®, and Homeward Bound®.

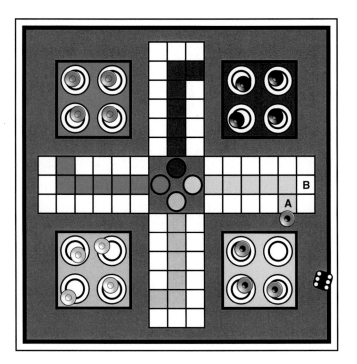

Diagram 14: Ludo starting position

Setup

The game is played with four counters per player on a cross-shaped board. In the beginning, all of the counters are kept in the players' yards, as shown in diagram 14. A counter may only enter the board when a player rolls a six, at which point it advances to position A. Thus, the game does not truly begin until the first player rolls a six, a number which, incidentally, entitles the player to another turn each time it is rolled.

Playing the Game

Once a counter is on the board, it can be advanced around the outer edge of the cross in a clockwise fashion according to the roll of the die. When a counter reaches position B, where it is protected from attack, it moves down the middle of the arm to the center of the board, where it is lifted out of play.

Strategy

Players may force enemy counters back to their yard by landing directly on top of them. If two of a player's own pieces occupy the same square, they can be piled and moved

as a single counter; however, they can also be captured as a single counter and sent back to the yard.

Two combined pieces form a block that cannot be passed or sent home except by two combined opponent pieces. Strategy-wise, it is best to get all four counters out due to the advantage of combining pieces. An additional rule to keep in mind is that three 6's in a row means the player's entire turn is forfeited.

Winning the Game

The first player to move all counters to the center of the board with the exact count is the winner.

SNAKES AND LADDERS (*see* CHUTES AND LADDERS)

Strategy Games

Intellectually challenging war games such as chess, which involve the cunning use of strategy in manipulating armies of opposing pieces, have been played since at least A.D. 600.

CHECKERS (DRAUGHTS)

NUMBER OF PLAYERS: Two

EQUIPMENT: Checkerboard and 12 pieces

DIFFICULTY: A simple game for all except very young children

DURATION: Around 10 to 30 minutes for a friendly game or two

A simple game where two players move pieces around a board and try to capture their opponent's pieces while at the same time promoting their own. Though the rules of checkers are simple, actual play may quickly lead into tangles of possibility and perplexity.

Setup

The game uses an ordinary chess board, laid out as in chess with a white square to the player's right hand. Each side starts with 12 discs, or *men,* set up in the back three ranks on black squares only (diagram 1). Players toss a coin for their colour, and black has the first move.

Playing the Game

In checkers, pieces move, one square at a time, only along the *diagonals*—the board's lighter squares have no part in the game. A piece can move only in the forward direction, at most a choice of two diagonal advances, unless it survives to reach the opposing back rank, where it is promoted, or *crowned,* a king. An additional disc, from the captured pile, is stacked atop the newly transformed piece to indicate its promoted status. Kings move by one diagonal step in any direction, forward or back.

The pieces, also called *checkers,* attempt by capture to remove opposing checkers from the board. To capture, a piece must leap, or *jump,* over an adjacent adversary and land on an empty square beyond. When presented with an opportunity, jumping is obligatory; if two different jumps or two ways of making the same jump are presented, a player chooses one. Sometimes a succession of jumps can be made in the same move; a player must continue capturing until no further jumps are possible. Promotion—to king, for example— immediately terminates a move.

The practice of *huffing*—removing a piece that has neglected to make all possible captures—is not a part of the standard game or its rules.

Winning the Game

Capturing all opposing pieces wins the game or, failing that, immobilizing the survivors, so that no move is possible for the

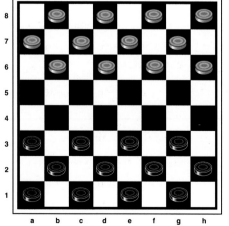

Diagram 1: Checkers starting position

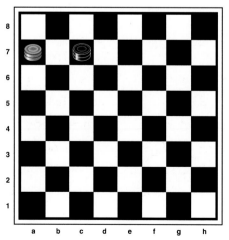

Diagram 2: Typical endgame position

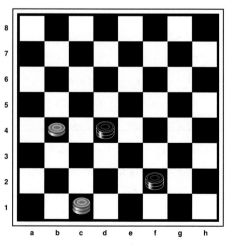

Diagram 3: Sacrifice play

opponent. However, experienced players frequently arrive at *endgames* that have no resolution: a few kings warily circling one another, without advantage to either side. Positions shown here in diagram 2 cannot be won—barring suicidal play by one side. Players can agree, at any time, to declare a game *drawn*.

Strategy

Players often look for ways of sacrificing a piece so that a crushing multiple jump results. In the example shown in diagram 3, Black throws a king in front of an advancing White piece (d4-c3; b4 x d2, which translates as d4 to c3; d4 jumps to c3). Next, moving the remaining king to e1 leaves White with only one—ruinous—legal move, c1-b2. The game is won with the resulting double jump. (Another notation is widely used, in which the dark squares are simply enumerated 1–32 beginning at bottom left.)

But thoughtful endgame tactics cannot help if a game has become locked up in a draw, by design, from its opening. The openings in checkers have been thoroughly studied, and many of them degenerate to drawn positions. A skilled player has little edge over an enterprising novice if a game's course can be steered, with a little memorization, to stalemate. At higher levels of play, to correct for these shortcomings, specific remedies can be adopted:

- **Eleven-man-ballot:** In this convention each player starts one man short, a piece selected at random (the same one for both players) but not from the rearmost rank.

- **Three-move-ballot (or three-move restriction):** Most major tournaments use this procedure, as do many serious players of the game. Cards are prepared, each showing a three-move opening sequence (Black, White response, Black), and one is drawn at random. First one player takes Black in the prescribed opening and, in the next game, White. Both, by turns, have the same chance to discover and exploit what advantages, if any, may follow from the opening. (There are about 152

useful and legal three-move possibilities.)

So popular have various 'assists' to the opening become that playing without preselection, freely choosing a first move, is often distinguished as go-as-you-please (GAYP).

Variations
Losing (or Giveaway) Checkers

In this form of the game, otherwise identical to ordinary checkers, players actively try to lose all their pieces. Although it may sound like a simple proposition, the obligatory capture rule complicates strategy in a similar way.

Moves and their forced consequences must be sifted for a successful strategy. Making kings should, of course, be avoided; it is a good idea to empty the relatively protected back rank as quickly as possible.

In this game, creating spaces between the pieces, making them more vulnerable to multiple jumps, is preferred play. First to suffer complete annihilation—or immobility—is the winner.

Italian Checkers

This game is similar to regular checkers, but has a few differences when it comes to capturing. Other ways of playing checkers have been around for at least as long as the standard modern game. Italian Checkers dates from the 16th century or perhaps earlier.

There are several twists in this variant. To begin, the board is set with a white square to each player's left hand, though pieces occupy the black squares, as in all checkers variations except Turkish (see page 50). The player with the lighter-coloured pieces moves first.

When capturing, if two or more opportunities are presented, a player must pursue the move that takes the most pieces. (When both a king and an uncrowned man are in position to make a jump, the king must be used.) All things being equal, if a choice is left that includes jumping a king on the one hand, but only uncrowned pieces on the

other, the king must be taken—
or the most kings, should there
be several possibilities. Rules for
capture in both this and Spanish
Checkers distinguish rank in
another significant way, as well:
Only kings may take kings; mere
men may not.

Spanish Checkers

This game is played like regular
checkers. All the rules for Italian
Checkers, including the board's orientation, are in force for
Spanish Checkers, but with enhanced mobility for a king.
Indeed, this somewhat chesslike innovation has been passed
along to a whole lineage of major checkers variants.

In this game a king can move any number of open squares
along a diagonal. It can also capture in this long distance
way as long as one or more vacant squares lie beyond the
piece to be taken and as long as it is unobstructed by its
own pieces (Diagram 5). If further captures are possible
along the same or different diagonals, these must be taken—
a king's landing squares after each capture must be those
that maximize the move's total captures; otherwise the king
may come to rest, ending a move, on any free square beyond
the last capture.

The move is completed only when all possible captures
have been made. Captured pieces are not removed, however,
until the end of a move; thus it may happen a king
encounters a piece already taken, but it cannot be jumped a
second time. Extending the move in this direction is
blocked.

Pool (or German) Checkers

Pool Checkers uses the far-ranging king of Spanish
Checkers, but further endows uncrowned pieces with the
power to capture in the backward direction. With this

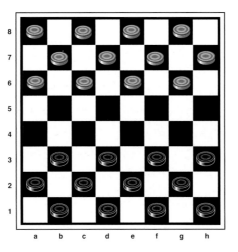

Diagram 4: Italian Checkers starting position

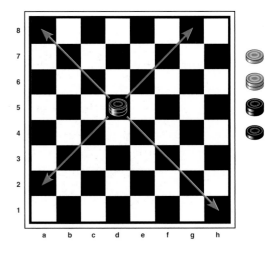

*Diagram 5: King captures in Spanish
Checkers*

ability a piece's promotion on reaching the back rank is not
automatic: Should a backward capture in the same move be
possible—and mandatory, as usual—the piece remains
uncrowned until it can return to the coronation rank and
rest there. Promoted pieces are called queens or dames in
this game, hence another common name for this variation,
Damenspiel.

Although making captures is mandatory, as in all checkers
games, a player is not forced into taking the move with the
maximum captures in any series of jumps (but all captures
must be made that follow from the selected line of play).
Captured pieces are not taken off the board until a move's
completion and may block progress in a multiple jump. The
board is positioned with a light square at each player's lower
right; the darker-coloured side moves first.

Frequently, in a strictly German variant, *a king-halt rule* is
observed. After each jump (sometimes modified after its
final capture) the king has no option but to land on the
empty square immediately beyond a capture.

Russian Checkers (Shashki)

Although set up like Pool Checkers, and using the same
basic rules, Russian Checkers differs in two ways: Upon
reaching the furthest rank a piece is unconditionally

The greatest ever

Few competitive endeavors have seen the likes of the Ohio-born mathematics professor and checkers player Marion Tinsley (1927–1995). He held the game's world title for 40 years, losing in that whole time a total of seven games. In fact, he had finished first in every tournament he entered for 45 years, but a championship was not bestowed until 1952.

In 1992, in London, Tinsley took on the most advanced checkers computer program of its day, called Chinook. By an ironic turn, it had earned the right in earlier matches to represent the rest of humanity against the champion. (This had caused some consternation for the game's governing bodies.) Chinook searched 20 moves ahead before posting a decision, reporting as well its view of the game's trend. On occasion, notwithstanding Chinook's calculation of advantage, Tinsley judged its moves flawed and proved himself the better analyst. Chinook's designer believed the program would have to look perhaps 60 moves deep to compete with the champion on an equal footing. The match ended 4-2 to Tinsley, but not before the adversaries had ground each other into 33 draws.

promoted and the move may continue—with backward captures, if the opportunity exists, on that turn. Secondly, the light-coloured side moves first.

A draw results when, with three kings remaining to one king, the player with three cannot achieve a win within 15 moves.

International (or Polish) Checkers

This game is played like conventional checkers with a few minor differences. This variant, which first appeared around 1725, has come to be known as Polish, International, or Continental Checkers and has adopted a larger board, 10 x 10 (diagram 6), as a complicating enrichment to the game. The so-called Polish variant is not well known in Poland; it probably originated in Paris, and it remains popular in French-speaking parts of Europe. International Checkers has a long tradition in the Netherlands and Russia.

International rules are the same as for Pool Checkers (see page 48), but each side starts with 20 pieces instead of 12, and the rule of maximizing captures is used. A draw results when, with three kings remaining to one king, the player with three cannot achieve a win within 13 moves. The board is oriented as in standard English Checkers, with a light square to each player's lower right, but the lighter-coloured side moves first.

For the Polish variant the rule about removing captured pieces may be modified, so that 'dead' checkers are taken off the board immediately and cannot bar progress of a move's continuation.

Canadian Checkers

Final enlargements to the checkerboard apparently occurred in Quebec, where early French-speaking settlers used a 12 x 12 array in a game that they called the Grand Jeu des Dames (literally, the great game for ladies). The rules are those of International Checkers (see page 49), but with 30 pieces on each side, arranged as shown in diagram 7.

Turkish Checkers

A radical departure from other forms of checkers, the Turkish game has no diagonal moves. Also, pieces make use of all squares, both light and dark.

Each player lines up his 16 pieces to cover his respective second and third ranks, as shown in diagram 8.

Uncrowned pieces move and capture straight ahead or laterally; jumping an adversary is mandatory when the opportunity presents itself. But only kings can move or capture backward—and they have the mobility of kings in Spanish or Pool Checkers. As in Spanish Checkers, if multiple captures are possible, the move is selected that takes the most. Captured pieces are removed immediately; they cannot block a move's continuation as they might in Spanish Checkers.

Winning in Turkish Checkers, as in all other variants, is by capturing all opposing pieces or hemming them in so that no legal move remains. There is, however, a third possibility in this game: A player loses if reduced to a single uncrowned piece.

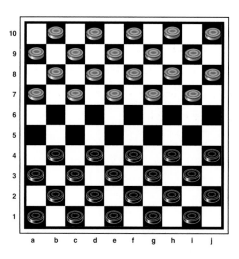

Diagram 6: Polish Checkers starting position

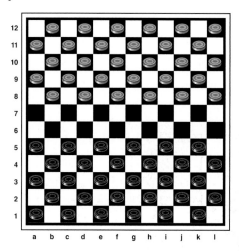

Diagram 7: Canadian Checkers starting position

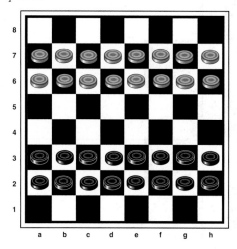

Diagram 8: Turkish Checkers starting position

CHESS

NUMBER OF PLAYERS: Two

EQUIPMENT: A checkerboard and 32 pieces

DIFFICULTY: Initially it can be difficult to master, but once that is achieved the game is enormously enjoyable and can be played by all ages

DURATION: A quick game can take 10 minutes; a longer one up to 30 minutes or an hour

Chess is a board game where players move 16 game pieces across a checkerboard to be the first to checkmate their opponent's king. This much-venerated game has absorbed the attention of devotees through the centuries. Today it is often played on a computer, with skill levels adjusted at will from beginner to expert.

Setup

A chessboard is an array of 64 alternating light and dark squares, arranged eight rows across and eight rows down. Taking as perspective a player's view when sitting at the board, horizontal rows are called *ranks*, vertical rows, *files*. The first rank should end at a player's right in a white square—otherwise the board must be rotated 90 degrees.

A standardized way of identifying squares, a coordinate-like notation, has been adopted. From the bottom left square, ranks are numbered in ascending order from 1 to 8; files proceed alphabetically left to right, A to H. Thus every square is pinpointed as the intersection of a rank and a file. It is assumed always that the lighter coloured pieces start at the bottom end of the board.

Playing the Game

Each player—referred to as White and Black—begins with 16 pieces: eight pawns, two rooks, two knights, two bishops, one queen, and one king. They are set up, as shown in diagram 9, so that the odd pieces, kings and queens, sit opposite one another. (White's queen occupies a light-coloured square; Black's a dark one.) The various pieces are given different powers of movement.

- **Pawn:** It moves only one square forward at a time, never backward. A pawn captures another piece diagonally, that is, just ahead and to the left or right one square. With a piece sitting directly in front, a pawn is blocked, unable to move until a diagonal capturing opportunity arises or the square ahead is vacated. Pawns have a special potential that often directs the course of a game or decides the outcome: Any pawn that has advanced finally to the opponent's back rank becomes instantly transformed into any other piece its owner wishes—called pawn promotion. (Usually it is nominated a queen, since that is the most powerful piece.)

- **Bishop:** The bishop moves only diagonally, through any unobstructed distance, forward or backward. Since one bishop necessarily begins on a light square and the other on a dark one, the board's diagonal confines them to squares of one colour—a white bishop and a black bishop. Together with the knights, bishops make up the game's minor pieces

- **Knight:** This is the oddest of chess moves, consisting of a straight one-square shift plus a diagonal one. The whole

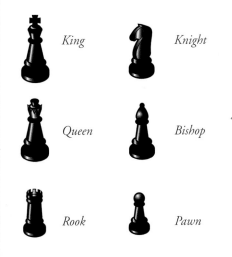

Diagrams 9 and 10: Chess starting position and chess pieces

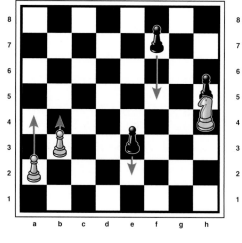

Diagram 11: Pawns in action

Diagram 12: The bishop in action

one square at a time. There is, however, a singular restriction in the king's case, that it may not move to a square—even though open—that lies in the path, the control, of an opposing piece. The king cannot be taken; the object of the game is to box it in, so that it is both exposed to capture and has nowhere to turn.

Scoring

As a rule of thumb, for judging the advantage of exchanging one or several

effect is a short L-shaped path, allowable in any direction (diagram 13). The knight cannot be obstructed; it may leap over other pieces.

- **Rook:** A rook moves straight through any unobstructed distance along the ranks and files, forward or backward, side to side (diagram 14). Along with the queen, it is one of the major pieces.

- **Queen:** This, the most powerful piece, combines the mobility of a bishop and a rook. Any diagonal or straight move, forward or backward, is allowed the queen (diagram 15).

- **King:** The king may move in any direction, but only

pieces for another, the pieces may be thought of as having the following relative values:

- Pawn = 1
- Knight = 3
- Bishop = 3
- Rook = 5
- Queen = 9

But these are only a rough guide. For example, having the two bishops, as against an opponent's bishop and rook, is usually reckoned an advantage even though in both cases the relative point sum is 6. And any piece occupying a strong, threatening position is obviously more valuable than if hemmed in or isolated at the edge of the board.

Diagram 13: The knight in action

Diagram 14: The rook in action

Diagram 15: The queen in action

Moves

White always moves first. The rules require that if you touch a piece, you must move it; and once a move has been made, it cannot be taken back. (A player may, however, touch and position a piece, saying *'j'adoube,'* 'I adjust,' beforehand.) Between friends these rules are often not strictly observed.

Capturing

All pieces capture opposing pieces in the same way, that is, by moving onto the square occupied by an opposing piece, whereupon the opposing piece is deemed taken and removed from the board.

Special Moves

Over time, two shortcuts have been adopted, as a convenience, to speed the opening stages of the game; one concerns initial pawn moves, the other aids the king in reaching early on a place of relative safety.

- **Initial pawn move:** Any pawn, on its first move only, may advance either one or two squares straight ahead. This two-square option can and does lead to positions in which a pawn seems to avoid capture by an opposing pawn—simply rushing past that square where it would have been in peril. When such a situation arises, an

opposing pawn is allowed, on its next turn only, the option of taking *en passant.* That is, it moves diagonally and captures on the square where the other pawn would have landed had it not been pushed forward the extra square (see diagram 16, where only the relevant pawns have been illustrated). The *en passant* rule is restricted in that it applies only to pawns, only after a two-square initial move, and only as an immediate reply by an opposing pawn.

- **Castling:** A king may, once in the course of game, exercise its option to *castle.* The castling move takes the king two squares to the side, either right or left, and brings the rook on that side across the king, to rest beside it (diagram 17). (Liberating the rooks, also called *castles,* from their remote corner positions had led, in centuries past, to laborious maneuvering. In one stroke, castling brings a rook past the king and more quickly into the thick of things.) A few conditions must be met, however, before castling is possible: The king and rook, on the chosen castling side, must not yet have moved, there can be no obstructing pieces between them along the rank, and the king cannot be in check nor cross a square, 'move through check,' controlled by an opposing piece.

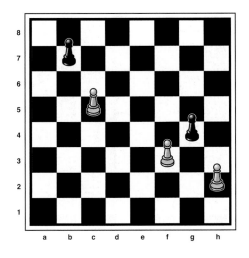

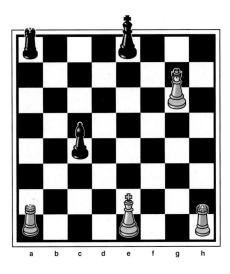

Diagram 16: The en passant *rule*

Diagram 17: Castling

Diagram 18: Exceptions to castling

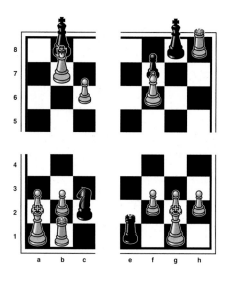

Diagram 19: Four possible checkmating positions

Check and checkmate

A king is in check when an opposing piece controls the square on which the king sits. Check must be countered immediately. Three responses are possible—moving the king out of check to an uncontrolled square; taking the piece that has put the king in check, or blocking the check by interposing another piece between the king and checking piece. (Remember, though, that check from a knight cannot be blocked.) If none of these solutions is possible, if the king is in check and has no legal move or protection available, the situation is *checkmate*, the end of the game.

Stalemate and draws

It may happen that the only possible moves left to a player would place the king in check. This condition is called *stalemate*, and the game is considered drawn. Draws may occur in other ways, too:

- **By agreement:** When players judge their positions and advantage to be equal, perhaps leading with steady play to insufficient material, one may offer a draw to the other.

Deep Blue

It is known, from a key mathematical result of game theory, that a best-possible chess strategy exists. But there is, as yet, no way of actually finding it, so that no one knows whether chess unveiled, like a hypercomplex form of tic-tac-toe, should result in a win for White, for Black, or in a tie. Meanwhile, computers have been turned loose on the game, allowing more positions and results to be evaluated than ever before.

The most famous of chess-playing computers, IBM's Deep Blue (successor to Deep Thought), looks ahead with 512 chess programs working simultaneously. It can mull several million chess positions per second. In its first match with World Champion Garry Kasparov, in February 1994, Deep Blue came off a respectable loser, having won two of the match's six games. Kasparov, incidentally, evaluates perhaps three positions per second.

After improvements Deep Blue triumphed in a 1997 rematch, 3.5 games to 2.5. (Draws count as a half-point for each player—or processor.) Before the critical game Kasparov had said he did not feel in top form; computers, of course, do not have good days and bad.

For the present it appears the human, 'intelligent' approach to the game is still a fair challenge for even the best of the 'crunchers.' In October 2002 the reigning machine, German chess 'master' Deep Fritz, tied World Champion Vladimir Kramnik 4–4.

- **50 moves:** One rule allows either player, at any time, to challenge the other to bring off checkmate within the next 50 moves, or the game is drawn.

- **Insufficient material:** Checkmate cannot be achieved without a certain minimum of force. A mere king and knight remaining, for example, have no chance of mating a lone, remaining king or king and knight. A draw is automatic.

- **Recurring position:** If attacking threats have reached a rather delicate balance, so that both players counter one another with the same move three times in a row, the

Diagram 20: The fork

Diagram 21: The pin

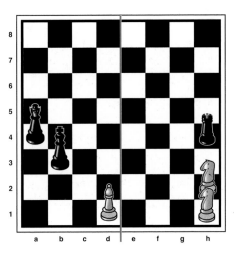

Diagram 22: The skewer

game is a draw. In a particular case, with one player driving the king into check again and again on the same series of squares, the draw is called *perpetual check.* (Obviously, it would be a player with losing prospects who hopes to arrange and spring a perpetual check and so prevent outright defeat.)

- **Time elapsed:** If a clock is used and both players have run out of their allotted time, the game is drawn.

Strategy

Chess is generally thought of as falling into three phases: the opening, middle game, and end game. In the opening, players do not seek obvious advantage or to attack; the object is economy: to move a few pawns, in concert, out of the way of the more powerful pieces on the back rank, and to place some of those pieces on important squares controlling the middle area of the board. The process, getting pieces into play, is called *development.* Thousands of openings have been described, probed, named, and filed away by chess masters. The moves are second nature for good players (and they must be players with good memories).

An opening blends, after perhaps eight to 12 moves, into the freer play of the middle game, in which opponents try to discover weaknesses and promising attacks. The middle game requires imagination and ability to look ahead into the consequences of possible lines of play.

When the attacks have spent themselves and play appears to have resolved itself into a few aims that might be achieved with the pieces remaining, the end game has been reached. Often players are calculating whose pawn can first reach the back rank to become a replacement queen; or whether a stalemate might be arranged; or indeed if checkmating possibilities still exist—after the gains and losses of the middle game.

Books by chess masters often generalize, as well, other strategic ways of viewing the game, such as theory of pawn structure and broad principles of development.

Experienced players look for ways to exploit certain situations, usually to snatch a piece at an advantageous price. The most elegant of chess tactics, the *combination,* is a planned series of moves, to each of which an opponent's reply is essentially forced, which leads inescapably to loss of material or even to checkmate. But caution is in order; a faulty plan generally results in disaster, and the deeper the combination the greater the chances of having overlooked its fatal defects.

Tactics and combinations

There are a few themes around which the plot is often hatched, and certain characteristics in a position that may be exploited. For example:

- **The fork:** It may happen that a piece directly attacks two others, or more, at the same time, 'forking' them. A protected pawn, for example, that advances to find a knight to its left and a bishop to its right will certainly get one of them, unless the opponent can counter with some equally frightening threat and forestall the loss.
- **The pin:** Here, an attacked piece is unable to move away because it would put the king in check; it has been 'pinned' to the king.
- **The skewer:** This resembles a pin, but does not involve the king. Unprotected pieces are caught along the same line of attack, presenting only the unwelcome choice of which is to be saved—for one of them is surely doomed.

Variations

Kriegspiel

This is the chess equivalent of 'Battleship,' with both players blinded in large measure to an opponent's location. Kriegspiel

will require a third participant, an umpire, who keeps track of both sides' moves and positioning.

Players are allowed to see only their own pieces; they use separate boards, out of view of one another. The umpire keeps a third, complete board, reflecting the whole state of the game. (The isolation of the opponents makes this game ideally suited to Internet play.)

Pieces act exactly as in normal chess, but each move is taken in the dark. If a move is not possible, the umpire simply says 'no,' and further attempts are made until a legal move has been accomplished. All umpire pronouncements are communicated to both players. In the course of probing and blundering across the board, players may begin to put pieces of the puzzle together.

A player, on any turn, can ask whether any pawn captures are possible. The umpire answers 'yes' or 'no.' If 'yes,' the player must then attempt at least one capture with a pawn. The umpire says 'yes' for a success, 'no' for any illegal result.

The umpire never identifies the pieces involved in a capture, but mentions only the player and the capture's location. For example: 'White has played and captured at g2.' Thus, White knows only which piece has done the capturing, and Black only the lost material's identity. One exception: When the umpire announces a capture has been made *en passant,* it will be clear to everyone that pawns were involved on both sides.

The umpire will specify the direction of a check, whether along a rank, a file, a diagonal, or by a knight; for instance, 'Black has given check along a file.' Commonly, in the case of a diagonal check, the umpire further indicates whether check has been given on a long or short diagonal segment.

Progressive Chess

In this chess variant players make a succession, or sequence, of moves in each turn. White makes one move, Black then makes two, White three, Black four, and so on. Other rules remain

Left: In a game of chess, the King can only move one square at a time.

Chess notation

Players frequently study their own past games—and those of the masters—often with comments and annotation provided by experts. Games are written down in the algebraic notation (A-H; 1-8) that replaced an older system in which the pieces, in setup order, lent names to their respective files: KB3 for third square on the king's bishop file, or QKt6 for sixth square, queen's knight file, and so on. Rather confusingly, White and Black moves were each reckoned from their own back ranks, so that, for example, White's K4 and Black's K5 were the same square.

The newer grid notation works from only one perspective, that of its origin at the board's bottom left. Only the piece and the square it lands on are given; if any confusion can result, for example, where either rook could move to the same square, the piece is compactly identified. Pawn moves specify simply the landing square. Here are some examples and special symbols:

- **Bd5 c6:** White bishop moves to d5; black pawn to c6.
- **Nxd5 Qxg2:** White knight takes the piece at d5; black queen takes at g2.
- **Rad1 Nc2+:** Rook on the a file to d1; knight to c2, giving check (+).
- **0-0 0-0-0:** White castles on king side; Black on queen side.

And some much abbreviated commentary:

!	good move	**!!**	excellent move
?	bad move	**??**	complete blunder
!?	interesting move	**?!**	dubious move

unchanged, though one addition is necessary: Giving check ends a player's turn, regardless of whether all allocated moves have been made. This is the case, at least, in the English variant. In the Italian variant, completing a turn is obligatory; if a player cannot finish an allotted sequence, stalemate results. Check in this version may occur only in the last move of a sequence.

An interesting provision of the English variant requires, in any turn, that all movable pieces be played once before any one of them can be moved for a second time; likewise for any third move, and so on. Generally, *en passant* captures are not allowed (English), or if allowed, only on the first move in a sequence (Italian).

Strategy often boils down to taking as much material as possible while trying to leave running room for the king. Pawns are promoted as in ordinary chess, but with frightening speed in this game.

Random Chess

The ritualized aspect of a chess game opening is dispensed with by setting up the pieces in a different order along the back rank. The brilliant, eccentric world champion (1972–75) Bobby Fischer promoted his own form of this variant, with the express purpose of putting thought back into the game's initial moves.

Pawns are lined up on the second rank, as usual, but some chance means is used to determine the positions of the pieces. One player, for

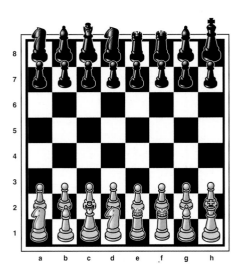

Diagram 23: Random Chess possible starting position

example, selects and holds a piece behind his back, while the other points to a rear-rank square. Positions once settled for one side are mirrored on the other. The game's only restrictions are that bishops must not be set up on the same colour and, for obvious reasons, castling is not permitted. Diagram 23 shows a possible starting lineup.

DRAUGHTS (*see* CHECKERS)

SHOGI (JAPANESE CHESS)

NUMBER OF PLAYERS: Two

EQUIPMENT: Board and 40 pieces

DIFFICULTY: Clear-thinking and strategic planning are necessary

DURATION: Around 30 minutes for a friendly game; several hours for a tournament

A game with many similarities to regular chess, Japanese chess is a thematic representation of battle—two armies facing each other across a game board—and has inspired chesslike games around the world. In Japan, the classic form is known as Shogi. It is played on a 9 x 9 board, of plain squares, with sides of 20 pieces each (diagrams 24 and 25).

Setup

Shogi pieces are flat, inscribed with rank, and identical for both sides; only the pieces' pointed ends, oriented

in the attacking direction by each player, distinguish the two forces. Though lacking any identifying colour, the two sides are usually referred to as Black and White. Black always moves first.

Playing the Game

As explained below, all but two of the pieces have the potential to be *promoted*, at which time they are flipped over to display insignia of their promoted status. Each side consists of:

- **King:** Can move one square in any direction.
- **Two gold generals:** Can move one square in any direction, except diagonally backward.
- **Two silver generals:** Can move one square diagonally in any direction or one step forward.
- **Two knights:** Can move one square to either side plus two squares forward; only a knight can leap over other pieces in the course of a move.
- **Two lances:** Can move straight ahead any distance, not sideways or backward.
- **Rook:** Can move any distance forward, back, or sideways in a straight (nondiagonal) line.
  - **Bishop:** Can move any distance forward or back along a diagonal.
  - **Nine pawns:** Can move one square forward.

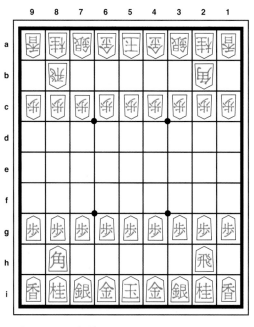

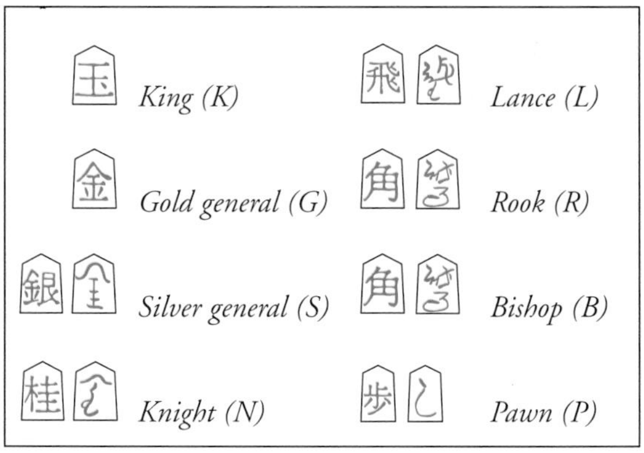

Diagram 24: Shogi starting position

Diagram 25: Shogi pieces

Promotions

All pieces but the king and gold generals are eligible for promotion after advancing into any of the last three ranks. Promotion is not obligatory, except when a piece has no further legal move: Pawns and lances must promote on reaching the last rank, knights on landing in either of the last two ranks. The option to promote exists at the completion of any move into the three-rank promotion zone, while inside, or when moving out of it.

Two kinds of *transformation* occur in promotion: Silver generals, knights, lances, and pawns all become gold generals; rooks and bishops retain their powers but acquire also the king's move.

Capturing and dropping

Pieces move, as in chess, onto the square occupied by an opposing piece, and the adversary is removed from the board. However, that is not necessarily the end of it. Pieces taken are kept aside by their captor and may become part of that army. On any turn, instead of moving, a player may *drop* one of the captured force onto any empty square—save that the piece must have at least one legal move open to it from the square on which it materializes. Other restrictions concern pawns: They cannot be dropped on any file that still has an unpromoted pawn (this results in immediate loss of the game), nor can they be dropped so as to cause immediate checkmate.

A captured promoted piece reverts to its unpromoted rank when dropped. Indeed, a piece can be dropped into the promotion zone, but it is not flipped over until the next turn

Winning the Game

Shogi ends in checkmate, exactly as in chess, or in a draw. Because captured pieces continually reappear on the board, draws almost never occur—even the rules on this subject are somewhat cloudy. Stalemate is a near mathematical impossibility, and the Shogi equivalent of 'perpetual check'

results in a loss to the checking player. Two drawing situations do occasionally arise: when both players repeat the same (nonchecking) moves four times in succession, and when both kings have advanced to the furthest rank where, with constant dropping of defenders, they have become too well protected to be checkmated. (The game may still be decided on the basis of a point count, but the procedure is not standardized.)

XIANGQI (CHINESE CHESS)

NUMBER OF PLAYERS: Two

EQUIPMENT: Board and 32 pieces

DIFFICULTY: Clever strategy is needed

DURATION: Around 30 minutes for a friendly game; several hours for a tournament

Similar to regular chess, Xiangqi (pronounced Jhangkee) uses a substantially different board. The object of the game is the same as chess, as are the rules governing check and checkmate. It is an ancient descendant of the earliest chess game—chaturanga—which originated in India. In this version the board is more directly suggestive of battle and territory: Palaces are marked off at either end and a river bisects the layout. Unlike other kinds of chess, pieces occupy the board's intersections, not the 64 open squares, so that play ranges over a grid of 90 (10 x 9) possible positions, called points.

Setup

Each side, Red and Black, starts with the 16 flat pieces shown in diagram 25, their rank identified by Chinese characters. The pieces are set up as shown in diagram 26.

Playing the Game

Red makes the first move. Pieces capture, as in chess, by moving onto a point occupied by an adversary—with the exception of cannons, explained below. The pieces, moves, and their relative values in play (expressed as points, 1 through 9) are:

- **King:** Can move one nondiagonal step at a time in any direction, but confined to its palace; it may not move onto the file in which the opposing king already sits—at the board's other end—unless some other piece, either Black or Red, lies between them on that file.

- **Two rooks (or chariots):** Can move any unobstructed distance vertically or horizontally, as in chess (9 points).

- **Two knights (or horses):** Can move one point straight followed by one diagonally, making a short 'L' in any direction; knights in Xiangqi are blocked by any piece adjacent, vertically or horizontally, from beginning a move that must pass through that point (4.5 points).

- **Two ministers (or bishops, elephants):** Can move two diagonal points at a time, but they cannot cross the river (4 points).

- **Two guards (or advisors, assistants):** Can move one diagonal point at a time, never leaving the palace (2 points).

- **Two cannons (or gunners):** A rook move, except that cannons can capture only by jumping over another piece and landing on an opposing piece. A screening piece, but only one of them, can be anywhere in the line between a cannon and its target (2 points).

- **Five pawns (or soldiers):** On their own

side of the board, they move and capture one point straight ahead; after crossing the river, one point ahead or sideways. Pawns are not promoted in Xiangqi, so that having reached the far end they may move only laterally along the last rank (before crossing the river, 1 point; after, 2 points).

Winning the Game

Check and checkmate come about just as in chess. But Xiangqi does not permit perpetual check or *perpetual chase*—driving a piece that has no other safe move back and forth to the same points, usually with the object of forestalling further play. A player initiating a perpetual check or perpetual chase must break it off within six moves or be declared the loser. Although many complex situations can arise, with detailed rules to describe them, it is generally the case that any combination of attacking pieces is barred from bringing about any recognizable form of a perpetual chase. Only kings and pawns are exempt and may undertake perpetual chase, even in concert with rooks, cannons, or knights.

Games are drawn when both players persist in initiating perpetual checks or chases; when the same pattern of moves seems likely to recur ('repeated moves,' as opposed to perpetual chase); when no further legal moves are possible or checkmate seems unobtainable with the material remaining; when king or pawn is engaged in perpetual chase; and when the game has reached a certain move count—often 100 without any pieces taken, or 400 total.

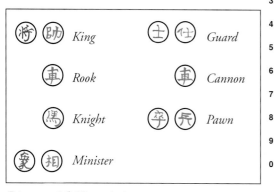

Diagram 26: Xiangqi pieces

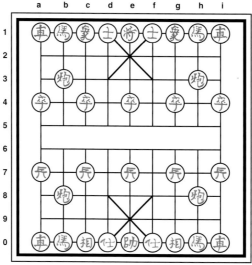

Diagram 27: Xiangqi starting position

Territorial Games

The object of territorial games, which include the ancient Chinese game of Go, is to capture a playing area or opponents' pieces, thus winning the game.

ALQUERQUE

NUMBER OF PLAYERS: Two

EQUIPMENT: Board and 24 counters (chips)

DIFFICULTY: Some forward-planning needed

DURATION: About 20 to 30 minutes

Similar to checkers, Alquerque is a board game for two that requires clever strategy to win.

Setup

The Alquerque board is a 5 x 5-point array (diagram 1), with every location connected to all those closest to it, vertically, horizontally, and diagonally. Two players each begin with 12 counters (chips), arranged as shown here. The object of the game is to remove all an opponent's counters from the board.

Playing the Game

Players may use any method to decide who will move first. Counters move by a single step to any vacant adjacent point, or by jumping. if any capture is available. To capture, a counter must be able to land on an empty point just beyond its prey—and captures are mandatory, just as in checkers/draughts. All exposed adversary counters, in whatever direction, must be taken in the course of a capture.

(Moves may zigzag around the board, like multiple jumps in checkers/draughts.) In one common usage of the rules, overlooking a possible capture results in the penalty loss of a transgressing counter; it is *huffed* from the board.

FOUR FIELD KONO

NUMBER OF PLAYERS: Two

EQUIPMENT: Board and 16 counters (in two different colours)

DIFFICULTY: Concentration needed

DURATION: About 20 to 30 minutes

Setup

Of Korean origin, Kono exists in five-field (5 x 5) and six-field (6 x 6) forms. The basic four-field game (see diagram 2), with 16 intersections (4 x 4), is played by two adversaries, each with eight counters (chips in the United States).

Playing the Game

Players may use any method to decide who will move first. The aim is to remove all of an opponent's pieces or to block them into immobility. Capturing is accomplished in only one way, by jumping over a counter of the same colour and landing on top of an opponent's counter. If no capture is possible, a counter must move along one of the board lines to an adjacent square.

GO

NUMBER OF PLAYERS: Two

EQUIPMENT: Go board, Go stones

DIFFICULTY: This simple game is fun for everyone

DURATION: About 30 to 40 minutes

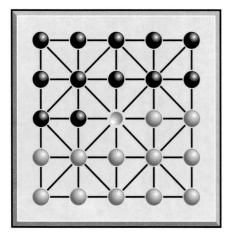

Diagram 1: Alquerque starting position

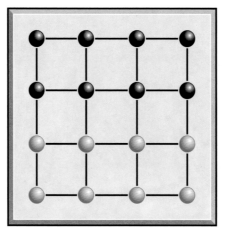

Diagram 2: Four Field Kono starting position

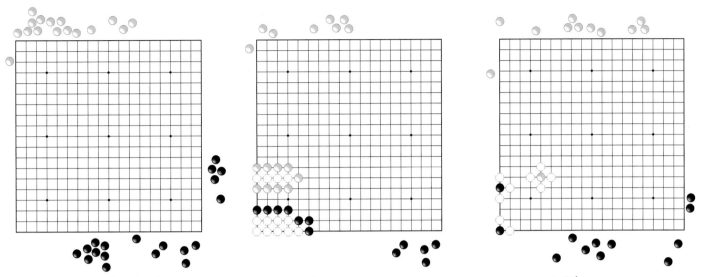

Diagram 3: *A Go board and stones*   Diagram 4: *Capturing territory*   Diagram 5: *Liberties*

Players in turn place stones on the board in an effort to surround territory. This game's rules are quickly absorbed, but beware: 'One minute to learn, a lifetime to master.' Immensely popular the world over, Go is of Chinese origin, with published copies of its rules dating back to the 7th-century Tang Dynasty.

Setup

Full-dress Go is played on a 19 x 19 square array of intersections (diagram 3), with the center point marked heavily for ease of reference, along with eight others symmetrically distributed nearer the periphery. Beginners might choose to practice on smaller boards, either 13 x 13 or 9 x 9—they result in a shorter game, too.

The Go pieces, called stones, are played onto intersections, not into the board's squares. One player is White, with lighter stones, the other Black, with darker stones. Black moves first, which is thought a slight advantage (thus the stronger player usually takes White).

Playing the Game .

By turns the two opponents play one stone at a time on any of the board's intersections, or *points*. Once played, stones remain where they are, unless captured and picked up, as shown in diagram 4. The object is to surround territory

Ancient descent

Games such as chess and Alquerque arrived in the West by way of the great Arabic civilizations around the time of Europe's Middle Ages. Chess came from India, where it was known as *chaturanga*, a battle game featuring war elephants and rajas.

Alquerque is often suggested as the parent of checkers/draughts. Although it is certainly possible, the game's principal features – a leaping capture and its mandatory nature – arose independently in many places, in many eras. Scholars guess that a more or less finished form of checkers was first played in France in the 12th century. But Alquerque has an unquestionable claim to greater antiquity: It appears recognizably incised in the roof tiles of an Egyptian temple at Kurna, dating from 1800 B.C.

Other games represented there include Nine Men's Morris and a version of Owari, from the mancala family of games, which have been played all over Africa for thousands of years.

completely, thus taking control of the areas within. Capturing stones is one way of taking territory; simply walling it off in an impregnable way is another.

Winning the Game

At the end of the game, when the last possible surrounding move has been made, when neither player can make further profitable moves, a winner is determined by adding up respective numbers of empty points within each player's various territorial holdings and subtracting the number of stones lost through capture. In practice, players usually neaten up their territories, making empty points easier to count, and then cover some of the points with their lost stones, leaving a correctly adjusted total of empty points.

Some terms

The language of Go includes many special ways of describing tactics, but understanding just a few terms is sufficient to start:

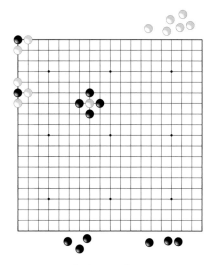

Diagram 6: Captured stones

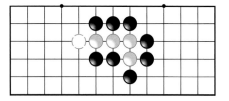

Diagram 7: Capture of a number of stones

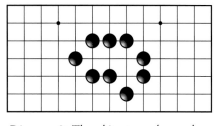

Diagram 8: The white stones shown above have been captured

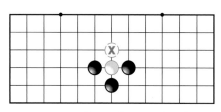

Diagram 9: White is threatened with capture

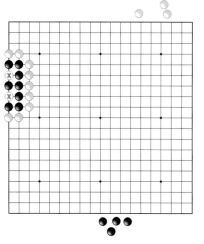

Diagram 10: The black stones are alive

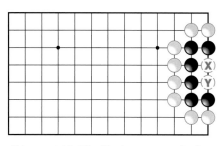

Diagram 11: The black stones are dead

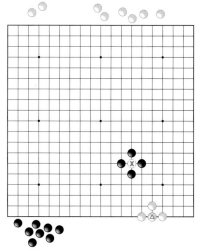

Diagram 12: White captures Black

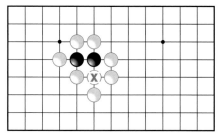

Diagram 13: Legal and illegal moves

Diagram 14: An illegal move

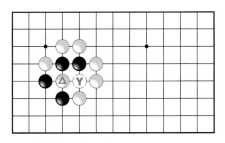

Diagram 15: *A legal move: Black captures White*

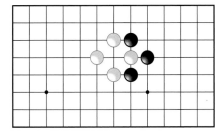

Diagram 18: *White recaptures*

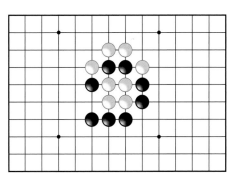

Diagram 21: *White captures Black*

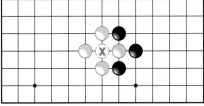

Diagram 16: *A white stone is in atari*

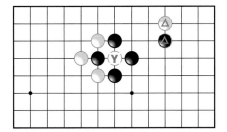

Diagram 19: *The rule of Ko*

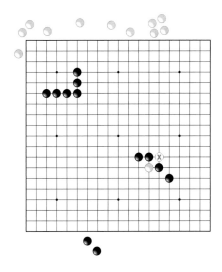

Diagram 22: *Connecting and cutting*

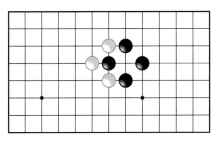

Diagram 17: *Black captures White*

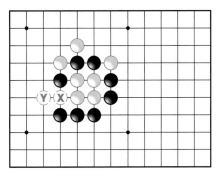

Diagram 20: *Attack and counterattack*

- **Liberties:** As a matter of definition stones are said to have a maximum of four liberties, that is, at most four adjacent vacant points. Note that stones positioned on the board's edge have three liberties; stones on corners, only two (diagram 5). When all a stone's liberties have been blocked by opposing pieces, it is captured (diagram 6). If stones are grouped, at least one in the cluster must have a liberty, or the whole group is captured (diagrams 7 and 8) . A stone can be played only onto points where it will have at least one liberty—which includes any liberty it might instantly create for itself if the move creates a capture.
- **Atari:** A threatened stone, with but a single liberty left to it, is said to be in *atari*. A clear case is shown in diagram 9.

- **Dead** or **alive:** Without liberties a stone, or a group, is *dead* and will be picked up by the capturing side. But it may happen that a group, though surrounded, has within it an open intersection, a liberty; such a group is considered still *alive* and cannot be removed. The black stones in diagram 10 are, and will remain, alive. White can play to neither open point because neither has a liberty nor creates one for a white stone—such a position is said to have 'the two eyes'; it is secure. In diagram 11 the black stones are dead: In the inevitable continuation, White can play to X or Y; if Black captures, the position in diagram 12 results. White has merely to place a stone at X to capture the group.

Legal and illegal moves

Stones of the same colour may share liberties, so that playing a white stone into the lower group in diagram 13 is legal—though pointless, as it merely wastes a turn while achieving no greater security. White could not play into the black cluster, however, as it would neither have nor create for itself any liberties after the move.

In diagram 14 Black cannot play to X though White could, if there were some reason to hasten this capture. Placing a black stone at Y (diagram 15) is perfectly legal: The black stone captures the white one marked by a triangle, thus gaining a liberty.

Ko ('eternity')

In a position such as that illustrated in diagram 16, a white stone is in *atari*. Black's play to its remaining liberty, to the left, captures and removes the white stone (diagram 17), but that now leaves Black in a complementary sort of *atari*, inviting the same response from White (diagram 18). Seesawing captures could go on indefinitely. The rule of *Ko* does not directly resolve the standoff, but requires each player to find other moves between captures in this perpetual swap.

Inasmuch as Black made the first capture in this example, White is forced first to leave the position. After playing somewhere else on the board, White can, on the next turn, come back to the *Ko* position and again capture (diagram 19). Black is then obliged to find some other move before returning and capturing, if so inclined. This rule ensures that the game will continue, in some region of the board, even if multiple Kos arise.

Flow of the game

Appearances shift constantly in Go; the attacker is counterattacked, the capturer becomes the captive. In a typical example (diagram 20), the central white group is in *atari*; play to X only forestalls capture from Black's play to Y. But, looking deeper, White sees that playing to another point (diagram 21) turns the tables, capturing two black stones and—for now—defusing Black's threat.

Strategy

Many learned volumes have been written on the game's tactics and strategy. In a most general way it is advised that players think in terms of walling off territory, not of captures, which are only necessary incidentals. They should attempt to make strong chains of connected stones. Unlinked stones are vulnerable.

The strongest chains form straight lines; diagonals are somewhat weaker. The upper left position in diagram 22 is quite difficult to attack. At the lower right, the situation is in flux: If Black can play to the point marked X all will be well; if White moves there, 'cutting' the chain, the black stones are in jeopardy.

HEX

NUMBER OF PLAYERS: Two

EQUIPMENT: Board and 122 counters (chips, as in gaming)

DIFFICULTY: A tactical approach is required

DURATION: About 1 hour

An elegantly simple but demanding two-player game, Hex was created in the 1940s by a Danish mathematician,

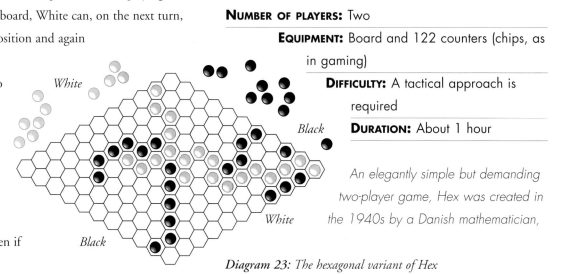

Diagram 23: The hexagonal variant of Hex

A worthy Dane

Piet Hein (1905–1996) invented other games, too, and did a great deal more than just think up new games. Trained as an architect and mathematician, he possessed a mind that tended to wander into geometrical mazes. During a quantum physics lecture by Werner Heisenberg, Hein found himself mentally assembling fractured pieces of things. The result was a first-class mathematical theorem and first-class game puzzle, the Soma Cube.

Hein even made the cover of *Life* magazine (October 1966) for thinking up a subtle blending of the properties of rectangles and ellipses in a shape he called the superellipse. It has been used in a very diverse range of designs, in city centers as well as for dining tables. Hein was also a prolific poet, and left these words, which can be as well applied to games as to mathematics and science: 'A problem worthy of attack, Proves its worth by fighting back.'

Piet Hein. In its original form the board consisted of equilateral triangles tiling a diamond-shaped area, counters occupying intersections. A later version covered the same area in hexagons, like a honeycomb, with counters inside the hexes (diagram 23).

Setup

One player has white counters, the other black counters. Each player tries to construct an unbroken chain of adjacent counters extending from one side of the board to the other. Black and White are each assigned two of the opposite sides as their goal lines. If, for example, White succeeds, it follows that Black must fail, for his path across the board is cleanly barred by White's completed bisection of the area. It follows, too, that a draw can never result, for in thwarting one player, the other necessarily completes a connection from side to side.

Playing the Game

Black moves first, placing a counter on any vacant point; White does the same in turn. Once played, counters are not moved again or captured. The board quickly fills with short assaults, blocked line segments, and serpentines of counters, black and white, trying to find a way around one other. The winning line can be any length; it can twist and turn and double back on itself. The four corner points belong to both sides, so that either may use them in making a cross-board connection.

HORSESHOE

NUMBER OF PLAYERS: Two

EQUIPMENT: Board and counters—two black, two white

DIFFICULTY: Easy to learn

DURATION: About 10 minutes

A short, simple game, Horseshoe requires no special equipment: A board can be sketched on paper and any handy objects—coins, buttons, and so on—will serve as counters.

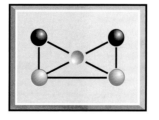 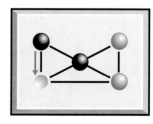

Diagram 24: *Starting position for a game of Horseshoe*   ***Diagram 25:*** *Achieving a winning position in Horseshoe*

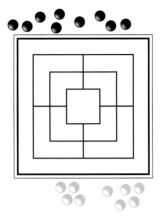

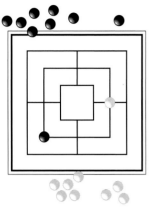

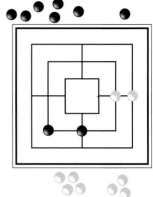

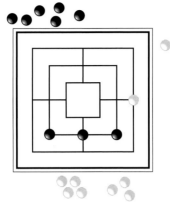

Diagram 26: Mill starting position

Diagram 27: The position after one move each

Diagram 28: The position after two moves each

Diagram 29: The position after Black's third move (forming a mill and capturing a White piece)

Playing the Game

Players may use any method to decide who will move first. From the starting position (diagram 24), one player moves into the layout's only vacant point, in the middle. By turns each player moves a counter onto the empty point until one of them is blocked and cannot move. In diagram 25, Black's next move will win the game, as the red counters are trapped (jumping over an adjacent counter is not allowed).

MILL (NINE MEN'S MORRIS)

NUMBER OF PLAYERS: Two

EQUIPMENT: Board and 18 counters (chips): nine black, nine white

DIFFICULTY: Some strategic skills are required

DURATION: About 30 minutes

Players move their nine playing pieces on the board's grid attempting to align three in a row, all the while preventing their opponent from accomplishing the same.

This game flourished in Europe during the Middle Ages, when it was often played on a layout drawn in the dirt. Cardboard or wooden sets are widely available for modern day players. In the United States the game is more usually known as Mill.

Setup

A board consists of three squares, each smaller one nestling inside the larger; a transverse line connects the squares, on each side, at their midpoints. This creates a total of 12 intersections, where a transverse meets a square, and these are the points used in play.

Playing the Game

Players may use any method to decide who will move first. Each of the two players begins with nine counters ('men'). By turns they may place a single man on any open intersection. Each tries to create a *mill* with some of his men, that is, three of them standing next to one another in a row. Completing a mill entitles that player to select and remove from the board one of his opponent's men, which is then 'dead' and permanently out of play. An opposing piece that is itself already part of a mill cannot be taken off, unless there is no other choice. Examples of a game's opening stages are illustrated here (diagrams 26–29).

When all the men have been played onto the board, turns continue by moving one to any open point, with the object usually of constructing a mill. A mill can be broken up and reformed any number of times.

Strategy

Especially desirable is setting up a configuration in which one man moves back and forth between two mills, breaking one and creating another with each turn: An opposing piece is knocked out of the game on every successive play for as long as this double mill can be sustained.

Winning the Game

The game is won when one player has been reduced to two surviving men or cannot make a legal move.

Variations

Hop

A common modification of the basic rules, this game allows a player with only three men remaining to hop over one of his own pieces, to land on any open point on the board. When both sides stand at three men, both have the Hop privilege. (Winning the game by blocking all legal moves is quite unlikely in this case.)

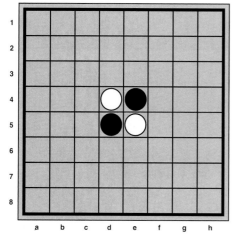

Diagram 30: Othello® starting position (and possible starting position for a game of Reversi)

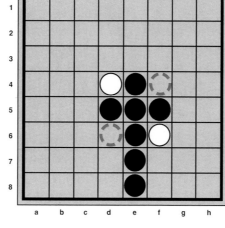

Diagram 32: Capture at a developed stage of a game

OTHELLO® (REVERSI)

NUMBER OF PLAYERS: Two

EQUIPMENT: Board and 64 discs with different colours on the reverse—generally black and white

DIFFICULTY: Complex; suitable for adults

DURATION: About 1 hour

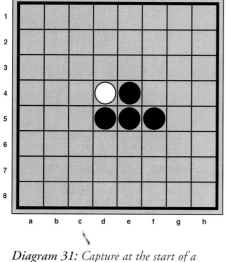

Diagram 31: Capture at the start of a game

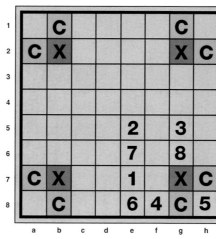

Diagram 33: Special squares

Like Go, this is a game of capture and recapture, but played with discs that are flipped over—reversing colours—with each change of ownership. The invention of Reversi, in the 1880s, is generally credited to the Englishman Lewis Waterman. Othello, a modern proprietary version with a slightly modified opening, appeared in 1971; it was created by Goro Hasegawa. (The game is highly popular in Japan, and most Othello champions have been Japanese.)

Setup

Both players have 32 reversible discs of black and white. Black begins. By turns discs are played into the four middle squares on a board with 64 squares. (Othello uses a prescribed starting position, shown in diagram 30; two of Reversi's possible openings are thus eliminated).

Playing the Game

The aim of each move is to place a disc adjacent to an opponent's disc in such a way that it is flanked on two sides—vertically, horizontally, or diagonally. A *trapped* disc is flipped, changing its colour to that of its captor. If no trapping move can be made, a player loses that turn and continues to forfeit turns until a legal move is possible.

In diagram 31, a white disc at e5 has just been trapped by Black's play to f5 and flipped. Further into the game (diagram 32), if White plays to f4, black discs at e4 and f5 will be flipped. Alternatively, playing to d6 will flip the discs at d5 and e6. As the game progresses each newly placed disc may result in many captures, with dramatic turnarounds on successive plays.

Note that only discs directly trapped by a move are flipped: It can happen that an uninvolved disc, as a result of neighboring colour changes, finds itself sandwiched. The disc is not turned over; 'chain reactions' of this sort are not allowed.

If a player has a legal move but has run out of discs, the opponent must supply one, turn after turn, until either no permitted move exists or all discs have been played. (In some versions, discs are simply drawn from a pool throughout the game.)

Winning the Game

Play continues until all 64 squares have been filled. The numbers of each colour are added up; highest total is the winner. (A tie is possible.) In Reversi, the game may end also if it happens that one player is left, after an opponent's turn, with no surviving discs on the board.

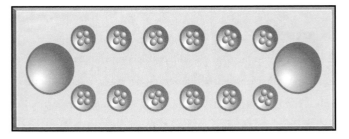

Diagram 34: Owari starting position

Strategy

In broad terms, good players believe it is not strategic to try for lots of captures on every move, especially in the early and middle game. The middle is changeable and volatile. Better to maintain fewer unflipped pieces, while concentrating on taking control of stronger points on the board, at the edges. The most vital are the corner squares, diagram 33, where discs are immune to capture. Without control of a corner, it can be hazardous to play into one of the adjacent squares (marked X and C), as discs exposed in this way can become stepping stones for an opponent's capturing move into the corner.

But the C squares have some strong points, as well. Note that X squares can take part in captures in only three directions (by playing the same colour to the squares marked 1, 2, or 3), but can themselves be taken in four ways. The C squares, by contrast, can be entrapped in only one way (for g8 this is by placing opposing colours at 4 and 5), while each may capture in three directions (for g8 this is by playing the same colour to the squares marked 6, 7, or 8).

OWARI

NUMBER OF PLAYERS: Two

EQUIPMENT: Board, 48 stones or beans

DIFFICULTY: Easy to learn, but requires close attention

DURATION: Around 20 minutes

Players take turns 'sowing' their stones tactically in the cups, according to the rules, and capturing their opponent's stones. The game originated in Africa thousands of years ago.

Setup

An Owari board consists of 12 small cups or bowls arranged in two parallel rows, with a larger cup at either end (diagram 34). A total of 48 stones, *sown* four to a cup, are the game's only pieces; they are not marked in any way as belonging to either of the two players.

Playing the Game

From the starting configuration, one player begins by picking up all the stones from any cup on his side of the board and redistributing them to the right, one at a time to each successive cup (not including the larger cups at the ends), moving counterclockwise. A move crosses onto the opponent's side of the board if necessary and ends only when the last stone is sown.

Players continue by turns in this way until it happens that one of them drops the last stone of a move sequence into a cup, on the opponent's side, that contains only one or two stones. With the addition of the last stone the cup's total, then, is either two or three—the condition that constitutes a capture. If the preceding cup also holds two or three stones, these too are taken, and so on in backward order until a cup is encountered with fewer than two or more than three stones. The turn ends; all captured stones are picked up and removed for storage to the large cup on the player's right.

The game ends when no more captures are possible (if both players still have stones, these are shared equally). The highest total of captured stones wins. Under certain circumstances a player may be left with no stones to place from his side of the board. If this cannot be remedied (see rules, below), the remaining stones are deemed captured by the opponent, the game ends, and totals are counted up.

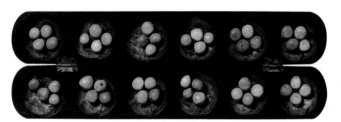

Above: *An original Owari board, with stones in the starting position. Any suitable receptacles can be used for the large cups.*

Special rules

If there are 12 or more stones in a cup, so that sowing them necessarily makes a complete circuit of the board, the original cup is skipped when the move sequence reaches it. The 12th stone is dropped one cup beyond, and placing continues from there, if any stones still remain to be distributed.

A move that would leave an opponent with no stones on his side—depriving him of any possible move—is not allowed if another move exists that would place at least one stone on the empty side.

Strategy

This rather simply ordered game requires close attention and some tactical ciphering. It is obvious that cups holding one or two stones will be vulnerable, but what to do about them? A player must decide whether to empty a vulnerable cup; to distribute stones from another into it; or to sow them ahead in opponent cups, leaving them with the wrong number to reach and capture one's own. Some moves, of course, may accomplish several of these objectives at once.

As a rough strategic principle, players often do keep their right-hand cups fuller, with capturing in mind. However, if stones are accumulating there, a canny opponent may try to sow stones in those cups—causing a prospective attack to overshoot, its last stone dropping harmlessly too far ahead. It is very difficult to separate the needs of attack and defense in this game; they blend fluidly in each new move.

REVERSI (*see* OTHELLO)

CARD GAMES

Card Games for Groups **73**

Card Games for One **100**

Children's Card Games **109**

Games of Chance **118**

Card Games for Groups

Playing cards first appeared in Europe in the 14th century. Columbus even carried a pack with him to America. Universally popular today, card games bring people together.

CANASTA

NUMBER OF PLAYERS: Four people play, two in each partnership

EQUIPMENT: Two decks of cards, including jokers

DIFFICULTY: Concentration and skill are required to play well

DURATION: 30 to 40 minutes

Canasta is a point-count card game played in pairs with the aim of being the first pair to gain 5,000 points. Imported from South America, the game was a major craze in the 1950s.

The object of the game is to gain as many points as possible, primarily through *melds;* these are combinations of three or more cards of the same rank that are laid down on the table— for example, 6, 6, 6 or J, J, J. All jokers and 2's are wild cards that can be used to stand in for cards of any rank when forming a meld. A meld must, however, have at least as many natural cards in it as wild cards.

When a meld has reached a length of seven cards, it becomes a *canasta.* It is gathered up and stacked to one side; its bonus points will be scored at the end of the game. (A natural canasta is stored with a red card on top—a 'red' canasta—and counts for more than a 'black,' wild-card, canasta.)
Additional cards may be *laid off on* (added to) an existing meld or completed canasta.

Card values

The basic value of a meld is the value of the cards it contains:

- **Jokers:** 50 points each
- **2s:** 20 points each
- **Aces:** 20 points each
- **K, Q, J, 10, 9, 8:** 10 points each
- **7, 6, 5, 4:** 5 points each
- **Black 3's:** 5 points each. They may only be melded when a player is *going out*—i.e., when a player has laid down all his cards in melds and there is no further play (see next page).

- **Red 3's** are not melded, but are laid down as soon as they are drawn. They earn bonus points in the final scoring. At the end, unmelded cards in a player's hand count against the partnership.

Setup

Each player is dealt 11 cards. The remaining cards are placed in the middle of the table, facedown, where they serve as the drawing pile, or *stock.* The top card, the *upcard,* is placed faceup beside the stock and begins the discard pile. If the upcard is a wild card or a 3, the next card from the stock is placed faceup on top of it.

Playing the Game

The player to the left of the dealer goes first, then play moves clockwise around the table. Each player in turn either takes the upcard or draws the top card from the stock. She may then meld or lay off cards on existing melds, if appropriate. Also, any red 3's must be laid down and replacement cards for each are drawn from stock. (An exception to the replacement rule is the case of a red 3

Diagram 1:
Melds and canastas

obtained by capturing the discard pile—see explanation below.) Finally, the player discards one card faceup on top of the discard pile.

Partners sit opposite one another, drawing to their own separate hands, but their melds are placed together on the table, in front of one of them, and either may add cards to any part of their joint meld.

A partnership can only have one meld of a particular rank. Care must be taken with melding, since an error incurs a penalty of 100 points for each exposed card that must be withdrawn.

The top card from the discard pile, if combined into a meld, also counts toward the initial value requirement.

Scoring

The first meld of each partnership, using cards accumulated in one of their hands, must meet a minimum point requirement, based on the team's score going into the hand. These requirements are:

- **Minus score:** 15 point minimum
- **0 to 1,495 points:** 50 point minimum
- **1,500 to 2,995 points:** 90 point minimum
- **Over 3,000 points:** 120 point minimum

If a partnership's first meld attempt has insufficient points, the player must either increase the value of the meld or take it back. In either case, a 10-point penalty is added to the partnership's initial meld threshold.

Unless a side *goes out* (see below), play continues until there are no more cards in the stock. If the last card drawn is a red 3, the hand ends after the drawer's turn, since no replacement card is available. Otherwise, when the stock is gone, play continues using only the discard pile. If a player can use the upcard on an existing meld she must take it. If not, taking the upcard is optional.

Once no player is willing or required to take the upcard, the hand ends.

The discard pile

Use of the discard pile is complicated in canasta. One universal rule is that if the top card on the discard pile is a black 3, called a stop card, the next player cannot take it, but must draw from the stock. Once the stop card is covered, the discard pile is available again. Another requirement is that a player may not draw from a discard pile containing only one card.

Capturing the discard pile

The main complexity involves *capturing the discard pile,* which is desirable because extra cards afford added opportunities to score. If a player immediately uses the top card of the pile in a meld, subject to certain conditions, she may then pick up the rest of the cards in the pile and add them to her hand. Officially, the ability to capture the discard pile may depend on whether it is *frozen* or *unfrozen*.

The pile is frozen to a partnership that has not yet melded, and is completely frozen if the first upcard was a red 3 that remains in the pile, or if the pile contains any wild card. Under these conditions, it can only be captured if a player melds by matching the upcard with a natural pair from her hand.

If the pile is unfrozen, it can be captured in two additional ways: The upcard can be laid off on an existing meld, or it can be combined with a matching card and a wild card from the hand.

In practice, many players do not use the official rule and play that the discard pile can only be captured by a natural pair.

Going out

A side must have at least one canasta before a player can *go out*. This is done by laying down all one's remaining cards in melds, which ends the hand. A final discard, to empty the hand, is optional. If the player going out has not previously made any melds, she *goes out concealed*.

A player has the option of asking, 'May I go out, partner?' She must then do as her partner says. The expected answer is, 'No.' The purpose of this procedure is to warn the partner to meld everything possible on her next turn so her cards will count for, and not against, the partnership. At the end of a hand, the *basic count* is first calculated based on these values:

- **Natural canasta:** 500 points each
- **Mixed canasta (has wild cards):** 300 points each
- **Going out concealed:** 200 points
- **Going out unconcealed:** 100 points
- **Red 3:** 100 points each
- **All four red 3's:** 800 points.

A partnership can end up with a negative score. If it has no melds, its red 3's score minus 100 each. Also, a red 3 left in anyone's hand counts minus 500.

Winning the Game

Each side adds to the basic count the points in its melds. The point value of all unmelded cards is subtracted, yielding the final score, which is added to the cumulative score from previous hands. The first team to reach 5,000 points wins the game.

CASINO

NUMBER OF PLAYERS: Two to four

EQUIPMENT: One deck of playing cards, jokers removed

DIFFICULTY: Game of skill, suitable for adults

DURATION: Half an hour

Casino originated in France in the Middle Ages and remains popular in Mediterranean countries. In this game, players capture as many cards as possible from the table by matching them with cards in their hands.

Setup

Play starts with a cut for deal—the player with the lowest card begins. He deals two cards facedown to each of the other players, then two cards faceup on the table, and finally deals two cards facedown to himself. He then distributes two additional cards to the players, the table, and himself in the same way.

Playing the Game

Players take turns playing one card faceup on the table, either to capture other cards, build sets, or add to the table cards, as detailed below. They score points at the end of the game for ending up with the most cards or the most spades, and for capturing the Big Casino (10 of diamonds), the Little Casino (2 of spades), or any ace.

Play options

For purposes of capturing, the ace through 10 have their face values (1–10). Face cards have no numeric value. The following plays can be made:

- **Capturing with a numeral card:** A numeral card can capture any card on the table that matches it in rank (unless it is part of a build—see below), as well as sets of cards whose combined value add up to the value of the numeral card. For example, in diagram 2, the 8 can capture not only the 8, but also the 5, 2, and 1.

Diagram 2: Capturing and a sweep in casino

Each card can be counted as a member of only one set, so that the 5 in this example could not also be combined with, say, a 3 to make another set.

- **Capturing with a face card:** Face cards can only be captured if they can be uniquely paired with a matching card. A face card in the hand can capture one on the table to make a single pair, or three on the table to make two pairs, but not two on the table. This rule exists because removing three face cards of a given rank would leave the fourth uncapturable.

- **Building:** If no immediate captures are possible, a numeral card from the hand can be combined with others on the table to form a *build* (see diagram 3). The player must announce the capturing number (which can never exceed 10) and must hold a card that can make the capture. For example, a player can play his 2 with a 3 and 4 on the table and say, 'Capturing 9's,' assuming he has a 9 in his hand. Cards that have been combined into a build may only be captured as a unit. If all goes well, the player will capture the build on his next turn—but his opponent may hold a 9 and take the build instead, or when possible add to the build (described below), changing its value. There are two kinds of builds: *Single builds,* in which the total value of the cards equals the value of the capture card. For example, a 3 from the hand combined with a 4 and ace on the table that is announced as capturing 8's is a single build. And there are *multiple builds,* in which the total value of the cards is a multiple of the capture card. The single build in the example above

would be a multiple build if the player announced, 'Capturing 4's.' The capture value of a multiple build cannot be changed.

- **Capturing a build:** This is done by playing the appropriate capture card. A player can capture a build made by an opponent.

- **Adding to a build:** The value of a single build can be changed by adding to it, so long as the player doing so has the relevant new capture card. Builds can also be played on by adding a card or cards equal to the capture value, so long as the player holds the needed capture card.

- **Trailing:** This refers to playing a card on the table without capturing or building. Trailing is not allowed if, on the player's previous turn, he has started or added to a build. In that case, he must capture, add to, or initiate a build.

Captured cards, along with the capturing card, are stored facedown in a player's pile. A *sweep,* capturing all the cards on the table, is worth a point. Sweeps are marked for later counting by turning the capturing card faceup in the sweeping player's pile.

When all players have played their four cards, a new round of four cards each is dealt. No new cards are dealt to the table.

The game ends when there are no cards left in players' hands or in the deck. All cards that are left on the table are taken by the player who made the last capture.

Diagram 3: Builds in casino

Scoring

- **Most cards:** 3 points
- **Most spades:** 3 points
- **Big Casino:** 2 points
- **Little Casino:** 1 point
- **Each ace:** 1 point
- **Each sweep:** 1 point.

Winning the Game

The player with the most points wins. If there is a tie for most cards or most spades, neither player gets the points.

CONTRACT BRIDGE

NUMBER OF PLAYERS: Four, in two pairs of partners

EQUIPMENT: Two decks of cards

DIFFICULTY: Skill and concentration are required

DURATION: About an hour

Contract bridge follows the same basic play for tricks as whist (see page 98), but has an opening auction in which players announce, in successively higher bids, how many of a hand's tricks the side will try to take. Tricks are cards played, one round at a time, to the center of the table: One player 'leads' and the others in turn follow until all have played. These cards make up one trick; its winner removes the small stack to one side, keeping each trick won separate. The winner also has the privilege of making the next lead.

Once set, a *contract* (the amount of the winning bid) is binding for the auction winners; they must win at least the number contracted, and will maximize their scoring by bidding up exactly to their hands' potential.

Setup

Partnerships are first established, either by agreement or by cutting cards: The two highest cards form one partnership, the

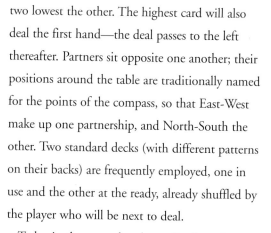

Diagram 4: Contract bridge's rank of suits

two lowest the other. The highest card will also deal the first hand—the deal passes to the left thereafter. Partners sit opposite one another; their positions around the table are traditionally named for the points of the compass, so that East-West make up one partnership, and North-South the other. Two standard decks (with different patterns on their backs) are frequently employed, one in use and the other at the ready, already shuffled by the player who will be next to deal.

To begin the game, hands are distributed clockwise, starting with the player on the dealer's left. All the cards are dealt out, one at a time, 13 to each player. Players arrange their hands in suits and calculate for themselves the relative strengths of their cards—this will play an important part in determining subsequent bids.

Scoring

Though modified guidelines are certainly used, the most basic scheme assigns points in the following way:

- **Aces:** 4 points each
- **Kings:** 3 points each
- **Queens:** 2 points each
- **Jacks:** 1 point each.

See also Keeping Tally on page 82.

Agreeable accidents of distribution may also have value in taking tricks and may be accounted thus:

- **Void (no cards in a suit):** 3 points
- **Singleton (only one card in suit):** 2 points
- **Doubleton (two in suit):** 1 point
- **All four aces:** 1 point.

Certain disagreeable features should be counted as deductions, lowering a hand's value:

- **No aces:** Minus 1 point
- **Each unguarded honor:** Minus 1 point.

An unguarded honor is one that very probably must fall without taking a trick because it is unprotected. A singleton king, for example, will likely fall to the ace. If the suit is longer, K-*x* (*x* = any lower card in suit) the king survives to become a winner when eventually led. Lower honors need more protection: Q-*x*-*x*, J-*x*-*x*-*x*.

To make an opening bid, a player is well advised to have at least 13 points in hand. A partner will usually respond, instead of merely passing, with as few as 6 points.

Bidding

As in whist, only those tricks are counted that are taken after the first six, or *book*. In bridge, players vie beforehand to name the trump suit, at the same time committing the partnership to a certain minimum trick score. The suit of the winning bid automatically becomes *trump*. For the duration of the hand any card in the trump suit outranks even the highest card of any other suit. Obviously, it is a great advantage for a partnership to establish the strongest suit the two hold between them as trump—but not at the cost of bidding to take more tricks than is likely possible. Sometimes the winning bid is in *no trump*—no suit is given special privilege.

Beginning with the deal, each player either passes or announces a number and a proposed trump suit, for example, two spades, three hearts, and so on. No further communication is allowed or should be tolerated—no winks, nods, or sharp kicks under the table.

Bidding works as a true auction: Each successive bid must exceed the last, until no player will venture a higher one. Suits are given a hierarchy (see diagram 4): Clubs are lowest, followed by diamonds, hearts, spades, and no-trump, in ascending order. A bid of one club can be topped by one diamond, for example, but one heart cannot follow one

spade. Players could conceivably make five successive bids at the 'one level' before necessarily reaching a bid of two.

Auction strategy

The auction proceeds with two aims in view, both to establish an achievable trick total and to share between partners, in this highly abbreviated code, as much information as possible about the makeup of their respective hands. When finally one player has bid a total that no one wishes to overmatch, so that three successive passes follow, the contract is set for that number of tricks, with the suit named serving as trump for the hand.

Two nonbid responses are possible during an auction: *double* and *redouble*. When a player has made a bid that seems unattainable, an opponent may, instead of bettering the bid, double it, which will multiply its scoring value, if made, or the resulting penalty, should the bidder fall short. An unfazed bidder or partner, confident of his estimates, may in turn redouble, further multiplying the points at stake.

Playing the Game

Once a contract has been set, the partner who first opened the contract's suit, the *declarer,* will play both of the team's hands. The first lead belongs to the player at the declarer's left. After the lead, the *dummy hand*—declarer's partner—is laid out faceup (and still organized by suit) at its table position. Whenever the turn comes around to the dummy hand, or if it has won the lead, the declarer chooses which card to play.

Strategy

Actual play of the tricks, particularly for the declarer, is one of bridge's routine challenges. A good deal is made clear, from the outset, when the dummy hand is exposed. The opponent who leads does not have the benefit of first examining the dummy hand and will try to play any sure winners or, mindful of previous bidding, a partner's best suit.

The declarer must plot the hand's course: whether to gather in trumps early, where to count upon losses, how to ensure the lead stays in the proper hand. Holding trump of sufficient length and strength suggests it should be collected first thing, preventing opponents *ruffing* (trumping) subsequent tricks. But it is a lamentable gaffe if the declarer's poor planning leaves the lead in the stronger hand.

Suppose, for example, with four tricks remaining, the dummy hand contains four spade winners, but the declarer is stuck with the lead and holds the last of the trump plus assorted losers in diamonds and hearts. Leading from the dummy, if it could have been arranged, wins all four tricks; from the declarer, only one (if the other side can avoid leading a spade).

Showing cunning

Of particular usefulness is the *finesse,* a play technique to force strong cards from an opponent's hand onto an unwinnable trick. To illustrate: As often happens, the declarer holds the ace of trump—and four others; perhaps the dummy has Q-J-10 of trump. The king, if guarded (very likely), would appear to be a sure winner for the opposition. However, if the declarer leads from the dummy, and the king is in the next hand, it is trapped. If played on the queen, the ace will take it; if reserved, it is eventually forced out and taken anyway.

The finesse is not guaranteed. Should the king lie in the hand across the table, it wins; or if adequately protected (with all four remaining trump in the example in diagram 5), it wins. Often the declarer has at least some expectations, inferences from the suits named during opponents' bidding.

Revoking or reneging

Cards played must agree in suit with the card led, unless a player has none of that suit. Otherwise, failure to follow suit entails a penalty: At hand's end, the offending side forfeits two tricks—if they won the invalid trick—to the other side; one trick if the opponents took it.

North

West

South

Diagram 5:

Finessing in contract bridge

Elements of bidding

Players hope in the course of bidding to hit upon the best contract they can make between them. If they are lucky, theirs will be the larger contract, the auction winner, and they will have a chance to try. Terse meanings, though sometimes fatally ambiguous, are generally to be understood from a bid or successions of them. (Advanced players may practice for a wider range of communication, adopting even more ways of signaling through their bids.)

As a general rule, it should be reckoned that bidding the hand all the way up to game in a *minor suit* (it would take a bid of five clubs or diamonds) usually requires a minimum of 29 points held between partners; in no-trump (a bid of three) or a *major suit* (a bid of four hearts or spades), 26 points. The much rarer opportunity for a slam will need from 33 points (small slam) to 37 points (grand slam). Here are some rough guides to opening:

- A 13-point hand is sufficient to open a partnership's bidding. Holding 13 to 21 points, with a five-card suit, bid one of this long suit. With two five-card suits, bid the stronger first; the other may come up later, after your partner's response.

- Without a long suit, 13-14 points (for example, distributed 4-3-3-3) should start at one no-trump (NT).

- Many players skip (or *jump*) a bidding level, going straight to 2NT, with 16-18 points in a no-trump distribution—but partners should ascertain beforehand that they are on the same wavelength.

- Holding 23 points, a very strong hand, the opener may jump straightaway to two of the best suit, or no-trump, requiring a partner response. Any response that involves the least possible raise signals weakness. Opening with a

The evolution of contract bridge

Whist was the preferred card game of mid-Victorian England, played everywhere on social evenings. Several novel game ideas transformed it by degrees into modern contract bridge. The first to appear, perhaps from Russia or India, was 'bridge-whist,' which introduced the notion of actually naming trump: The dealer chose it, rather than relying on chance, and played the partner's hand as a dummy. ('Trump' derives its name from a very old French game, *Triomphe,* that is a closer ancestor to euchre than to whist.)

In the early 20th century, bridge-whist acquired another refinement, competitive bidding to name trump, and became auction bridge. Though recognizable to any modern bridge player, the auction form did not fully metamorphose into contract bridge until a decade or two later, with the adoption of three elements now central to scoring and strategy.

Contract bridge added to the game the requirement to bid all tricks scored toward game, or below the line. *Overtricks* no longer accumulated toward game. The *vulnerable* condition was established, as well, and large bonuses added for *slams.* These modifications sharpened the penalty for failure while at the same time providing a sufficient reward for success—the game's drama was much heightened.

point or two less than 23 but holding a six- or seven-card suit is also worth a jump.

- The two club open, a jump bid to two clubs (holding at least 23 points), forces the bidding all the way up to game. Even if unable to signify any support, a partner must continue the bidding so that a game contract is reached. Responsibility belongs completely to the opener.

Pre-emptive bids

More often a sacrifice than not, a player with a weak hand but a long suit (seven or more cards) may choose to open at the three level. If the other side is only a trick or two shy of game, it may not wish to risk taking a contract at this level. The opener may 'go down,' but with exceptionally long trump the loss will not be large.

Responses

A hand may need to be somewhat revalued in the light of a partner's opening bid: Only three in the bid suit is a poor matchup, making a 1-point deduction; voids and singletons in other suits become more significant, worth a point more. As to responding:

- **With fewer than 6 points, pass:** If a forcing bid opens, the reply should be weak, the least permitted at that stage of the bidding.
- **6 to 10 points:** Make the smallest realistic bid, perhaps naming a five-card suit with an honor, but only if the bid need not thereby climb to the two level. Otherwise, 1NT. Raise a partner's opening to two in his suit when holding four of them or three with an honor.
- **13 to 19 points:** A game contract is very likely. With at least four of the bid suit, jump one level to three; the opener is thus informed of strength. If there is no biddable suit, but 16 points or more, jump to no-trump.
- **19 points or more:** A rare distribution—perhaps pointing to slam (see page 82). The best response is a jump with change of suit, a game-forcing bid, or with a

balanced hand, a jump naming no-trump. Jump-bids should always elicit a rebid from the opener, leaving it up to the bidder to reach or stop at game level.

Cueing

When partners have agreed on a trump suit, particularly after a confirming jump bid, they continue in *cue bids* to explore their strengths. After a jump, for example, to three hearts the response might be four clubs, meaning, 'We have a fit in hearts, I also have the ace of clubs; what do you have?' But it could instead mean, 'I have a void in clubs.' The point is, in either case, the partnership has first-round control in that suit—with the ace or with a trump.

Slams

If the bidding reveals sufficient strength, partners going on to slam (six or seven tricks) may resort to special conventions to ascertain the number of aces and kings they hold between them. In *Blackwood,* a popular convention, one player bids 4NT ('How many aces do you have?'); the other responds five clubs ('I have none or all four'), five diamonds ('I have one ace'), five hearts ('I have two aces'), or five spades ('I have three aces'). Using *Gerber*—querying from a safer, lower level— a player bids four clubs; responses are graduated as in Blackwood, one bid upward per ace. The intent must be unmistakable, however, announced circumstances where four clubs could mean nothing else.

Defensive bidding

The weaker side bids, too, communicating its better suits or simply trying, with fine judgment, to force the stronger hands to their highest supportable contract—or beyond. An *overcall* in a bid suit, for instance one heart countered by two hearts, gets everyone's attention. It means a *stopper* in the bid suit and strong cards in all others; a partner should respond accordingly, as if

the overcaller had in fact opened with a forcing bid.

Doubling in the first round is not an authentic challenge; it indicates a generally good hand, without a clear best suit, and requires a partner to respond, naming best suit.

Keeping tally

One hundred points makes a game; two games a *rubber.* Generally, one member of each partnership records the scores, jotting them on a special bridge pad or a piece of paper ruled appropriately.

Scoring makes use of two important conventions: First, points are recorded either *below the line,* counting toward the game outcome; or *above the line,* bonuses to be included only in a rubber's grand total, determining an overall winner. Secondly, a side that has won a hand, said to have a *leg up* toward winning a game, is *vulnerable; overtricks* (see below) score higher when vulnerable, and even more when doubled or redoubled. Penalties are greater, too, for failing when vulnerable.

Overtricks

Any tricks taken in excess of the number bid are scored above the line as bonuses; their value does not depend on suit:

- **Each overtrick, not vulnerable:** 50 points
- **Each overtrick, vulnerable:** 100 points.

Again, points are multiplied by two if doubled, by four if redoubled.

Contract tricks and game

Because tricks in different suits have different values, reaching game score (100 points) is more difficult in, for example, clubs than hearts. These are the only points scored below the line. Trick values are:

A	B
500	500
150	150
30	500
40	
90	
	120
120	
930	1270

Diagram 6: The bridge score sheet

- **Clubs, diamonds:** 20 points
- **Hearts, spades:** 30 points
- **No trump:** 40 points for first trick, 30 for each subsequent trick, so that a contract of three makes game.

When doubled, all values are doubled; redoubled, they are doubled again.

Undertricks

Penalties for failing in a contract are also scored above the line as points awarded to the opposition. The scales, not vulnerable and vulnerable, are uneven: Falling short by more than one trick, when doubled or redoubled, invites a ruinous scoring result:

- **Each trick, not vulnerable:** 50 points
- **First trick, doubled:** 100 points
- **Second and third tricks, doubled:** 200 points each (300 points for the fourth and any further undertricks)
- **First trick, redoubled:** 200 points
- **Second and third tricks, redoubled:** 400 points each (600 points for the fourth and any further undertricks)
- **Each trick, vulnerable:** 100 points
- **First trick, doubled:** 200 points
- **But, subsequent tricks, doubled:** 300 points each
- **First trick, redoubled:** 400 points
- **Subsequent tricks, redoubled:** 600 points each.

Slam bonuses

Bidding and taking all the scoring tricks—seven of them—is called a *grand slam;* taking all but one, a *small slam.* Both win bonus scores, entered above the line:

- **Small slam:** 500 points
- **(And vulnerable):** 750 points
- **Grand slam:** 1,000 points
- **(And vulnerable):** 1,500 points.

Honors

The five top cards (A, K, Q, J, 10) in the trump suit are its

Above: A game of contract bridge

honors. Bonuses apply only to honors held in one hand (not between the partners, as in whist); they score above the line:

- **Five honors:** 150 points
- **Four honors:** 100 points
- **No-trump honors (four aces):** 150 points.

Odds and ends

A few other bonuses, above the line, may apply. Most add value to a won rubber:

- **Winning rubber if opponents have won a game:** 500 points
- **Winning rubber if opponents have not won a game:** 750 points
- **Winning one game in an unfinished rubber:** 300 points
- **Having the only leg (part score) in an unfinished rubber:** 50 points
- **Making a doubled contract ('for the insult'):** 50 points.

CRAZY EIGHTS

NUMBER OF PLAYERS: Two to five

EQUIPMENT: Deck of cards

DIFFICULTY: Easy

DURATION: 10 to 15 minutes

In Crazy Eights players aim to get rid of all the cards in their hands.

Setup

After shuffling, the dealer gives each player five cards, one at a time. (If only two are playing, seven cards are dealt to each.) The dealer stacks the remaining cards facedown in the middle of the table, then turns the top card faceup and places it beside the stack to start the discard pile.

Playing the Game

On each turn, a player tries to reduce his hand by playing one card faceup on top of the discard pile. To be eligible for discard, a card must match either the suit or the rank of the card showing on top of the pile. Eights, the 'crazy' cards in this game, may be discarded onto the pile regardless of what card is showing. Also, when playing an 8, the player declares what suit must be played next, an option that can be used for tactical advantage.

If a player has no eligible card, he draws one card at a time from the stack in the middle of the table until he can play.

Diagram 7: A cribbage board

Drawn cards that cannot be discarded are added to the player's hand. The game continues until one of the players has no remaining cards.

CRIBBAGE

NUMBER OF PLAYERS: Two to four

EQUIPMENT: One deck of playing cards, jokers removed, cribbage board or paper and pencil for scoring

DIFFICULTY: An intricate game, more suitable for adults

DURATION: Half an hour

The most distinctive elements of this game are its scoring system and its ancient roots. It is thought to have been devised by an English poet in the 17th century, based on an earlier game about which little is known.

Setup

The object of the game is to be the first to reach 121 points, which is twice around a cribbage board. Points are scored both while a hand is played and when the hands are *shown* after play.

In a two-player game, players cut for the deal; low card wins. After a shuffle and cut, six cards are dealt facedown to each player. Each then throws two cards facedown into a pile called a *crib*. Cards in the crib will be scored for the dealer during the *show* phase of the hand. The cards are then recut, and the top card below the cut is turned up and placed faceup on top of the pack. This card is the *starter*.

Playing the Game

Each player, beginning with the nondealer, places a card faceup on the table in front of him and announces the numerical total of the cards showing. Kings, queens, and jacks all count 10, and aces are low. For example, if the first play is a 10, and the next player plays a 7, he says 17 while doing so. The total may go to a maximum of 31. If a player cannot lay down another card and stay below 31, he says 'Go,' and the other player then has a chance to play as many cards as he can without exceeding 31. When no more cards can be played while staying under 31, the total is reset to zero and the hand continues until all cards in both hands have been played.

Scoring

The following scores are logged as soon as they are made, on a cribbage board or otherwise:

- **Two for his heels:** Dealer turns up a jack for the starter—2 points
- **Last:** Playing the last card without hitting or going over 31—1 point

---

The cribbage board

■ ■

The standard board consists of two sets of two rows of holes (See diagram 7). Holes are divided into sets of five, to make counting easier. Each player uses one side of the board. The first score is recorded by counting one hole per point and placing a peg in the hole corresponding to the number scored.

A player's next score is recorded by counting from the first peg the number of holes corresponding to the new score and placing the second peg at that point. The third score is recorded by moving the back peg the appropriate number of holes past the front peg, and so on through the game.

Pegs are moved up the outside and down the inside of the board. One trip up and down the board is 60 holes, but each end has a finishing hole as well. Thus a standard cribbage game is twice around the board (120 points) plus the finishing hole (121 points).

- **Thirty-one:** Hitting 31 exactly—2 points
- **Fifteens:** Playing a card that brings the cumulative total to 15—2 points
- **Pairs:** Playing the second card in succession of the same rank—2 points
- **Pairs royal:** Playing the third card in succession of the same rank—6 points
- **Double pairs royal:** Playing the fourth card in succession of the same rank—12 points
- **Runs:** Playing last of three or more cards that form a sequence—1 point per card in the sequence. Cards need not have been played in rank order (for example, playing a 5 after a 6 and a 4 scores 3 points). A 4-point run can be scored after a 3-pointer, and a 5-point run after a 4-pointer.

The show

After the play, players show and record the score for the different scoring combinations that can be built from the cards in their hands plus the starter card, which counts as a fifth card in each hand. Cards can be used in more than one combination. For example, the same 6 could be combined with a 9 for a 15, with another 6 for a pair, and with a 5 and 7 for a run. The nondealers go first, then the dealer scores his hand, and finally, the dealer scores the crib. Point values for combinations scored in the play are the same in the show.

The scores available during the show are:
- **Fifteens:** All possible combinations of cards that make 15 may be used. For example, a player with a two 7's and one 8 could make two combinations, pairing each 7 in turn with the 8, for a total of 4 points.
- **Flushes:** Four cards in one suit score 4; five in one suit score 5. Only the longest flush counts.
- **Muggins:** An optional rule specifying that if a player fails to claim any potential points in his hand, the other player can claim them.
- **One for his nob:** Holding the jack in the same suit as the

starter scores 1 point.

- **Pairs and pairs royal:** Same as during play, except that only the largest combination is scored.

- **Run:** Cards can be part of more than one run. For example, a hand with 6, 6, 7, and 8 plus a 9 starter could score 2 runs of 4 for a total of 8. Only the longest run is counted.

Winning the Game

Once both hands and the crib have been shown, the hand ends. The other player becomes the dealer for the next hand and the game continues until one player reaches the winning score. After each player has had a chance to deal, players cut for the deal in the next hand. When the winning score is reached the game ends immediately; the other player does not get to record any further points, even if he would have ended up with more points than the winner.

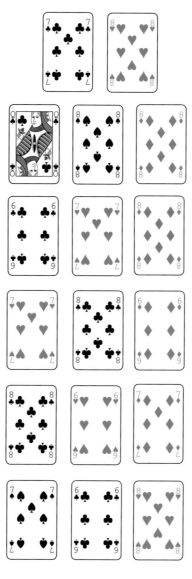

Diagram 8:

Scoring combinations for cribbage

Three or four players

A few special rules apply when more than two players are in the game. In the three-handed game, each player gets five cards and discards one into the crib, and the show begins with the player to the dealer's left.

In the four-handed game, players play as partners, combining their scores, and five cards each are dealt, and one goes into the crib.

The nondealing partnership shows first.

EUCHRE

NUMBER OF PLAYERS: Four, in two pairs of partners

EQUIPMENT: One deck of cards with 2's to 8's taken out; one joker (*benny*) is left in the deck

DIFFICULTY: Tactics required

DURATION: About 1 hour per round

Although Euchre's play and terms may seem rather old-fashioned, it remains popular in many parts of the English-speaking world.

Trump order

Once a trump suit is established (see below), both jacks in the same colour become important cards. Trump seniority, descending, follows the order: joker, jack, jack in suit of same colour, ace (the ace is high, but not as high as the joker and like-coloured jacks), king, queen, 10, 9—eight trump in all. The jack in suit retains its archaic name, the *right bower;* the other of the same colour becomes the *left bower.* With the exception of the jacks, the rest of the deck ranks in the usual order, aces down to 9's.

Setup

The object in euchre, as in bridge or whist, is to win tricks (explained below). Bidding precedes trick play, as in Bridge, but here the similarities end.

To begin, an initial dealer is chosen—by cutting for high card, for example. (The deal moves one player to the left with each new hand.) The dealer shuffles; the player to the right cuts. Cards are dealt clockwise to each player in two rounds: three cards in the first, two in the second, and the remaining five placed facedown in the middle of the table. The top card of the central pile is turned faceup (diagram 9), whereupon the bidding can begin.

Playing the Game

The upturned card's suit is nominally trump, unless all players pass in a first round of bidding. There will then be a second bidding round, in which a different trump suit is named by the winning bidder (bidding is explained below). Cards in the trump suit rank higher than any cards of other suits. Thus, even a lowly 9 of trump beats an ace of another suit. A curious twist of the rules allows the dealer, in the first round only, to take the central card into his hand after bidding is complete. The dealer replaces it with one from his hand; his discard is put facedown at the bottom of the pile. (If the joker has been turned up in the center, the dealer announces a suit before looking at his hand.)

The player to the dealer's left starts. Only two kinds of bid are possible: to pass ('I pass') or to announce, 'I order it up,' by which it is understood that the player will attempt to take three tricks (explained below) and the bidding is over. By bidding, a player becomes the hand's *maker,* and must further specify whether the three tricks will be won playing alone or

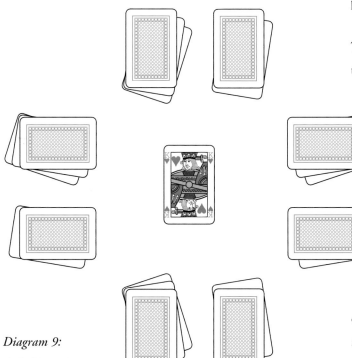

Diagram 9:
A deal in euchre

How the joker got its name

Euchre seems to have arisen in the region of Alsace, a border *département* of France with long cultural ties to Germany. The name probably comes by way of the outdated German *juchs,* for a joke or game. Anglicized slightly, the extra card became a joker, introduced into standard card decks in the 1850s expressly for the purpose of playing euchre. Left and right bower are also of German origin, taken straight from *bauer,* a farmer or peasant.

Because euchre caught on with sailors, it traveled widely—and spawned a welter of variant rules. Though the game is played today from New Zealand to Nova Scotia, no completely standard set of rules exists.

in partnership. If alone, the maker declares 'up, down'; if in partnership, simply 'up.'

Should all players pass in the first round, a second begins. The three-trick contract will be won by the first to bid, as in the first round, except that the maker names the trump suit and whether playing alone: for example, 'spades, down,' or in partnership, 'spades, up.' When a hand is to be pursued alone, a partner's hand lies facedown on the table, out of play. An opponent, a *defender,* may also announce, 'I will play alone,' in which case the other defender drops out, reducing the hand to two players. Most rules conventions allow the dealer to be included even if the central card was taken.

Tricks are played in the usual way: One player *leads* a card (plays it to the center of the table) and the others in turn follow until all have played a card. These cards make up one *trick;* its winner removes the small stack to one side, keeping each won trick separate. The winner also has the

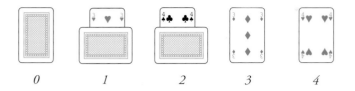

0   1   2   3   4

Diagram 10: Each partnership uses two 3's and two 4's to score— the number of pips exposed denotes the number of points scored.

privilege of making the next lead. For the other players following suit is mandatory when possible (a trump may be played only when a hand has no remaining card in the suit led); highest card or highest trump wins. The opening lead belongs to the player on dealer's left or, if the maker plays alone, to the lone hand's left.

Scoring

The first person to reach 10 (in some variants 11, and in others as little as 5) points wins the game. In an extended scoring

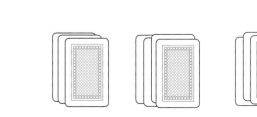

Diagram 11: Dealing for three-handed Five Hundred

system, the best two out of three *legs,* each played to a score of 21, make a match. Points are awarded as follows:

- **Taking three tricks:** 1 point
- **Taking all five tricks, a *sweep* or *march:*** 2 points
- **Taking all five, playing alone:** 4 points
- **Failing to take three tricks, that is, *euchred* by the defenders:** 2 points, to defenders
- **Two makers euchred by a lone defender:** 4 points, to defenders.

Some of the deck's unused cards, two for each partnership, keep a running score (diagram 10). Here, the numbers 0-4 are displayed in exposed *pip* count; that is, in the number of visible card spots. Commonly, the facedown card when turned crosswise (instead of covering pips lengthwise) can denote 5, so this sequence might also be read 0, 6, 7, 3, 4. A crosswise card laid faceup can denote five plus its face value— to reach higher numbers.

FIVE HUNDRED

NUMBER OF PLAYERS: Two to six

EQUIPMENT: One deck of cards

DIFFICULTY: Some skill is needed

DURATION: About 20 to 30 minutes

This game dates from 1904, when it was first introduced by the U.S. Playing Card Company—with evident success, for it is widely played in the United States and became practically the national game in Australia.

Setup

A standard deck is modified according to the number of players in a hand, so that ten cards per player are left, plus three extras, the *widow* cards. (Two-handed play, not described here, involves a rather more complex deal, with starting layouts.)

With four players, 2's, 3's, and black 4's are removed; for three players, 2's through 6's are extracted; with five players, the whole deck is used. A single joker, the *benny* (as in euchre), is added in all games. Six-handed games may use a special 63-card deck, obtainable from game suppliers, or make up such a deck from two ordinary ones.

Trump

One of the outcomes of the bidding (see below) will be to name one suit as *trump:* For the duration of the hand any card in the chosen trump suit outranks even the highest card of any other suit. Sometimes the winning bid is in *no trump*—no suit is given special privilege.

As in euchre, the trump suit ranks its jack, the *right bower,* just behind the benny, which is always highest. The like-coloured jack, the *left bower,* ranks third, the ace fourth, and so on, descending through the usual card order. In a no-trump hand, only the joker has trumping power; jacks revert in rank to their normal value, between queen and 10.

Dealing and bidding

After cutting for deal—high card wins—hands are distributed, beginning at dealer's left: three cards facedown at a time to each player, three into the middle (the widow), then four to each player, and finally three to each.

Dealer then opens the bidding, naming a number of tricks to be taken and a trump suit (for example: six, spades). Bids may be for as few as six or as many as ten tricks (the maximum). Each bid in turn must exceed the last, the auction principle. A player may pass instead of making a bid; after two passes in succession, the bidding is closed. Normally, once a player has passed he has no further opportunity to bid; often this rule is suspended by agreement.

Suits have a rank, as in bridge, so that a bid of, for example, six hearts is higher than six spades. Suits rank from no-trump (highest) through hearts, diamonds, clubs, and spades (lowest).

Two special bids are possible, which have their own rank within the auction's bidding. *Nullo,* or *misère,* signifies that a player intends to take no tricks in a no-trump hand. It has the effect of raising the bidding to a level between eight spades and eight clubs. An *open misère* outranks all other bids, so that it automatically closes the bidding. A player declaring open misère lays his hand down faceup; the contract must be made with all other players fully aware of the hand's makeup. Though a formidable challenge, a successful open misère scores highest of all contracts, alongside ten no-trump. (But scoring variations do exist.)

Playing the Game

The highest bidder has the privilege, before making the first lead, of taking the widow's three cards, at the same time discarding three facedown to the table. Trick play then proceeds in the usual way: One player *leads* a card (plays it to the center of the table), and the others in turn follow until all have played a card. These cards make up one *trick;* the highest card, or highest trump, in a trick wins these cards. The player who supplied the winning card removes the small stack to one side, keeping each won trick separate. The winner also has the privilege of making the next lead. Players must follow suit and may bring out a trump when *void* (that is, when holding none of the suit that was led). Two restrictions apply to playing the benny: In a no-trump hand, it can be laid only on a trick in whose suit the player is void; and if the benny is led, the player must announce its suit—which cannot be a suit in which the player was void at the hand's beginning.

Even in unpartnered games of Five Hundred, it makes sense for opponents informally to combine, whenever possible, in their play against the bidder. Each player retains any won tricks, which are worth 10 points each when tallied at the end of the game. A bidder's points are awarded—or deducted—according to the value of the bid.

Scoring

The first player to reach 500 points wins. If two make 500 in the same hand, the win goes to the player who has the bid. In any other case, the player who first reaches 500 during the course of a hand—by taking tricks—is the winner. A failed bid results in a minus score equal to the bid's value. Bid values are:

Tricks bid:	6	7	8	9	10
Spades:	40	140	240	340	440
Clubs:	60	160	260	360	460
Diamonds:	80	180	280	380	580
Hearts:	100	200	300	400	600
No-trump:	120	220	320	420	520
Misère:	250				
Open misère:	520				

Variations

Four-handed, or Australian, Five Hundred

Played in partnerships, this variation differs in several particulars from the basic game.

The widow is formed one card at a time, at the end of each three- or four-card distribution. (All 2's, 3's, and black 4's have been removed from the deck.) In playing a misère or open misère, the partner is inactive, hand laid out faceup. Although open misère may be bid at any time, misère is allowed only if the bid level has reached 7.

Bidding is closed after three successive passes. Its winner is referred to as the *contractor*. The widow, if picked up by the contractor, is not shown to other players. In misère or open misère, the joker must be played if it cannot be used in a suit that has been led. The joker can be led, and its suit named, only if that suit has not been previously led. Finally, scores are kept jointly for each partnership. If one side accumulates a score of minus 500, the game is lost ('going out the back door').

Five-handed Five Hundred

In this variant, played with a full deck, a contractor may choose for the course of a hand to form a temporary partnership. Points for such a hand are divided equally between partners, but individual scores are kept.

Taking on a temporary partner may cloak the play in mystery, at least for a while. The contractor names a card, and its holder automatically becomes a partner. Depending on agreed rules, a partner either announces the fact or remains silent, playing secretly to support the contractor.

Under the rule of silent partnership, a contractor may name a card in his own hand—opponents will not discover that he is competing alone until the partnership card itself is played.

Misère is usually barred in five-handed games; open misère is worth only 230 points. There may be, however, an option to bid *super open misère,* a bizarre contract in which the bidder's hand, faceup on the table, is actually played by the opponents. The bid scores 430 points.

Six-handed Five Hundred

Rules follow the five-handed version, but partnerships comprise three players, in alternating positions around the table. A special six-handed deck contains additional denominations—11's, 12's, and red 13's—that rank between 10's and jacks.

Alternatively, the 2's, 3's, and red 4's may be used, taken from a second standard deck. When one partner plays alone, both of the others and their cards are out of the hand.

GIN RUMMY

NUMBER OF PLAYERS: Two

EQUIPMENT: One deck of playing cards, with jokers removed; pencil and paper

DIFFICULTY: Some skill is needed

DURATION: Up to 10 minutes per hand

A popular pastime that originated in Spain, gin rummy reached the United States by the 19th century and many variations developed. The object is to make a ten-card hand containing only sets and sequences of cards: three or four of a kind and/or sequences of three or more in the same suit.

Setup

Players cut for the deal, and the high card can choose to deal or not. The dealer shuffles the cards and the nondealer cuts. Ten cards are dealt to each player. The next card is turned up and placed next to the remainder of the deck, stacked facedown in the middle of the table. The *upcard* begins the discard pile, while the remainder serves as a drawing pile.

Playing the Game

The nondealer goes first and has the option of taking the upcard or drawing the next card from the drawing pile. She must then make a single discard, faceup on the discard pile. The dealer may then take the top card from the discard pile or draw from the drawing pile. Play continues in this way until either a player has completed a *gin hand* in which every card in the hand forms part of a set (indicated by playing the last discard facedown); or a player chooses to *go down,* or knock, rapping her knuckles on the table. This can be done whenever the *deadwood*—the cards not part of a sequence or set—in her hand have a value of 10 points or less or there are only two cards left in the drawing pile. If play stops because there are only two cards left to draw, the hand is a *washout.* Neither player scores; the cards are reshuffled and redealt.

Scoring

A player with a gin hand earns points equal to the value of all the deadwood in an opponent's hand. Face cards count 10, aces count 1, and numbered cards count their rank.

After a player has knocked, both players lay down their

A	B
15	12
27	61
31	68
58	
88	
115	
75	
100	
290	
−68	
222	

Diagram 12: A score table for a game of gin rummy; A has won 3 more hands than B, for a net 75 point bonus plus 100 points for reaching 100.

hands. The opponent of the player who has knocked may play off any matching cards from her hand onto the sets and sequences in the knocker's hand. Following this procedure, the player with the lower value of deadwood in her hand scores the difference between the value of her deadwood and that of her opponent. A tie goes to the nonknocking player.

Bonus points

Several bonuses are also awarded:

- A player with a gin hand gets 25 points.
- If the opponent of the knocker wins, a situation called an *undercut,* she scores 25 points.
- The winner of a hand gets an additional *line bonus* of 25 points that is added to her total at the end of the game.
- The player who first reaches 100 points gets a *game bonus* of 100 points.

Winning the Game

Scores are recorded cumulatively over the course of the hands on a score sheet like the one in diagram 12. The game is over when a player reaches 100 points, excluding line bonuses. If the opponent has not won a single hand, referred to as a *blitz* or *washout,* the winner's score (excluding the line bonuses) is doubled. After all other scoring, line bonuses are added. The loser's score is subtracted from the winner's score, and the winner's final score is the difference between the two.

Variations
Hollywood

This version was invented in California. It involves three or more simultaneous sets of scores on a score sheet ruled into

Diagram 13: A set and a sequence in gin rummy

three sets of columns. The first scores in the game are entered in the first set of columns. After the second hand, scores are entered in both the first and second columns. After the third, the scores are entered into all three columns.

When one player reaches 100 in one of the columns, the column is closed and no further scores are entered. When one of the players reaches 100 in each column, total scores for each column are calculated, and then combined. The winner is the player with the highest combined total score, and the winning margin is her total minus that of the opponent. The only other scoring difference from standard gin rummy is that the doubling from a blitz includes the line bonuses.

Partnership Gin Rummy

This version for four people uses two packs of cards, with one member of each partnership playing against a member of the other partnership. At the end of the game the partnership combines its individual scores to give a final partnership total. Partners change places between hands, so that each plays against both opponents. The game is usually played to 150 points.

HEARTS

NUMBER OF PLAYERS: Three to seven

EQUIPMENT: One deck of playing cards

DIFFICULTY: Concentration needed

DURATION: About 20 to 30 minutes per round

The very aims of whist and bridge, to win tricks by dint of planning and finesse, are turned upside down in Hearts. In this game, players avoid certain tricks like the plague. With each heart taken, a player adds a point toward losing the game. (Tricks are cards played, one round at a time, to the center of the table: One player leads a card to

7 points

10 points

13 points

Diagram 14: Penalty cards for Black Maria

the table and the others in turn follow until all have played a card. These cards make up one trick; its winner removes the small stack to one side. The winner also has the privilege of making the next lead.)

Setup

Players cut for deal (lowest wins), and the entire deck is distributed clockwise beginning at dealer's left. Hearts can accommodate from three to seven players—as a rule there are no partnerships. To arrange an even distribution of cards, one or more deuces are removed from the deck (but never the 2 of hearts): one deuce for three players, two for five players, and three for seven.

Playing the Game

The player at dealer's left leads first; each trick's winner leads thereafter. With the lead, any card may be played at any time—except for hearts. Other players are obliged to follow suit, if they can. (Revoking, that is, not following in suit when able to do so, incurs a 13-point penalty.) The highest card of the suit led always takes the trick. Before a heart can be led, however, hearts must be 'broken,' that is, someone void in a suit led must already have played a heart.

A little experience in the game quickly shows the wisdom of jettisoning a hand's 'losers' (that is, sure trick-winners) early on, before other players have voids and begin to rid themselves of hearts. Long suits, even hearts, need not be a disadvantage, so long as a player can dodge the lead. Sometimes, of course, a hand is just too strong—a bridge player's dream—and all efforts to pass the lead off will prove futile.

Scoring

Each heart taken counts as one penalty point. Players agree

beforehand on a game limit, usually 50 or 100 penalty points, and deal new rounds until someone accumulates the point limit.

Winning the Game

A game ends when any player reaches the limit; the player with fewest points wins.

Variations

American Hearts, or Black Lady

This variant, best suited to four players, is nearly universal in the United States. As with Black Maria, three cards are passed before play commences, but in the American game cards are directed in successive hands to different players.

The sequence begins with a pass to the left; in the next hand to the right; then across the table; and finally 'hold,' no pass at all. Hearts are worth one penalty point each; the queen of spades (the Black Lady) counts 13.

In American Hearts a player may deliberately try to take all the penalty tricks (that is, the queen of spades and all the hearts), or 'shoot the moon.' Success costs each opponent the full 26 penalty points; failure, on the other hand, confers up to 25 points and much embarrassment on a rash plotter.

Winning all the penalty tricks usually requires some subterfuge, holding back some high cards while others gladly play theirs onto early tricks. Soon enough someone notices uncharacteristic play and becomes suspicious. Players freely discuss their misgivings and whether one of them should, for the good of all, absorb some points before it is too late. No one, of course, wants to be the Samaritan—it often results in a point drubbing once the lead is snatched.

Tactics

The threat of someone 'going all the way' causes players to consider their initial passes with care. Getting rid of losers is all very well, but not if they make a powerhouse of another hand. Creating a void while keeping the queen of spades, if

 *1 point*

 *2 points*

 *11 points*

 *12 points*

13 points

Diagram 15: Penalty points for Spot Hearts

it is well guarded, is often a good idea: it can be selectively played, perhaps to forestall a shot at the moon.

Black Maria

A popular European version, Black Maria (British slang for a police van) is scored differently from basic hearts and uses an interesting exchange of cards among players. Not only do hearts bring unwanted points, but also do the ace, king, and queen of spades. They are substantial penalties: 7 points for taking the ace, 10 for the king, and 13 for the queen (the Black Maria).

In this variant, after the deal but before the first lead, each player prunes three cards from his hand and passes them facedown to the player on the right. Replacements are picked up only after a player's selection and pass are completed.

Spot Hearts

Played as basic hearts, scoring in this variant assigns penalty points to each heart according to its face value; the ace equals 1 point, the king 13.

PINOCHLE

NUMBER OF PLAYERS: Two

EQUIPMENT: Two decks of playing cards with identical backs; pencil and paper

DIFFICULTY: Complex

DURATION: 1 hour to several hours

Descended from a German game, binokel, two-, three-, and four-handed versions of pinochle have been immensely popular, particularly in the United States. The two-handed game falls into two trick-playing phases, the first with melds, card combinations that score points. The second phase is straightforward trick play, without melds.

Setup

Special decks are available for pinochle, but two standard decks will serve. All cards numbered 2 to 8 should be removed; pinochle uses only 9's through aces. Aces rank highest, as in most card games, but 10's come next in pinochle. So, in descending order, rankings are: ace, 10, king, queen, jack, 9.

Players cut for deal; highest card wins. Cards should be dealt facedown four at a time, in three sets, giving each player 12 cards. Each player looks at his own cards. The deck's next card should be turned up in the middle; its suit names trump for the hand. For the duration of the hand, any card in the trump suit outranks even the highest card of any other suit. (If the upturned card is a 9, called a *dix*—see below—it scores

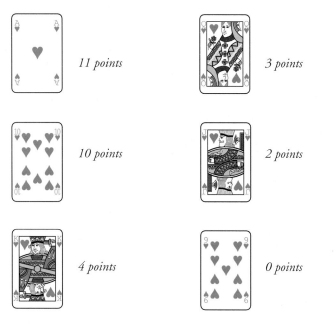

11 points

10 points

4 points

3 points

2 points

0 points

Diagram 16: *Scoring in pinochle*

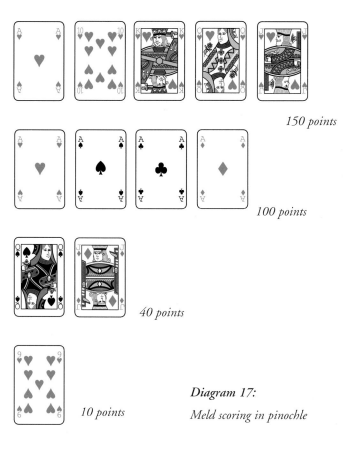

150 points

100 points

40 points

10 points

Diagram 17:
Meld scoring in pinochle

10 points immediately for the dealer.) The rest of the deck, the *stockpile,* goes crosswise across the trump.

Playing the Game

First phase

The nondealer leads. In the first phase, players need not follow suit; in other respects tricks are won or lost in the usual way, with the highest card in the suit or a trump. (Tricks are cards played, one round at a time, to the center of the table: One player *leads* a card to the table and the other in turn follows. These cards make up one *trick.* The winner removes the trick to one side, making a pile of all won cards. The winner also has the privilege of making the next lead.) For example, the jack of hearts is led; the opponent might choose to play the 9 of clubs, even though he holds the king of hearts—but wishes to reserve it as part of a meld. In the first phase players are eager to win tricks, and thus the privilege of making a meld, but not at the cost of playing away valuable cards before they have been melded.

Replacement cards are drawn from stock after each trick round—the trick's winner goes first—so that a player's hand always contains 12 cards.

After winning a trick and before making the next lead, a player may lay down a meld and score its value. Melds, it should be noted, are not out of play; melded cards can be picked up and played on a trick—with replacement from stock, just like any other card in the hand.

When stock has shrunk to one facedown card and the original faceup trump, melds are no longer allowed. The trick winner who draws when only two cards remain in stock may choose either but, if it's the facedown card, it must be shown to the other player. This concludes a game's first stage.

Second phase

Players begin each holding 12 cards—all meld is taken up—the last trick's winner leads. There is no stockpile. Players maintained a 12-card hand through the first phase, and thus begin the second phase with 12. In this round players must follow suit. If void and holding any trump, a trump must be played: Playing a trump is mandatory if void in the suit led. A trump remains the same throughout the first and second phases. Only tricks are scored in the second round; there is no melding.

Melds and Scoring

At the end players go through their trick piles, sorting out all the *counters* (A, K, 10) taken. They are worth 10 points each, a total of 240, plus 10 points automatically earned for taking the last trick, for a maximum of 250 points achievable in second-round trick play. Games are generally played to 1,000 points, except that if both players break 1,000 in the same hand, the game continues to 1,250—and onward by 250-point increments until there is a clear winner.

Diagram 18: Melding rules: (a) marriage was the first meld; (b) three queens added to the marriage give 60 queens as a second meld

Meld points are recorded as each is laid down. Combinations that score points include:

- **Flush** (one of each trump rank, except 9): 150 points
- **Four aces, one of each suit** (100 aces or aces around): 100 points
- **Four kings, different suits** (80 kings or kings around): 80 points
- **Four queens, different suits** (60 queens or queens around): 60 points
- **Four jacks, different suits** (40 jacks or jack around): 40 points
- **King and queen of trump** (a royal marriage): 40 points
- **King and queen, other suits** (a marriage): 20 points
- **Spade queen plus diamond jack** (a pinochle): 40 points
- **Double pinochle** (both spade queens and diamond jacks): 300 points
- **Nine of trump, by itself** (a dix, pronounced *deece*): 10 points

Though some systems greatly multiply the value of a *double around*—for example, all eight aces—the more usual method is to score just twice the points.

Melding rules

There are three things to keep in mind when melding: A meld is possible only after winning a trick; only one meld can be laid down in a turn, and unplayed melds do not score points.

Melded cards may be played in more than one way, as a part of a different kind of meld. Thus, in diagram 18, three queens played to an existing marriage form a new meld of 60 queens. Three kings might later be laid down as well, making 80 kings with the marriage. But the melds must be of different kinds: An extra jack of diamonds played, for example, to an existing pinochle does not yield a second pinochle.

In a melding turn (that is, after winning a trick) existing melds may not be merely rearranged for a new score; at least one new card must be played from the hand to the table before new melds are possible.

Once a card has been played from a meld onto a trick, a similar card may not later be added to that meld, scoring it again. The original meld's points are deducted if a player mistakenly attempts to form the meld again.

The king and queen of trump, a royal marriage, can be augmented on a subsequent turn to become a flush. Both melds are scored.

Playing a dix is not considered a complete meld. The first dix to be melded immediately replaces the central trump, and that card is taken into the player's hand. The player remains eligible for a further meld in that turn. Likewise for the second dix: It is played alone and may be followed by another meld.

Three- and four-handed games

In the four-handed, partnered version each player receives 12 cards. There is no trick play in the first, or melding phase. Instead, there is a round of bidding: The player to dealer's left goes first, either passing or opening for at least 250 points (declaring a minimum the partnership must score). In turn players may raise the bid, in increments of at least 10 points, or pass, until three players have passed in one round. The winning bidder, or *declarer,* has the right to name trump and to lead the first trick. Also, the declarer's partner selects and passes four cards to the bidder, who reciprocates, sending four replacements to the partner. All scoring meld combinations for both sides are then simply laid out, recorded, and gathered back up, after which trick play commences.

A three-handed game follows the same bidding and

straightforward meld procedure, without trick play in the first phase. Players receive 15 cards each; the three extra cards are delivered into a pile in the center, the *kitty,* at any time during the course of the deal. The winning bidder chooses trump and receives the three kitty cards. (They are shown to the other players and put into hand. The declarer then selects and removes any three cards from his hand, thus starting his trick pile.) Both of these variants are usually played to a winning score of 1,500 points.

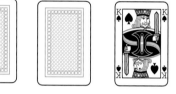

Diagram 19: A Scopa sweep

matches the value of the hand card. Only one matching card or set can be captured per turn. If both a pair and a set are possible, the pair must be captured.

Capturing all the cards on the table is a *sweep.* If no capture can be made, the hand card is left on the table, or *trailed.* Players consolidate their captured cards into a facedown pile, except that the hand card from a sweep is left faceup so that a point for the sweep can be counted at the end of the game.

Whenever both players run out of cards, three more are dealt, and play continues until the deck is exhausted and players have no more hand cards. The player of the last card gets the cards left on the table, but this is not a sweep.

SCOPA

Number of players: Two

Equipment: One deck of playing cards

Difficulty: Fun for children and adults

Duration: Half an hour

Setup

This Italian game uses a deck of cards with the 8's, 9's, and 10's removed. Like casino, players capture cards from the table by matching them with cards from their hands. Jacks count as 8, queens as 9, and kings as 10, with the rest of the cards taking their face values for purposes of capture. Aces are low.

Playing the Game

Players cut for the deal, with the lower card dealing. Each player is dealt three cards facedown. Four cards are then dealt faceup on the table. On each turn, a player places a card from his hand, the *hand card,* faceup on the table. If he can, he either *captures* a table card by pairing it with the hand card, or captures two or more cards by combining them into a set that

Scoring

At the end of each hand, each of the following scores 1 point:

- Capturing 21 or more cards
- Capturing 6 or more diamonds
- Capturing the 7 of diamonds (the *sette bello*)
- Primiera: From the pile of captured cards, each player finds his highest card in each suit based on the following values: 7 = 21; 6 = 18; ace = 16; 5 = 15; 4 = 14; 3 = 13; 2 = 12; face cards = 10. The player whose four high cards give the larger total gets the point.
- Capturing a sweep.

Winning the Game

New hands are played until one player reaches 11 points and wins the game.

SLOBBERHANNES

NUMBER OF PLAYERS: Three to seven

EQUIPMENT: One deck of cards

DIFFICULTY: A fairly easy game

DURATION: About 20 to 30 minutes

In Slobberhannes, a predecessor of hearts (see page 92), players try to avoid taking the first or last trick or the trick containing the queen of clubs. The curious name comes from the German for 'Slippery Jack.'

Setup

All cards below 7 should be removed from a standard deck, and the shuffled remainder dealt one at a time, facedown.

Playing the Game

The person to the dealer's left plays the first card. Other players must follow suit, if possible. The highest card in the suit wins the *trick,* and the winner plays the first card of the next trick. Each player starts with ten counters (chips). One counter must be placed in a central pool by the person taking the first trick, the person taking the last trick, and the person taking the queen of clubs. If the same person takes all three tricks, an additional counter must be forfeited. Play continues with the deal passing to the left from round to round.

A player who runs out of counters is out of the game. The last remaining player, or the player with the most counters when play is stopped, wins the pool.

WHIST

NUMBER OF PLAYERS: Four, in two pairs

EQUIPMENT: A deck of cards

DIFFICULTY: Complex

DURATION: About 1 hour for two games

In this fairly complex card game players aim to gain as many points as possible by playing the highest cards. A very social game—the gin rummy or hearts of centuries past—whist waned in popularity as contract bridge displaced it in drawing rooms and clubs in the 20th century.

Setup

Players cut for partners. The higher and lower two are paired or they may agree beforehand on partners. They cut again for the initial deal, high card winning (an ace is low in this draw, but high otherwise throughout the game). Partners sit opposite one another. Beginning with the left-hand player, the dealer distributes all the cards clockwise around the table to each player, turning the last faceup in the middle. The middle card's suit will serve as *trump* for the hand. That is, that suit will win over all others.

Playing the Game

Once a trump has been determined, the first to play (at the dealer's left) must select and place a card in the middle, as do the other players in turn. Cards played must agree in suit with the first; if a player has none of that suit, a trump may be chosen or a card of any other suit. Each round of four cards make up a *trick,* which is won by the highest card played in suit, or the highest trump (the trump is higher). The winner then leads any card to the middle, to begin the next trick.

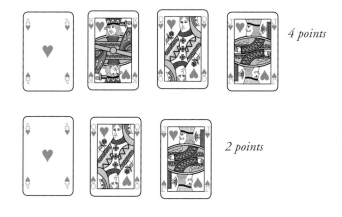

4 points

2 points

Diagram 20: *The English system of scoring for honors in whist*

Usually one partner keeps all tricks taken by the side; they will be counted and scored at the end. Failure to follow suit, when a suited play is possible, is a serious infraction, called *revoking*. The penalty for this is described below. A player who catches his error may repair the mistake before a trick is gathered up, though the misplayed card remains faceup, and opponents may demand it go on the next trick in that suit.

Scoring

Two scoring systems, American and English, are in common use. In both, only the excess over six tricks taken by a partnership is counted—a maximum, therefore, of 7 trick points. For example, if one side has taken eight tricks, it collects two points; the other side, with five tricks, scores nothing. Games are played to a score of 7 in the American system, to 5 under English rules. Winning two games completes a *rubber,* worth two additional points to the partnership. Overall scores are tabulated at the end of each rubber.

Regarding the penalty for revoking: In American scoring 2 points are taken from the offending side and added to the other; the English system deducts 3 or, if that would result in a negative score, adds 3 to the opponents' tally.

Using the English method of scorekeeping, as shown in diagram 20, extra points are awarded for *honors,* that is, when two partners hold all, or all but one, of the A, K, Q, and J of one suit. Having all four honors scores 4 points; three honors, 2 points. Because this convention introduces a significant element of luck into scoring, many players prefer to do without it.

West

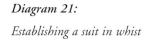

South

North

East

Diagram 21:
Establishing a suit in whist

Choosing leads

Partners would very much like to know how their hands complement each other—what suits to lead that will put their opponents at a disadvantage. Unlike contract bridge, where bidding allows some information to be traded, whist has no opening discussion of a hand's potential. By common understanding, a whist player will indicate a hand's longest, strongest suit by leading a card in that suit. Good players may agree on more refinements in their choices to help a partner gauge the other's holdings more accurately.

As a general rule, unless holding very strong honors, a player leads with the fourth highest card in his best, longest suit. Once a trick is taken, a player continues leading in his strongest suit or leads back in the suit played by his partner—this is called establishing a suit. In the game example here (diagram 21), the hands have been stripped down just to spades in order to consider one possible distribution and the outcomes. The player at the top has just led the 7 from a very long suit in hand. With a little luck, particularly if trump has already been exhausted, the partners will have only one loser in this suit, to the king or queen.

Of course, the distribution may not favour them; the opponents may hold all four missing spades in one hand and win two tricks—or more if one of them leads a low spade to a partner's void (that is, the partner has none of the suit that was led), with trump still in hand. North's good spades would fall to the trump in this case. Trump outranks any cards of other suits.

Establishing a void, clearly, can have tactical advantage, particularly when partners are able to lead by turns to one another's voids and trump each trick.

Card Games for One

Napoleon spent his exile on St. Helena playing a version of solitaire. Solo card games have remained a popular way of whiling away the hours, especially with the advent of computer solitaire.

CLOCK PATIENCE

NUMBER OF PLAYERS: One

EQUIPMENT: Deck of playing cards with jokers removed

DIFFICULTY: Easy to play

DURATION: 10 to 15 minutes

The object of this game, also known as Four of a Kind, Hidden Cards, and Sundial, is to arrange the cards in 13 piles, one for each rank. Play it with a standard card deck, minus the jokers.

Setup

Shuffle the cards and deal them facedown into 13 piles of four each, 12 in the shape of a clock and the 13th pile within the circle, as in diagram 1.

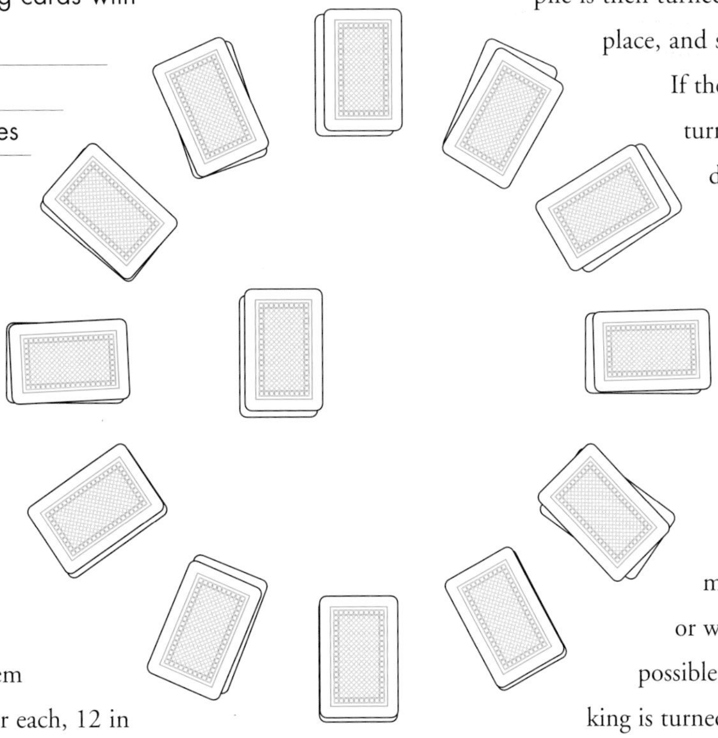

Diagram 1: Layout for clock patience

Playing the Game

Turn over the top card from the pile in the middle—the kings' pile—and place it faceup on top of the pile corresponding to its correct place on the clock face—for example, a 9 would go on the pile where the hour hand would point at 9 o'clock. Jacks take the 11 spot and queens the 12 spot, and aces the 1 o'clock spot. Then turn up the uppermost facedown card from

the pile to which the first card was added and place it in its correct place, faceup on top of the pile. A card from that pile is then turned up and moved to its correct place, and so on (see diagram 2.) If the last facedown card in a pile turns out to belong to that pile, draw the first available facedown card in the next clockwise pile to keep the game going.

Ending the Game

The game ends when all cards have been successfully moved to their proper places, or when no more plays are possible. This occurs if the fourth king is turned up before the end of the game, because there is no fourth card to draw from the kings' pile.

Variation
Watch Solitaire

This version is played in the same way, except that if the fourth king is turned up before the end of the game, the player is allowed to replace it in any other pile and take a replacement card from that pile. The replacement may only be done once, but the chances of completion are increased fivefold.

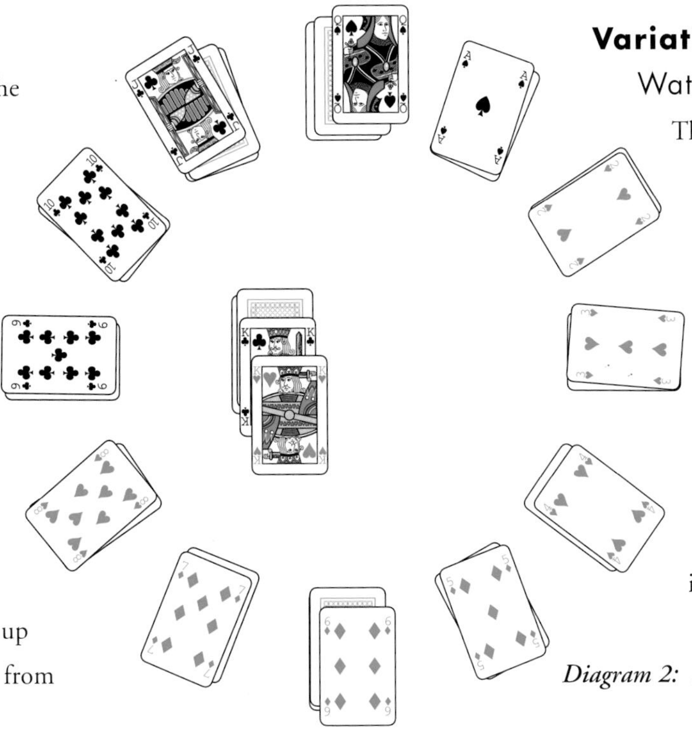

Diagram 2: Playing clock patience

Diagram 3:
Layout of the cards for
The Four Corners

grid with the depot cards (see diagram 4).

During the initial layout, any aces or kings turned up are moved to the middle and replaced in the depot columns. Kings are lined up with the top two rows of depot cards, and aces with the bottom two rows. The kings form the beginnings of suited sequences of cards building down (king, queen, jack, and 10 of clubs, for example, and so on). The aces start suited sequences that build up (ace, 2, 3, and 4 of hearts, for example, and so on).

First stage play

When the 12-card layout of depot and corner cards has been completed, the player can move any corner card to a central pile where it is in proper suit and sequence. A depot card can only be moved to a central pile if it is in the same horizontal row as the pile on which it is to be played. Cards moved to the middle are not replaced. After all available moves have been made, one card is added to each depot and corner pile,

THE FOUR CORNERS

NUMBER OF PLAYERS: One

EQUIPMENT: Two decks of playing cards without jokers

DIFFICULTY: Some skill is needed

DURATION: About 15 minutes

The object is to build both ascending and descending suited sequences. Based mostly on luck, it is difficult to win.

Setup

Shuffle two packs of cards together. Then lay 12 cards out as shown in diagram 3: two columns of four cards, which are the beginnings of eight piles called *depots*, plus four corner cards laid diagonally at each end of the two columns. The space in the middle must be wide enough for four additional columns of cards, which will eventually form a 4 x 4

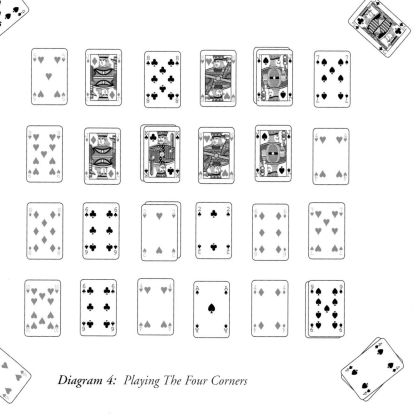

Diagram 4: Playing The Four Corners

Diagram 5: Layout for Grandfather's Clock

If available moves are again exhausted, the player can pick up all of the corner and depot cards in the order in which they were first laid down and re-deal them around the layout. This may improve the situation, for example, by converting an ascending pile, the 4, 5 and 6 of hearts, into a descending pile, the 6, 5, and 4 that can be played on the 3 of hearts in the middle. The corner and depot cards can be picked up and re-dealt twice, but no more than twice, during a game.

GRANDFATHER'S CLOCK

NUMBER OF PLAYERS: One

EQUIPMENT: A deck of playing cards

DIFFICULTY: An easy game

DURATION: 5 to 10 minutes

This solitaire game also has a clock layout, with the aim of shifting cards to the appropriate place on the dial.

with aces and kings being moved to the middle as before. Then any permissible corner or depot card moves are made, after which cards are dealt to the depot and corner piles again. This process continues until all the cards have been dealt out.

Second stage play

After the first stage, the rules change. Corner cards can be moved as before, but now the top card from any depot pile can be moved to the middle, regardless of which row it is in. Also, the top card from any depot or corner pile can be moved to any other depot or corner pile on which it can be played in either ascending or descending sequence on a card of the same suit. At this point, the player must consider moves on the basis of how future opportunities will be affected.

Setup

Remove 12 cards from a standard 52-card deck in a sequence from 2 to king. The numeric sequence must also be in sequence by suits: for example, 2 of spades, 3 of hearts, 4 of diamonds, 5 of clubs, 6 of spades, 7 of hearts, and so on. Place the 12 cards in a circle, with the 9 at 12 o'clock and the remainder following clockwise, as shown in diagram 5. Shuffle the rest of the cards and lay them out faceup in eight columns of five overlapping cards.

Playing the Game

Any card may be moved from the top of a pile onto the preceding card in the same suit on the clock—the 7 of hearts on the 6 of hearts, for instance. Moves can be made on the columns as well. Regardless of suit, one top card can be

Diagram 6: *Playing Grandfather's Clock*

played on the top card of another column to form a descending numerical sequence—a 6 on a 7, for example. Also, if a column becomes empty, its space can be filled in by any card from the top row of another column.

Continue play until each of the piles on the clock face has the right card at the top—an ace at 1 o'clock and a queen at 12, or until no more moves are available.

KLONDIKE

NUMBER OF PLAYERS: One

EQUIPMENT: A deck of playing cards without jokers

DIFFICULTY: Some strategic skills help

DURATION: About 10 minutes

The aim of this game, invented according to legend during the Alaska gold rush, is to build four piles of cards, one for each suit, in order from aces to kings.

Setup

The tableau, or initial layout, consists of a row of seven piles of cards. The first has one card, the second has two, the third has three, and so on. The top card on each pile is turned faceup, and the rest are facedown. The remaining 24 cards form the reserve (see diagram 7).

Remove any faceup aces to begin one of the four foundation piles, the ones to be built up in sequence by suit. To uncover more cards for play onto the foundation piles, move cards in the tableau, building them down in numerical sequence in alternating colours (red on black; black on red).

Playing the Game

You can also move a sequence of cards from one pile to another. When all faceup cards are moved off a pile, the top facedown card can be turned up. If a blank space is created in the tableau, it can be filled in only with a king. Cards played to a foundation pile may not be removed and used again.

Once all moves are exhausted, play cards from the reserve either directly on the foundations or onto the tableau. Two different methods are available. In the first, cards in the reserve are turned up one at a time, and the reserve may only be gone through once.

Diagram 7:
Layout for Klondike

Diagram 8: A game of Klondike

Agnes

In this variation, after the tableau is formed, the next card is dealt faceup above it and forms the beginning of the first foundation. All the other foundations must begin with a card of the same value. The last card in each foundation pile will be the card immediately below the first card in sequence. If the pile begins with an 8, for example, the last card will be a 7.

After the first foundation card is dealt, a row of seven cards is dealt below the tableau to serve

In the second, cards are turned up three at a time, but only the top card can be played. In the three-card method, the reserve can be gone through three times. Play continues until all cards have been moved to the four foundation piles, or until there are no moves left and the reserve has been used as many times as permitted.

Strategy

The three-at-a-time method is strategically more useful, because you can learn which cards are in the reserve deck, and where they are, during the first time through. You can use this knowledge on subsequent passes through the deck. Examine the tableau with care, too, to discover whether whole sequences could be transferred from one pile to another to free up cards that can move to the foundations or to expose new cards.

Variations

Two-player Klondike

In this variation, players each have their own decks, tableaux, and reserve piles, but can play on any of the eight foundation piles. They take turns; the player with the lowest card in the one-card column goes first. A turn ends after a player resorts once to the reserve pile, or after a player is called for failure to play an ace to a foundation pile when he could have done so.

Computer solitaire

The age of computers has created a solitaire renaissance. Klondike, which was probably already the best-known solitaire game, has become even more familiar in recent years because it is included with every copy of Microsoft Windows under the name Microsoft Solitaire.

Many other solitaire card games are widely played on computers. Because the application takes over the tedious job of laying out the cards, play is easier and faster than with real cards. Free Cell, another solitaire card game packaged with Windows, has become an addictive pastime for many personal computer users, and has several websites devoted to it.

Hundreds of other computer solitaire card games are available online, either free or for sale. There are even websites that allow people to bet on their solitaire skills.

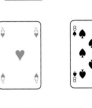

Diagram 9:
Laying out the cards
for Agnes

as the reserve. When there are no more moves, a second row of seven cards is dealt to the reserve. A third row can also be dealt when moves are again used up. (The two extra cards left after the last seven-card reserve row is dealt are added to the final row.)

Blank columns begin not with kings, but with whatever card goes last on the foundation piles.

LOVELY LUCY

NUMBER OF PLAYERS: One

EQUIPMENT: A deck of playing cards without jokers

DIFFICULTY: Some strategy needed

DURATION: About 15 minutes

Originating in France as La Belle Lucie, this form of solitaire has the aim of building four ascending suited sequences of cards from aces to kings.

Setup

Deal shuffled cards three at a time faceup into 17 *fans* of three cards, plus one single card alone, as in diagram 10. Then move aces to one side to begin the foundations

where the ascending sequences will be built.

Playing the Game

Only the top cards of the fans and the singleton are playable. Cards can be played only one at a time, either on the foundations in ascending suited sequence, or on the top card of another fan in descending suited sequence. Once a card is on the foundation it cannot be moved. When all three cards of a fan have been played, the space is simply left vacant (see diagram 11).

Once a card has been moved to a fan, it cannot be moved again except onto the foundation. Therefore the cards

Diagram 10: Laying out the cards for Lovely Lucy

Diagram 11: Vacant spaces

aces are removed from the pack and set out to begin the foundations before the cards are dealt. The initial deal is then 16 three-card fans.

Shamrocks

This game is laid out like Lovely Lucy, but is played with these differences:

- Any king that is above another card of the same suit can be moved just beneath it.
- The player can build either up or down on the fans, and need not follow suit.
- A fan may only contain three cards.
- No redeals are allowed, and there is no merci.
- It is not always best to move a playable card immediately to the foundation, since it may be of better use to the fans.

MONTE CARLO

NUMBER OF PLAYERS: One

EQUIPMENT: Deck of playing cards, jokers removed

DIFFICULTY: Easy

DURATION: 5 to 10 minutes

This is a simple game of chance, the aim of which is to arrange the deck into 26 pairs of equal rank.

Setup

Shuffle and lay out a 52-card deck, left to right and faceup in five rows of five cards.

Playing the Game

Pairs of cards may be picked up from the array if they adjoin one another horizontally, vertically, or diagonally. For example, in the layout in diagram 12, the queen of clubs could be paired either with the queen of diamonds or with

beneath an unplayable card in the fan, and any cards that could play on those cards, are blocked. So take care to avoid burying needed cards.

When all moves are exhausted, pick up the remaining cards in the fans, shuffle, and redeal them in threes. Two redeals in all are permitted. Once the redeals have been used up, the player can make one additional play to open up the game: the *merci*. On the merci play, any one blocked card can be moved out from under the cards above it to any permissible location.

Variations

Trefoil

This game is exactly like Lovely Lucy, except that the four

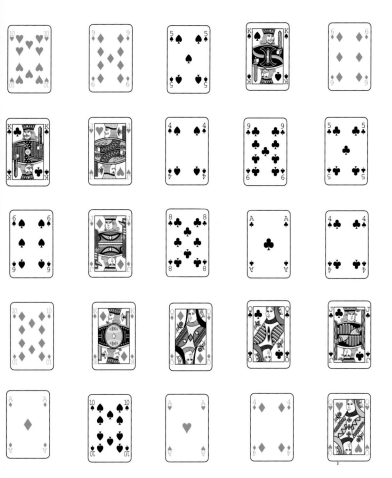

Diagram 12: Laying out the cards for Monte Carlo

NINETY-ONE

NUMBER OF PLAYERS: One

EQUIPMENT: A deck of playing cards, with jokers removed

DIFFICULTY: It helps to be good at mental arithmetic

DURATION: Several hours—or until patience runs out!

The object is to make a tableau in which the total value of the top cards add up to 91. Numbered cards have their face value. The ace is 1, the jack is 11, the queen is 12, and the king is 13.

Playing the Game

To start, lay the shuffled deck faceup in 13 piles of four cards, as show in diagram 13. To change the total, move a card from the top of any pile to the top of any other pile. The only qualification is that each pile must retain at least one card. The game ends when the tableau totals 91 or when the player quits.

the queen of hearts.

Fill in any gaps created in the array by sliding cards from the right, or up at the end of a row, so that it will preserve the order in which the cards were first laid out. Then deal new cards to the end, restoring the array. Again, remove adjoining pairs. When no more pairs can be made, rebuild the array as before.

Continue play in this way, even after all cards are dealt: Each time no plays remain, fill gaps by moving the remaining cards.

Winning the Game

The game ends when all cards have successfully been discarded, or when no plays are left (for example, a sequence of 3-5-3-5 in the only remaining row).

Diagram 13: Laying out the cards for a game of Ninety-one

Children's Card Games

Simple card games such as Go Fish and Donkey will provide
hours of entertainment—especially on rainy days.

BEGGAR MY NEIGHBOR

NUMBER OF PLAYERS: Two or more

EQUIPMENT: One deck of cards, or two decks for four or more players

DIFFICULTY: The game depends more on luck than skill

DURATION: About 5 to 10 minutes

A simple card game where players try to win a pile of cards. Whoever runs out of cards first loses. Although this game requires no skill, children will find its pace exciting.

Setup

To begin, shuffle the cards and deal them around until none remains; a four-handed game or higher will need two decks. Hands are stacked facedown and unseen in front of each player.

Diagram 1: The cards played in Beggar my Neighbor

Playing the Game

Beginning at dealer's left, players turn up the top card and place it in the middle. Cards with face values from 2 to 10 are of no account; the turn passes. When an honor card—jack through ace—appears, the procedure changes.

After an honor is turned up, the next player must transfer to the middle pile a number of cards equal to the value of the honor: Jacks are worth one card, queens two, kings three, and aces four. If in the course of adding these cards to the stack no new honor appears, the original player takes possession of the middle cards, stacking them beneath his hand.

The shoe is on the other foot, though, when another honor card does turn up. Play stops again, even if all cards due the first honor have not been added. Now the original player must surrender cards equal to the new honor's value. This time, if yet another honor has not shown up, the stack is taken by the second player, the one who added the last honor.

Winning the Game

The chance to win the pile can pass back and forth between two players for as long as honors continue to turn up, after which the game continues as before. Anyone who runs out of cards is out of the game. The player who has finally taken all the cards wins.

CHEAT (I DOUBT IT)

NUMBER OF PLAYERS: Three or more

EQUIPMENT: One deck of cards

DIFFICULTY: Easy to play

DURATION: 5 to 10 minutes

Deception is the method and object of this game; good players keep opponents guessing about their credibility at every stage.

Setup

Shuffle the cards and deal the entire deck around. It does not matter if some players have an extra card. Players should guard their hands closely so that others cannot catch a glimpse.

Playing the Game

The player to the dealer's left begins, placing a card of his choice facedown in the middle and announcing its rank. This may be the truth, or it may not. Subsequent players, in clockwise order, must do the same, claiming a higher rank for each card laid on the growing central pile.

At any time a player may call out 'Cheat!' (or 'I doubt it!'), signifying a challenge. The card in question is turned up: If the verdict is truth, the challenger must pick up all the cards in the middle; if falsehood is revealed, the one who played that card picks up the central pile.

Pressure builds, clearly, as a card's supposed rank climbs toward ace, since the next player in turn will have no choice but to allege fraud—and the card may even prove to be genuine. Depending on the ages of participants, strategies may become highly convoluted. Should the opener choose a low or middle rank, encouraging a larger pile to grow? Or begin pre-emptively higher, forcing a challenge earlier? This game greatly resembles poker in the range and importance of tactical deceptions.

Winning the Game

The winner is the first to run out of cards.

Variation
Double Cards

The rules may be modified to allow play of more than one card (of the same value) at a time. An opportunity exists, thus, of intensifying a bluff: Having nicely calculated his chances, a player might, for example, play two or three cards in the middle at once, naming them queens. Potential challengers must weigh the risks, as always, but with more in the balance.

CONCENTRATION (PELMANISM)

NUMBER OF PLAYERS: Two or more

EQUIPMENT: One deck of cards

DIFFICULTY: Concentration needed

DURATION: 5 minutes or more

This is one children's game that may actually be more difficult for adults. The challenge is to remember where the cards are after they are turned up briefly, two at a time, on the table.

Playing the Game

Lay out all 52 cards facedown, either in ordered rows or in random disarray. The first player turns up any two; if they happen to

Diagram 2: Concentration

match, the player keeps them and takes another turn.

When, as more often happens, there is no match, the two cards are turned facedown but without shifting their positions in any way. The opportunity then passes to the left. Other players have a chance to study any upturned cards, to try to remember them and their places on the table.

Winning the Game

The game continues by turns until all cards have been paired and taken. The player with the most cards wins.

DONKEY

NUMBER OF PLAYERS: Three to six

EQUIPMENT: Four cards of equal value for each player

DIFFICULTY: Easy

DURATION: 5 to 10 minutes

This is a short, fast game for younger children. The object is to collect all four cards of the same face value.

Setup

First, strip a complete rank from a standard deck for each player. With four players, for example, aces through jacks might be removed; they will constitute the game's deck.

Playing the Game

Shuffle the cards and deal four to each player. They should examine their hands and pass one facedown to the left. Naturally, players will want to keep any pairs or triples they already have and pass an unmatched card.

Winning the Game

The game continues with successive passes until one player unceremoniously lays down a finished set of four. On seeing what has happened, the others lay down their cards as well, no matter what they have. The last to notice, and lay down

his hand, loses and becomes the 'donkey' until the title is passed along to someone else in a subsequent hand.

Variation

Pig

With a subtler ending than Donkey, Pig uses all the same rules, except that a player who has completed a collection of four merely touches his nose. The last to react—by also touching his nose—is nominated 'pig.'

EARL OF COVENTRY (*see* SNIP SNAP SNOREM)

GO BOOM

NUMBER OF PLAYERS: Two to 12

EQUIPMENT: One deck of cards (two decks are needed for six or more players)

DIFFICULTY: Very simple

DURATION: 15 minutes

All children, particularly the very young, will enjoy this simple, noisy game.

Setup

Seven cards are dealt to each player; the remainder are put in a stockpile in the middle of the table.

Playing the Game

Beginning at the dealer's left, a player puts one card in the middle of the table, faceup; then each player in turn must place a card in the middle that matches the last in either rank or suit. (Aces are high.) A player who cannot follow in rank or suit must begin drawing from the stockpile, taking one card at a time until a playable card turns up. If the stock is exhausted, the thwarted player must pass.

When a round has been completed—everyone has played

or passed—the cards in the middle are examined. Whoever played the highest card wins the privilege of leading first in the next round.

Diagram 3: Go Boom

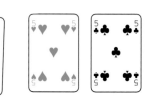

Winning the Game

If the highest card is tied by one or more of equivalent rank, the first to have played its kind wins. The game's object is to be first with an empty hand and, thus, to announce triumphantly, 'Boom!' Should it happen in a round that everyone must pass, the game ends; the player with fewest remaining cards wins.

GO FISH

NUMBER OF PLAYERS: Two to five

EQUIPMENT: One deck of cards

DIFFICULTY: Luck is needed

DURATION: 5 to 10 minutes

There is some strategy to this simple game. Players must decide on which sets of four (books) to collect, sometime changing course as the game progresses.

Setup

For two or three players, seven cards each are dealt out; with four or five, each receives five cards. The deck's remainder is placed in the middle, facedown, becoming the *fishpond.*

Playing the Game

After all players have examined their hands, the player to the left of the dealer begins, asking the right-hand player for any desirable card; for example, a queen. If that player has any of the rank named, those cards must all be handed over. If not, he announces 'Go fish,' and the other takes the top card from the fishpond, ending his turn.

Should it happen, however, that the drawn card matches the original request, the player must say 'I fished upon my wish' and continues the turn, making a new demand of the player to the right.

Winning the Game

In the course of the game, when a player has made a book (a set of four of a kind), it is laid down immediately—which entitles the player to ask again for a card. Play goes around the table clockwise in this manner until someone succeeds in emptying a hand by converting it completely into fours. The winner, therefore, is the player who puts down on the table all his cards in sets of four, or who has the most sets when the fishpond dries up.

Diagram 4: Go Fish

I DOUBT IT (*see* CHEAT)

MY SHIP SAILS

NUMBER OF PLAYERS: Four to seven

EQUIPMENT: Deck of cards

DIFFICULTY: Suitable for older children and adults

DURATION: About 10 minutes per game

The object of this easy card game is to be the first to collect seven cards of one suit.

Setup

From four to seven players are dealt seven cards each, facedown, one at a time, from a shuffled 52-card deck. Cards that are not dealt are set aside.

Playing the Game

Each player examines his hand and chooses one card to discard, placing that card facedown on the table. When all players are ready, the discards are passed to the left, each player thus receiving a new card from the player on his right. Players again choose a discard and pass it to the left.

Winning the Game

Discarding and passing continues until one player has managed to collect seven cards of one suit. As soon as this happens, the player calls out, 'My ship sails!' and wins the game. If several players make suited hands at the same time, the first one to finish saying the phrase is the winner.

OLD MAID

NUMBER OF PLAYERS: Three to five

EQUIPMENT: One deck of cards

DIFFICULTY: An easy game

DURATION: About 10 minutes

In this game, cards are paired off and discarded until only the unpairable Old Maid is left, in the losing hand.

Setup

The queens of hearts, diamonds, and clubs are removed from a standard 52-card deck; cards are then shuffled and all are dealt. Players examine their hands and remove all the cards that they can pair with another of the same rank and colour.

Playing the Game

The player to the dealer's left draws a card from the player on his right. If he can pair this card with one from his hand, he removes the pair and places it faceup on the table; otherwise the drawn card becomes part of his hand.

The next player to the left then draws a card from the player on his right, and the game continues, with players removing pairs from their hands until finally all the cards are paired off except for the Old Maid (the Queen of Spades). The player who ends up with the Old Maid loses.

Variation

Le Pouilleux

A more politically correct version of this game is played in France, where the Jack of Spades, called Le Pouilleux ('the lice man'), is the odd one out.

PELMANISM (*see* CONCENTRATION)

ROLLING STONE

NUMBER OF PLAYER: Four to six

EQUIPMENT: Deck of cards

DIFFICULTY: Easy for older children and adults

DURATION: About 15 minutes

In this simple card game players aim at matching cards by suit until one hand is emptied.

Setup

The number of cards used depends upon the number of players. Each player must have eight cards and each suit must be equally represented. So for six players, one rank is removed (for example, all the 2's); for five players, two ranks are removed; and for four players, three ranks are removed.

Playing the Game

Cards are shuffled and dealt, and play is begun by the player to the left of the dealer. She may play any card; the other players in turn must play a card of the same suit, until one player cannot play. This player must pick up all the cards that have been played and add them to her hand. She then continues the game by playing a card from any but the suit just used, with the other players following suit as before.

Winning the Game

The game ends when one player wins by running out of cards.

SLAPJACK

NUMBER OF PLAYERS: Two or more

EQUIPMENT: One deck of cards (two decks are needed for four or more players)

DIFFICULTY: Very simple

DURATION: About 10 minutes

This is a physical game for quick reflexes.

Deal cards around until the deck is exhausted; it does not matter if some hands have an extra card.

Hands are gathered up, unseen,

into facedown piles. The player at dealer's left begins by laying his hand's top card faceup in the middle. By turns the other players do the same until a jack appears. The first person to slap a hand over the jack wins the pile. The game ends when one player has won all the cards.

As long as two players remain in the game, any others who have run out of cards can continue to play and replenish their supply by winning a pile.

SNAP

NUMBER OF PLAYERS: Two or more

EQUIPMENT: One deck of cards for two to three players; two decks for four or more players

DIFFICULTY: An easy game

DURATION: About 5 minutes

This simple game requires only that players pay attention and react quickly.

Cards are dealt around until none remains—it does not matter if some players have an extra card. Hands are stacked facedown in front of each player.

Playing the Game

The first to play, at dealer's left, turns up one card, placing it faceup next to his hand. The next player does the same with his hand, and so on around the table.

Faceup cards are neatly stacked, too, so that only the last one played is in plain view. When a card of matching rank to one already visible is turned up, the first player to call 'Snap' wins both piles and adds them to the bottom of his facedown pile. Suits do not matter, only rank.

Diagram 5: Snap

The game continues until one player has taken all the cards.

Running out of cards does not take a player out of the game, so long as two others remain active. Temporarily emptied hands may still call a matchup and win a new supply of cards. Should a player mistakenly utter 'Snap' when there is no match, a facedown card is forfeited to each player and added to their facedown hands. Disputes naturally arise over precedence in announcing Snap; it is wise to have an adult on hand to referee close calls.

SNIP SNAP SNOREM (EARL OF COVENTRY)

NUMBER OF PLAYERS: Three to ten

EQUIPMENT: Deck of cards

DIFFICULTY: Easy for adults and older children

DURATION: About 20 minutes or longer

An old game, sometimes known as Earl of Coventry, Snip Snap Snorem has the simple object of making discards until a hand is emptied.

Setup

Using a shuffled standard 52-card deck, cards are dealt to each player, facedown, one by one, until the deck is exhausted.

Playing the Game

The game begins with the dealer playing a card from her hand faceup in the middle of the table. Players, in turn from the dealer's left, have the opportunity to play a discard of the same rank as the card in the middle. The first to have a matching card plays it on the middle pile and calls 'Snip!' Play continues until the next person with a match calls 'Snap!' as she plays. The third person with a match plays and calls 'Snorem!'

Players without a match cannot discard. The Snorem

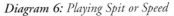

Diagram 6: Playing Spit or Speed

player starts the next round by playing any card faceup in the middle. The game continues until someone wins by having no cards left.

SPIT (SPEED)

NUMBER OF PLAYERS: Two

EQUIPMENT: One deck of cards

DIFFICULTY: The game can become very frantic

DURATION: 10 minutes

The layout and mechanics of this game have features in common with solitaire, but two players are pitted against one another in a frequently frenzied race to rid themselves of cards.

Setup

After cutting for the deal, cards are shuffled and the whole deck distributed. Both players then construct identical layouts. To begin, a row of five single cards is laid out; only the first is turned faceup. Beginning with the row's second card, the action is repeated: an upturned card plus three added in succession to the other piles.

This continues until a last, faceup card completes the fifth pile (see diagram 6). Players place the remainder of each hand in the middle of the table, forming two stockpiles, with the top card of each turned up and placed alongside, to start a stack called the Spit pile.

Playing the Game

When the layouts are finished, players count aloud, 'One, two, three, spit!' to open the game. Working quickly—and manipulating cards with just one hand—they play faceup cards from their respective layouts onto either of the upturned cards in their stockpiles.

Each card played must go in order, either up or down in rank, atop the other. (But an ace can only be covered by a 2, because it is low only in value; a king, similarly, connects only to a queen.)

As each card is removed from a layout pile, the card beneath is turned faceup. Each may elect, as well, to play onto any of the upturned cards within their own layouts, thus exposing a new card.

In keeping with the game's kinship to solitaire, some players adopt the rule that cards can be played only in alternating red and black order.

If neither player can lay a card down, a fresh starter is turned up from each stockpile, and the game resumes with another unison count. The round concludes when both stockpiles are exhausted. Both players should try to capture the smaller of the two discard piles; the one who first slaps a hand over it, shouting 'Spit,' takes possession. Each player's pile and any layout cards still remaining are shuffled, new layouts are dealt from each, as in beginning the game, and play restarts. When one player finally has fewer than 15 cards, he will have no Spit pile and his new layout will be incomplete; play continues as before, but now with both players competing to discard onto a single Spit pile.

A variant procedure, which often shortens the game, awards the smaller pile to the player whose own stock is first exhausted.

Winning the Game

The point of the game is to get rid of all cards, both from stock and layout; the first to do so wins.

WAR

NUMBER OF PLAYERS: Two

EQUIPMENT: Deck of cards

DIFFICULTY: Easy for adults and children

DURATION: About 20 to 30 minutes

This fun game is based entirely on luck.

Setup

A standard 52-card deck is shuffled and dealt out so that both players receive a facedown stack of 26 cards.

Playing the Game

Without examining the cards, each player turns up the top card from his stack. The player with the higher card takes the pair and puts it facedown in a separate winnings pile. He then turns over the next card in his stack and plays as before, until it happens that each player turns up a card of the same rank. At this point, a *war* ensues.

Each plays the next two cards from his stack facedown on top of his tied card, then plays the third card faceup. The player with the higher third card wins all the cards in the two warring stacks. If there is a tie at the end of the war, another war is played, with the eventual winner taking all the cards.

Winning the Game

When a player runs out of cards in his stack, he makes a new stack of his winnings pile. The game continues until one player, the winner, has all the cards.

Games of Chance

Whether betting for small change, candies, or peanuts, these games will entertain you while testing your powers of deduction and bluffing.

BLACKJACK (TWENTY-ONE)

NUMBER OF PLAYERS: Two to seven

EQUIPMENT: One or more decks of cards

DIFFICULTY: Suitable for adults and older children

DURATION: From 1 hour to several hours

Offered in casinos around the world, blackjack is an entertaining card game also played at home. Although distinctions are occasionally drawn between blackjack and twenty-one, none really holds up in common usage. It is sometimes said that blackjack denotes the noncommercial game and twenty-one the casino form, but casinos themselves use both terms, usually to signify how many decks are used in the game. In any event, basic playing rules are the same.

Setup

The game's *banker*—the house, in casino games—and up to six players try to make hands totaling 21 points, or as close as possible without exceeding 21. Cards count as their face value, except that kings, queens, and jacks are each worth 10 points, and an ace counts as either 1 or 11.

Any combination, in two cards, of an ace and 10-point card (K, Q, J, 10) is called a *blackjack;* it is an automatic winner, unless tied with a banker's blackjack, in which case the bet is returned. A player's blackjack wins, however, if the banker makes 21 points in three cards or more.

Playing the Game

One or two decks may be used. (They are shuffled often, at the dealer or player's request, so that remaining cards cannot

favour either side.) A banker is chosen, who also deals out the hands. Because the banker has an edge in this game, the position should be passed along to other players. Commonly, the bank moves to a player with blackjack, though other methods of assignment may be agreed upon.

Players place wagers in front of them—any gaming chips or tokens will do—before any cards are dealt. Beginning at banker's left and dealing around one card at a time, each player and the banker receive two cards. Player hands are facedown; dealer's second card is faceup.

Players and the dealer examine their hands. If anyone

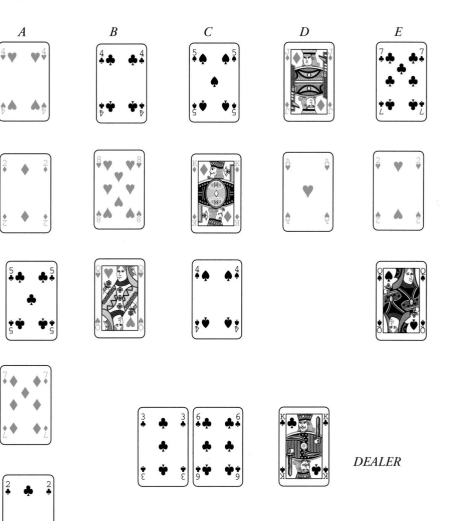

Diagram 1: The end of a blackjack round. Dealer's hand (with 19 points) loses to A and D (who has a blackjack) and ties or 'pushes' with C and E; B is bust.

Pontoon

An 18th-century French game, *vingt-et-un,* spawned many gambling variants, including blackjack and a closer descendant, pontoon.

In many ways similar to blackjack, pontoon betting is perhaps too complex for widespread casino popularity. The object is the same, but with an additional winning hand, the *five-card trick,* interposed in rank between a *pontoon* (blackjack) and mere multicard 21's. Any five-card hand of 21 or fewer points is an immediate winner, except against a pontoon.

Pontoon's structure is like blackjack, except that players may double their bets before receiving the second card. (In some versions, the banker has an opportunity first to double all bets, and players can then redouble.) And before taking a third or any subsequent cards, a player may again bet, saying 'I'll buy one.' The stake may be any amount up to the total wagered thus far.

A player also has the option of saying, before any draw, 'Twist me a card,' which signifies the player will offer no further bets; the card and any that follow are free. Twisted cards are dealt faceup; if bought, facedown. 'Sticking'—taking no more cards—is allowed when a player's count reaches 15 or more.

Five-card tricks and multicard 21's pay double, and a pontoon triple the amount wagered, but in this game players too are at risk: They must pay out to the banker on the same terms. In addition, tied hands win for the banker.

holds a blackjack, it is turned up immediately and remains exposed until paid off at the end of the hand. The dealer now asks each player in turn, starting again at the left, whether they will take a card. A player who wants an additional card says 'Hit me,' or makes a light sweeping motion with the cards against the table. Having taken a card, the player is entitled to continue, taking one at a time until satisfied with a hand's point total. Then the player announces 'Stay' or 'Stick,' or merely slides the original two facedown cards under the chips wagered.

Of course, another outcome is possible, indeed even probable: In seeking to improve, for example, a 13-point hand, a player might draw a 2, making 15. That is, under most circumstances, not a good hand. With misgivings, the player might feel compelled to ask for another card. If it is a 9, it raises the hand total to 24—too many. Anything over 21 points is a *bust* and must be turned faceup at once. The banker sweeps up the losing bet and losing cards.

When all players have acted, either standing or busting with the cards drawn, the dealer then attends to his own hand. The facedown card is turned up, so that players can see the dealer's hand and assure themselves it is played according to the game's special dealer requirements. These are as follows:

- The dealer/banker must hit any hand of 16 points or less
- The dealer must stick with 17 points or more
- The dealer must hit a *soft* 17.

A *soft* total is one added up with an ace in it, counting as 11. 'Soft 17,' therefore, would be A-6 (in two cards), which makes both 7 and 17. Because the soft-17 rule slightly increases the overall banker advantage, the game is seldom offered without it.

The dealer makes settlements after completing his hand. If the dealer busts, all surviving hands are paid off. Otherwise, bets are individually won or lost against the bank, depending on hand values. Tied hands are called *pushes;* wagers are returned.

Special player options

There are other special opportunities that can offer some advantage to a player:

- **Doubling down:** Perceiving the dealer to have worse-than-average chances (for example, showing a 5 or 6), a player may double the bet, at the same time announcing 'Double down.' For this privilege, however, a player forgoes the right to choose how many cards to take: A mandatory single card, facedown, is dealt to the hand (this is in addition to the two he already has). In many games—and most casinos—doubling down is permitted only when a player holds 10 or 11; under freer rules, the choice is open to any hand, regardless of value. Doubling down is sometimes allowed on a split hand—a potentially large advantage.

- **Insurance:** When the dealer hand shows an upturned ace, players may be asked if they wish to buy insurance against the chance of a dealer blackjack. If yes, another bet equal to the first wager is posted. Should the dealer in fact have a blackjack, the insurance bet is paid off, the other is swept up, netting nothing for the player but avoiding a loss. When no blackjack materializes, the insurance 'fee' is forfeited and the hand continues in the normal fashion.

- **Splitting:** In the event that a player is dealt a pair (in the original two cards), they may be turned up and bet as two separate hands. An additional bet, equal to that already placed, must be wagered on the second hand. Each hand is first completed, receiving its second card, and then each is played out, one after the other. If one of the hands is paired, it may be *resplit*. A third wager is posted and the hand played separately, like the others.

Above: Shuffling the cards

Often, house rules do not allow aces to be resplit, or impose limits on how many times any other rank may be resplit.

- **Surrender:** Faced with unpromising cards and a strong dealer showing (an upturned 10-pointer, for example), a player may be permitted, at some cost, a way out. By saying, in the playing turn, 'I surrender,' half the wager is forfeited outright without further proceedings.

Limits and payouts

Normally, the banker sets lower and upper limits for any single wager, but these may be agreed upon before the game. All bets are paid at even odds except for blackjack, which wins one-and-a-half times the wager (universal in casinos) or twice the wager (in some private games). A dealer with blackjack, however, collects only the original player bet. Frequently, blackjacks that are made from split hands, especially from split aces, are paid at only one-to-one odds.

Strategy

A great deal has been written about maximizing a player's odds in blackjack, with crucial subchapters analyzing the effects of subtle rules variations. Another approach favours card counting, trying to keep a tally of cards already played. Because a deck that has become relatively rich in remaining ten-pointers favours a player, such a tactic has solid value, but it makes demands of ordinary memory that most people cannot sustain. And casinos have generally adopted a counter-strategy of shuffling eight decks together and distributing them from a shoe. In a general way, though, guides can be laid out for deciding when to hit or stay (and these are somewhat streamlined):

- Stay if holding 17 or better.
- Always hit, obviously, with 11 or less, or with a soft 17.
- Dealer hands are considered weak when showing 2 through 6; a player holding 12 through 16 should never hit against a weak dealer hand. (Hitting 12 against a

dealer 2 or 3 is one possible exception.)
- A player with a weak hand (12 through 16) should hit against a dealer showing 7 or more.
- Always double down when holding 10 or 11, except when the dealer shows a 10-pointer.
- Holding 8 or 9, double down against a dealer showing 5 or 6.
- Split any pairs that are likely to improve (because so many of the deck's cards are 10-pointers). In a nutshell, this comes down to aces and 8's—which should always be split—and 7's, which are split unless the dealer shows 8-10. Paired 4's, 5's, and 10's are never split. Two 6's, already weak, have good odds to become even worse (two 16's), though some authorities recommend splitting them against a dealer's 2 through 6; likewise 3's and 2's versus a dealer 4 through 7.

MICHIGAN (NEWMARKET)

NUMBER OF PLAYERS: Three to eight

EQUIPMENT: Deck of playing cards plus four extra cards, chips

DIFFICULTY: Easy to follow

DURATION: About 15 minutes per round, depending on the number of players

This card game is played for chips, which can be gained both by winning rounds and by playing certain cards during a round. It uses a standard 52-card deck, as well as four specific cards from a second deck: the ace of hearts, king of clubs, queen of diamonds, and jack of spades (the boodle cards), which serve only as receptacles for chips.

Setup

The four boodle cards are placed faceup on the playing surface. Prior to each round, the dealer places two chips, and the other players one chip, on each boodle card. The dealer then deals hands facedown, one card at a time, to each player, as well as one extra hand, which is not used. All of the cards in the deck are dealt, regardless of whether the number of cards per hand comes out even. Players examine their own hands, but the extra hand stays facedown, its main function being to foil a sequence.

Above: Poker players show down their hands.

Playing the Game

Cards are played faceup and remain in front of the person playing them. The player to the left of the dealer begins by selecting a suit and playing the lowest card of that suit in her hand. (The ace is always high.) The player who has the next highest card in that suit must then play it, then the player with the next card above that one, and so on, until the ace is reached, or until no player has the next card in sequence. The last card played in an unfinished sequence is called the *stop card*. The player of the ace or stop card continues the round by playing the lowest card she holds in another suit, following which play continues until the ace or a stop card is reached. The round ends when one of the players wins by running out of cards.

Scoring

Each losing player must pay the winner one chip for each unplayed card remaining in his hand. Also, in the course of the round, if a player matches a card corresponding to one of the boodle cards, he wins all the chips on that boodle card. Chips on the boodle cards that are not won remain in place, and chips for the next round are added to them. The deal changes for each round, passing to the left.

POKER

Number of players: Five, six, or seven

Equipment: One deck of playing cards, with jokers removed, gambling chips

Difficulty: A game of skill, but can be played at a simpler level

Duration: About 1 hour, but sometimes far longer

There are countless poker variants played around the world, but nearly all are built from three basic kinds: draw, stud, and widow. The ranking of hands and betting procedures, too, have a universal nature.

Setup

The aim in any poker game is to complete a hand that outranks all others, thus winning all bets, that have been thrown into the middle of the table, called the *pot*. As shown in diagram 2, hands fall into ten categories, each with its own descriptive name. These are, in ascending rank:

- **High Card (a):** A hand whose value is rated card by card from highest to lowest, there being no other valuable quality, such as pairs, present. When comparing two high-card hands, start with the highest card and work down: A-Q-J-3-2, for example, beats A-Q-10-9-8.

- **One Pair (b):** As between two one-pair hands, the highest pair wins; if pairs are tied, then high cards are accounted; for example, 9-9-K-8-3 beats 9-9-K-7-6.

- **Two Pair (c):** The highest pair determines the winner; for example, Q-Q-2-2-8 beats J-J-10-10-A. If both pairs are the same, the hand's lone remaining card becomes the tie-breaker. The first hand might be announced as 'queens and 2's' or 'queens over 2's.'

- **Three of a Kind or Trips (d):** The highest three of a kind wins. In games where similar trips are possible (widow and wild-card variants), the other two cards in a hand are compared, and high card takes the pot.

- **Straight (e):** Any five-card sequence is a straight. Unless otherwise specified, the lowest straight is the *wheel* (or *bicycle*), A-5; the highest is 10-A. Players sometimes agree among themselves to count the ace as a high card only, so that 2-6 becomes the lowest straight.

- **Flush (f):** Five cards in one suit make a flush. Among two or more flushes, rank is established as for a high-card hand, comparing them card-by-card to find the winner.

- **Full House (g):** Three of a kind plus a pair is a full house. The rank of a hand's trips is first considered in the event of a tie; for example, J-J-J-2-2 beats 10-10-10-A-A. The winning hand here would be described as 'Jacks full of 2's.'

- **Four of a Kind or Quads (h):** Ties can only occur in

wild card and widow games; the fifth card's value resolves the contest.

- **Straight Flush (i):** Five cards in sequence and in the same suit—a hand very seldom seen.

- **Royal Flush (j):** The highest kind of straight flush, 10-A, and the best (and rarest) hand in poker.

In poker, if competing hands tie in all respects, the pot is split equally among them. Suits are never used in poker to settle precedence among cards of the same rank. Wild card games

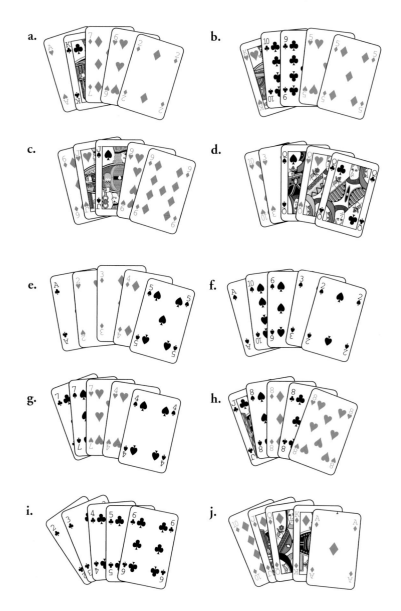

Diagram 2: Poker hands

usually recognize one further hand, *five of a kind,* which outranks all others.

Note that in one form of poker, *low ball,* the list must be stood on its head, and the worst becomes the best.

Betting

Poker players, in both public and private games, have adopted the general betting framework known as *table stakes.* This means that only chips on the table—before a hand is dealt—may be wagered, and that a player's *stack,* or any part of it, cannot be removed from the table until the player leaves the game. In other words, chips once placed on the table are committed to the game; they may not be sheltered from risk by stuffing a few into a pocket. A minimum buy-in amount is usually agreed upon, with minimums, too, for further buys.

When a player has bet the last of his chips, gone *all in,* he remains eligible to win all of the bets he has covered; any further betting in the hand is among players who still have their chips; their subsequent bets accumulate in a *side pot,* to which the all-in player can have no claim. By this means, in table stakes, no player can be driven out of a hand merely because of a dwindling supply of chips; he competes in the pot for only as much of it as he can match.

To begin, before each hand, players all contribute some fixed minimum bet, the *ante,* to the pot. In Hold 'Em, described farther on, the procedure is somewhat different.

In turn and depending on any preceding action, a player is expected to choose one of six options:

- **Bet:** A number of chips is wagered, put into the pot.
- **Call:** A player only matches the amount bet, or *sees* the bet, without adding an additional bet.
- **Check, or Pass:** If no bets have yet been made, and wishing to make none, a player may simply pass the turn on to the left.
- **Fold:** If unwilling to call a bet or raise, a player drops out of the hand, turning his cards facedown and pushing them away.
- **Raise:** An additional bet, over and above any amount already bet. (The other players are obligated to match this to stay in a hand.)
- **Reraise:** Generally, the total number of raises in any single round is limited by agreement to three or four. (When only two players remain, *head to head,* raising restrictions are often dropped.) As a rule, raises must be at least as much as the previous bet.

When either everyone has passed or all bets and raises have been met, the round is over.

Players agree beforehand on a minimum and maximum bet amount, such as one to five chips. In a *pot-limit* game, any player may wager up to as much as the pot contains on any

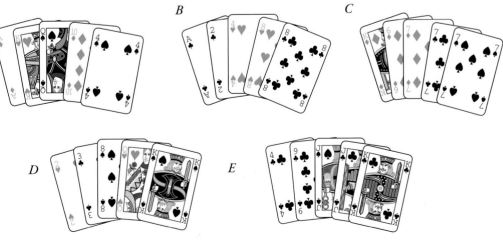

Diagram 3: An assortment of hands in Five-card Draw after the deal: Player D, with no pair, should fold. Player A, also holding a weak hand, might draw to his A-K, or keeping all but the 4 try, unwisely, to complete a single-ended straight.

given turn. A *no-limit game,* as the name implies, has no betting constraints.

Structured games prescribe a single bet amount in specific rounds; for example, two chips in the first two of four rounds, and four chips in the last two. (Raises are always by increments of the allowed bet. For instance, two chips are raised by two, to four; four can then be raised by two, to six, and so on.)

Playing the Game
Outline of play

Once a dealer has been chosen, usually by cutting for high card, deal passes in each new hand to the left. In the most popular form of noncasino play, *dealer's choice,* the dealer nominates the hand to be played, any variant known to the group, and distributes the cards accordingly.

No matter what the special form of the game, it will have betting rounds (generally from two to five) at several stages of the deal. When the last round is completed, and all bets have been made, the players *show down* to determine the winner: All surviving hands are turned up and compared. If at any stage all but one player have folded, the hand ends immediately; cards are not shown, and the pot belongs to the remaining player.

Rules and etiquette

Following are some of the rules common to all forms of poker:

- **Plays should be made in turn.** Disclosing intentions prematurely can, and often does, unfairly influence play—and the damage cannot be undone.
- **A bet announced is a bet made.** Once an action is declared aloud, it is binding.
- **Bets are made in one motion.** It simply is not permitted to move a few chips into the pot, look around for reactions at the table, and then announce that more are coming (a string bet or string raise). A bet must either be announced—and the chips can be fumbled into the pot in any manner—or placed in the pot all at the same time.

- **Cards declare themselves (cards 'speak').** Unless otherwise agreed, a hand turned up in a showdown competes at its actual best rank, regardless of whether the player has overlooked its value, for example, by calling 'pair' when a straight is also present.
- **The hand in play should not be discussed.** Relevant remarks about certain cards or suits may unfairly disclose information to other hands.
- **The last to bet or raise goes first in a showdown, and others in turn.** Players sometimes balk at turning over their hands. If it must be used, the rule exists. Should everyone pass in the last round, the first to have passed must show first.
- **Players must guard their hand.** It is outright cheating to try for a glimpse of another player's cards. But each player must take care not to expose cards through carelessness.

Variations
Draw Poker

Players are dealt five cards facedown. There is a round of betting, after which everyone, in turn from the dealer's left, has an opportunity to throw away some cards after examining them and take replacements, the *draw.* The draw is followed by a final betting round and showdown.

Rules vary concerning the number of cards that may be drawn. Up to three are always permitted, often with eligibility for a fourth if the hand contains an ace (which should be shown after a hand is over). Players may agree, however, that four or even five replacements can be taken in any draw.

Draw Poker, one of poker's older games, is more often seen today in its low-ball form. Straights are often excluded as low hands in this variant, so the perfect low would be 6-4-3-2-A (aces are usually nominated '1'). If straights are allowed, a wheel (5-A) is then an unbeatable low sequence, which is useful when the lowest and highest hands are dividing the pot equally (see next page).

Well-known Poker variations

- **Chicago:** Seven-card Stud; the high spade in the hole is wild.
- **Indian:** Five-card Stud, except the hole card is held to the forehead, exposed to everyone but its owner.
- **Low Hole Card Wild:** Seven-card Stud; the low card in the hole is wild and all like it received in subsequent rounds. The last card (down) may alter a hand's value dramatically, invalidating the previous low.
- **No Peek:** Seven cards dealt facedown; players may not look at their hands. Starting at dealer's left, one card is exposed, followed by a betting round. The next player turns up cards until the first is beaten, and so on, with each successive player flipping cards until the last has been bettered. Each time a new leader is established, betting commences with that hand. If all seven are turned up without beating the leader, the player is out; the option to bet passes to the left.
- **Roll Your Own:** In stud format, either Five- or Seven-card, but all cards are delivered facedown. Players choose which one to flip up in each turn, acting either simultaneously, on cue, or in succession.

Stud Poker

In this most numerous family of poker variations, some cards are dealt faceup, others facedown *(hole cards)*. The simplest form, *Five-card Stud,* has four betting rounds: Players first receive two cards, one down, one up, and bet. The highest hand visible—the highest card, necessarily, in the first round—always acts first. A third, fourth, and fifth card are dealt around, with betting after each.

Wild card options and other gadgets are often tacked onto basic stud games. Popular variants in Five-card Stud include making the hole card wild or allowing players to buy a replacement card at the end, usually paying the pot twice as much for a card dealt down as for one dealt faceup. The buy option adds one more round of betting to the game, as well.

Stud games might be nominated *high-low:* The best and worst hands divide the pot equally between them after the showdown. It must be understood beforehand which is to be the best low hand. Generally, low straights and flushes are allowed to compete as both high and low (so that 5-A is the best low). The same hand could, therefore, take both halves of the pot.

It must also be agreed how hands are to compete, that is, whether hands at the showdown declare themselves—a straightforward approach—or must be specifically designated high, low, or high-low before the showdown. This alternative requires a separate declaration round (usually with another, final betting round): Players take two chips in hand under the table; one clinched hand emerges holding either no chips (low), one chip (high), or two chips (high-low).

On signal, all hands open, revealing the binding intention of each player. No matter that a declared high turns out to be lowest, it cannot take the pot's low end. Also, a high-low declarer must win both ends, or none at all. (Ties are generally accounted wins, so that one end of the pot is halved again between its two winners; multiple ties may lead to bothersome and untidy fractions.)

Seven-card Stud

By far the most popular of stud types, Seven-card Stud is played high, low *(razz),* high-low, and with every conceivable appended gimmick and gadget. Players are initially dealt three cards, two down and the last faceup. A betting round ensues—the highest cards visible always act first. The next three cards arrive faceup, with betting after each card is dealt. The seventh, the *river card,* is dealt facedown, *down and dirty.* After a last

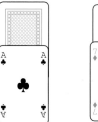
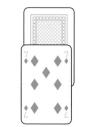

Diagram 4: An initial deal in a game of Five-card Stud, before the first round of betting.

round of betting, remaining hands show down for a winner.

High-low games of Seven-card Stud often incorporate a special restriction, a *qualified low* that limits low hands to 8 or less; that is, a valid low assortment may contain no card higher than an 8.

Texas Hold 'Em

Texas Hold 'Em is the dominant poker widow game. (The term widow is encountered in several card games—some predating poker—that utilize a *community* card, or cards. Doubtless the metaphorical reference is to the widow card's unattached status and its eventual integration into the most suitable hand.)

Some cards, to be held in common by all players, are dealt faceup to a layout in the middle of the table— known as the *flop.* All players first receive two cards facedown, the *pocket.* After a betting round, three cards are

Right: A royal flush in poker

placed side by side in the middle, faceup. Players bet again; a fourth and fifth widow card is dealt, each followed by betting, and remaining hands show down.

Players form the best five-card poker hand from the seven cards available—pocket plus flop. Any combination is valid, even using only the five flop cards. Cards speak for themselves, as usual.

Blinds and order of play

Instead of antes, only the player to the dealer's left makes a bet, the *blind,* before any cards are distributed. Usually the amount required equals a minimum bet. This tactic is necessary in a widow game to get the action started, because no one holds any visible cards. The player at dealer's left acts first in every round and is deemed, before cards are dealt, to have made an opening wager.

In the first round the player to the blind's left will have to fold, call, or raise this built-in starter bet. Thus, there can be no passing (except for the blind) in the first round. The blind is *live,* that is, having posted a forced bet, the player has the

A primer on Seven-card Stud strategy

Nothing but long experience or an intuitive gift can tip a player to an opponent's true strength or weakness, so bluffing is a requisite skill in poker. In keeping with the odds and reasonable expectations, however, some opening standards may prove useful:

- **Assess your odds:** Relative long shots (for example, three-card suit or sequence) are profitable only when several players have stayed to contribute, multiplying a pot's profit for the winner. Partake in two- or three-way action only if already holding good cards (a high pair or better).

- **Consider staying the course** with an ace or king in the first three cards, especially against uninspired opposition. With a pair of either, play aggressively from the outset.

- **Remember the poker adage:** 'The best hand going in wins.' The better the cards you decide to play, the more you may expect to win—with many heartbreaking setbacks along the way.

- **Stay for two more cards** if the first three cards are matched in suit or form a sequence. Receiving a fourth in suit or sequence, continue to the river; otherwise (and holding no other prospects), fold after the fifth card.

- **Watch the betting action:** A pair in the hole (a *wired* pair) is a promising hand, but not if the pair is probably beaten by cards already visible elsewhere. The betting action may guide the decision to call or fold.

option of raising or passing when the turn comes back around, after all other players have acted.

Two blinds are sometimes employed: The player immediately to the dealer's left puts up half a bet *(little blind)* and the next a full bet *(big blind);* in turn, all players must match the blind (or raise it, if so inclined) or else fold.

Terminology

The initial three widow cards make up the flop—though all five upcards may be intended by this term. Context must decide. The fourth is the *turn;* the fifth is the *river.* Following are some additional terms:

- **Dealing:** In this and other widow games, the deck's top card is usually discarded, or *burned,* before any card or group of cards is turned faceup (one burned before the flop, one each before the turn and river). The deal passes to the left after each turn. In casino games, with a dealer provided by the management, an imaginary dealer position is passed along by means of a *button,* a large disc in front of the dealer-player.

- **Kills:** Before the deal the player at the blind's left is normally allowed to raise, or *kill,* the blind (doubling it); the next may add one more bet increment, and so on, until the limits are reached. All kills are live, with an option to raise when the turn comes around. Another form of this gadget, applied in Stud Poker, doubles the game stakes in any hand that follows two successive wins by the same player. A marker of some kind can be used to keep track: It passes with the pot to a winner and is flipped over, to the 'on' side, only in the event of a second win; otherwise it returns to the middle.

- **Omaha:** This is a widely played Hold 'Em variation in which four pocket cards are dealt instead of two. A valid hand must combine two cards, and only two, from the pocket with three from the flop to compete. Often encountered as a high-low game, it invariably employs the 8-low restriction (see Seven-card Stud).

PARTY GAMES

Children's Party Games **131**

Family Party Games **139**

Old-Fashioned Parlor Games **146**

Racing Games **149**

Super Party Games **153**

Children's Party Games

Organizing a children's party can seem like a nerve-racking affair, but with a little planning and a great selection of games you can make it work.

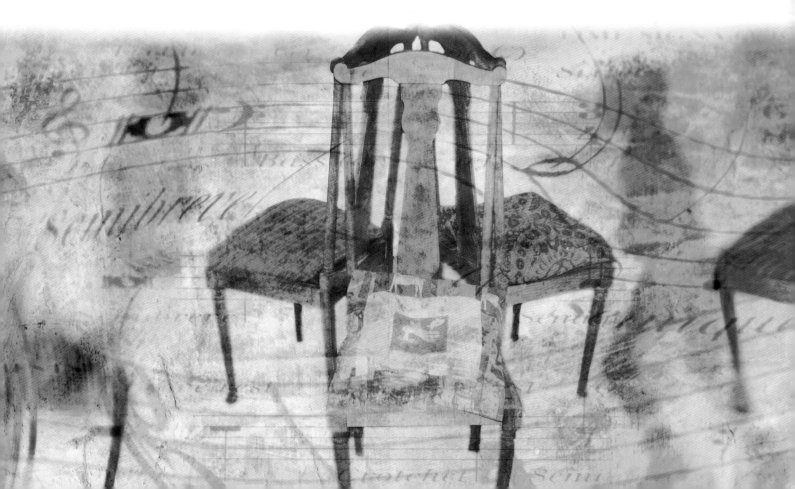

BLINDMAN'S BLUFF

NUMBER OF PLAYERS: Six or more

EQUIPMENT: Only a blindfold is required

DIFFICULTY: Easy for adults and children

DURATION: From 30 minutes to an hour

A simple game that requires one blindfolded player to chase and catch another player. This lively pastime has been around for centuries and comes in several different versions.

Playing the Game

In the simplest version, the player chosen to be the 'blindman' is blindfolded, led to the middle of the room and spun around three times while the other players position themselves around the room. The blindman must then search for the other players, who may contort their bodies to escape his touch but are not allowed to move their feet. Once the blindman has come into contact with another player, he must attempt to establish his or her identity by using his hands. If he guesses correctly, that player becomes the blindman in the next round. Otherwise, the blindman must try to find someone else.

Variations

Blindman's Circle

In this version, the players start by walking in a circle around the blindman. When he claps three times, the players come to a halt and the blindman points to the edge of the circle. Whoever the finger selects, or most nearly, must then enter the circle and be pursued by the blindman for a period of two minutes. If the blindman successfully touches his victim, he or she becomes the next blindman. Otherwise, the player returns to the circle and play resumes from the beginning.

Blindman's Staff

Again, the players start by walking in a circle around the blindman, but this time he carries a long stick. When he points the stick toward the edge of the circle, everyone stops walking, and the the nearest player grabs the end of the stick. The blindman asks 'Who's there?' and the player, trying to disguise his or her voice as much as possible, answers 'It's me.' If the blindman correctly identifies the voice, its owner must become the new blindman. Otherwise, play continues as before.

Seated Blindman's Bluff

Players begin by sitting in a circle of chairs gathered tight around the hapless blindman, who is required to sit carefully on one of the nearby laps and attempt to identify its owner without making any additional contact with the body. Any giggling will no doubt help with his guesswork.

BOBBING FOR APPLES (APPLE DUCKING)

NUMBER OF PLAYERS: Any reasonable number

EQUIPMENT: Large tub, apples

DIFFICULTY: Assist small children to play, otherwise it is a matter of dexterity

DURATION: From seconds to minutes

Players using only their heads duck into a tub of water to retrieve apples. This game has been around for centuries.

Setup

Place a large tub of water on a floor capable of withstanding splashes and drop in a dozen or so apples. Have players gather around the tub.

Playing the Game

The object of the game is to get as many apples as possible out of the water using only your head and mouth—no hands or elbows are allowed, so be prepared to get wet.

Winning the Game

If everyone plays at once, the winner can be either the first person to get an apple out of the tub or the person who gets the most apples out in a set amount of time. If players take individual turns, the winner is the person who gets an apple out the fastest.

DEAD LIONS

NUMBER OF PLAYERS: At least four

EQUIPMENT: None

DIFFICULTY: Fun for even tiny children

DURATION: A few minutes

Playing the Game

The children all lie on the floor and pretend to be dead lions. If a child moves at all he is out. The last child left on the floor wins. The disqualified children can help to spot any movements from the children still on the floor, and even encourage them to move or try to make them laugh. Touching is not allowed. This is a good cool-down game if the party—and the children—are becoming slightly overheated.

THE FARMER IN THE DELL

NUMBER OF PLAYERS: At least nine

EQUIPMENT: None

DIFFICULTY: Age 3 and up

DURATION: About 5 minutes

Playing the Game

One child is chosen to be the farmer and the other children hold hands and form a circle around him. They skip around the farmer chanting:

The farmer in the dell, The farmer in the dell,
Hi-ho, the derry-o, The farmer in the dell.
The farmer takes a wife, The farmer takes a wife,
Hi-ho, the derry-o, The farmer takes a wife.

The child playing the farmer picks another child from the ring to be his wife. The other children skip around them, chanting:

The wife takes a child, The wife takes a child,
Hi-ho, the derry-o, The wife takes a child.

The wife picks another child to be the child. The other children skip around them, chanting:

The child takes a nurse, The child takes a nurse,
Hi-ho, the derry-o, The child takes a nurse.

The child picks another child to be the nurse. The other children skip around them chanting:

The nurse takes the cow, The nurse takes the cow,
Hi-ho, the derry-o, The nurse takes the cow.

The nurse picks another child to be the cow. The other children skip around them, chanting:

The cow takes a dog, The cow takes a dog,
Hi-ho, the derry-o, The cow takes a dog.

The cow picks another child to be the dog. The other children skip around them, chanting:

The dog takes a cat, The dog takes a cat,
Hi-ho, the derry-o, The dog takes a cat.

The dog picks another child to be the cat. The other children skip around them, chanting:

The cat takes a rat, The cat takes a rat,
Hi-ho, the derry-o, The cat takes a rat.

The cat picks another child to be the rat. The other children skip around them, chanting:

The rat takes the cheese, The rat takes the cheese,

Hi-ho, the derry-o, The rat takes the cheese.

The rat picks another child to be the cheese. Then all the children in the circle rejoin the group, except for the cheese. The other children skip around him, chanting:

The cheese stands alone, The cheese stands alone,

Hi-ho, the derry-o, The cheese stands alone.

GUESS THE SMELL

NUMBER OF PLAYERS: At least three

EQUIPMENT: Blindfold, objects with different smells

DIFFICULTY: Suitable for children 6 and up

DURATION: A few minutes per person

Setup

Collect a number of smelly objects, which players will try to identify by scent alone. Things with strong scents, such as oranges, garlic, or vinegar, should be used along with objects that have subtler smells, such as flowers, bubble bath, or cucumbers. Slightly unpleasant smells, such as sour milk and menthol cough drops, always raise a giggle.

Playing the Game

Blindfold the child who is 'it' and hold each of the objects under his nose one at a time. The child tries to guess what the object is without touching it. He gets a point for each correct guess. The next contestant has different objects to identify. The child with the most points at the end of the game is the winner.

MATCHBOX RACE

NUMBER OF PLAYERS: Six or more

EQUIPMENT: Two matchbox covers

DIFFICULTY: Easiest for those with small noses

DURATION: About 15 minutes

This silly party game is the most fun when played by a large group of children.

Setup

To begin, divide players into two teams, and have each player stand in a line with his hands clasped behind his back. Then, find two appropriately sized matchbox covers and slip them onto the noses of the first player in each line.

Playing the Game

On the call of go, each team will attempt to pass a matchbox cover all the way to the end of the line by transferring it from nose to nose, as shown below. Hands may not be used. If a cover falls to the ground, it must be returned to the first person in line and its journey starts all over again.

Winning the Game

The first team to pass the matchbox cover to the end of the line wins.

MUSICAL CHAIRS

NUMBER OF PLAYERS: Six or more

EQUIPMENT: Chairs, a music source, small prizes (optional), coloured paper if playing a variation

DIFFICULTY: Easy, even for very young children

DURATION: As long as the players want to keep going, but about 15 minutes is enough for very small children

This game requires a source of music, such as a radio, tape, or compact disc player. With very young children, even fewer than six players can make a game.

Setup

Set out a line of chairs, one less than the number of people playing, with alternate chairs facing opposite walls.

Playing the Game

The children (or adults) march around the line of chairs as the music plays. When the music stops everyone must find a chair to sit on. The person left standing is out. After each round, a chair should be removed until there are only two children and one chair left. The child who manages to sit in the remaining chair is the winner.

Variations

Musical Bumps

In this version, the children dance to the music. When it stops, they drop to the ground and sit cross-legged. The last one to sit down is out. The rounds continue until one child is left.

Musical Statues

In this version, the children also dance to the music. However, when it stops, they must stand as still as statues. Anyone who moves is out. The rounds continue until one child is left.

Musical Spots

Cut out circles of coloured paper, one less than the number of people playing. The children dance to the music, then, when it stops, they must find a circle to sit on. The child still standing is out.

The rounds continue until one child is left on a circle.

Organizing a children's party

It is up to the adults to set the pace for a children's party. Children love lively, active games, but it is a good idea to include quieter, calmer activities as well so that the fun does not peak too soon. Plan to offer some games, then some food, and then more games—starting with a few quiet pursuits to let the food settle.

Organize in advance, making sure that prizes are wrapped and music and props are prepared. Adults have the final word on rules and winners—so make sure the children understand this. Watch that the fun does not get out of hand, and that smaller children do not suffer at the hands of bigger ones.

Finally, always prepare more games than you think you may need as it is hard to predict how long each event will last.

ORANGES AND LEMONS

NUMBER OF PLAYERS: About ten

EQUIPMENT: A long rope

DIFFICULTY: Suitable for children 5 and up

DURATION: About 5 to 10 minutes, depending on the number of players and how long the tug-of-war goes on

This game is ideal to play in a large room, park, or yard.

Playing the Game

Choose two children to joins hands and raise their arms to make an arch. They must secretly decide between them which one will be orange and which one lemon.

The other children march in a circle passing under the arch and singing:

Oranges and lemons, Say the bells of Saint Clements
I owe you five farthings, Say the bells of Saint Martins
When will you pay me, Say the bells of Old Bailey
When I grow rich, Say the bells of Shoreditch
When will that be? Say the bells of Stepney
I'm sure I don't know, Says the great bell of Bow
Here comes a candle to light you to bed
Here comes the chopper to chop off your head, Chop, chop, chop!

As they sing the final line, the two children forming the arch bring their arms down to trap one of the other children. In a whisper they ask the trapped child if she wants to be orange or lemon, and she lines up behind the appropriate child.

The game continues until all the children are lined up. Then there is a tug-of-war between the two sides to decide the winning team.

PASS THE BALLOON

NUMBER OF PLAYERS: About ten or more

EQUIPMENT: Two balloons

DIFFICULTY: Suitable for children 5 and up

DURATION: A few minutes per race

Playing the Game

The children line up, one behind the other in two teams. Each child at the front has a balloon. At the starting signal he passes it over his head to the child behind, who continues to pass it back. When the person at the back receives the balloon, he runs to the front and starts to pass the balloon backward again.

Winning the Game

The game is over when the child who started the game is again at the front with the balloon. The team to do this first wins.

PASS THE PACKAGE

NUMBER OF PLAYERS: At least five

EQUIPMENT: A small gift, tissue paper or newspaper, sticky tape, and a radio, tape, or compact disc player

DIFFICULTY: Fun for both young and older children

DURATION: About 5 minutes per round

Setup

Wrap a small gift in at least ten layers of tissue paper or newspaper, securing each layer with tape.

Playing the Game

The children all sit or stand in a circle, and as the music plays they pass the package from hand to hand. When the music stops the child who is holding the package at the time unwraps a layer of paper. The music starts again and the game continues until all the layers have been removed. The child to take off the final layer of paper keeps the present.

Variations

Start the Music

The adult controlling the music can decide to start the music again before a layer of paper has been removed, in which case the package must be passed on and the layer completely removed by the next player holding it when the music stops.

Small children in particular love receiving presents, so you could wrap a few little tokens between the layers of paper so that everyone finds a little gift.

RING-AROUND-THE-ROSY (RING-A-RING-A-ROSES)

NUMBER OF PLAYERS: Any number

EQUIPMENT: None

DIFFICULTY: Age 3 and up

DURATION: A few minutes per song

This is an ideal game for small children who love to sing along to the easy rhyme.

Playing the Game

Players hold hands and dance around in a circle, chanting the rhyme below. As they sing the last line they all drop down to sit or lie on the floor:

Ring-around-the-rosy, A pocketful of posies,
Ashes, ashes, We all fall down.

This is the most popular and common verse, but these verses can also be chanted:

The king has sent his daughter, To fetch a pail of water,
A-tishoo, A-tishoo, We all fall down.

The bird upon the steeple, Is singing to the people,
A-tishoo, A-tishoo, We all fall down.

The wedding bells are ringing, The boys and girls are singing,
A-tishoo, A-tishoo, We all fall down.

SIMON SAYS

NUMBER OF PLAYERS: Four to ten

EQUIPMENT: None

DIFFICULTY: Not as easy as it first seems

DURATION: About 10 to 15 minutes

A follow-the-leader game that is lots of fun for lively kids.

Playing the Game

One person is designated Simon, and the others line up in front of him. Simon tells the players to do something, such as touch their heads or jump up and down while also doing the action himself.

If the instruction is preceded by 'Simon says,' all players must perform the act or be eliminated. If it is *not* preceded by

The tales of Mother Goose

Nursery rhymes and children's chants are believed to have been around for thousands of years, but they were not recorded in book form until the 1700s. *Mother Goose's Melody* was published in London in 1781 and later reprinted in the United States. It was so hugely popular in the United States that even today rhymes for young children are called Mother Goose rhymes.

Some rhymes are believed to reflect events of the day in which they originated. 'Ring-around-the-rosy' may hark back to the plague of the 1600s and refer to the number of people who died. An alternative version of the rhyme ends: 'Hush! Hush! Hush! Hush! We've all tumbled down.'

these words, players must not perform the act, and anyone who thoughtlessly copies Simon is eliminated. The last person in the game wins and takes Simon's place for the next round.

SQUEAK, PIGGY, SQUEAK!

NUMBER OF PLAYERS: At least four

EQUIPMENT: Blindfold, chairs, cushion

DIFFICULTY: Fun for all ages

DURATION: A few minutes per game

This game can be enjoyed by very young children as well as older players.

Playing the Game

The children sit on chairs in a circle. One child is chosen to be blindfolded. She is put in the middle of the circle, given a cushion to hold, and turned around a few times. Then the blindfolded child puts the cushion on the lap of any child in the circle and sits on it, saying: 'Squeak, piggy, squeak!' The child who is being sat on squeaks like a pig, and the blindfolded child must try to guess whose lap she is sitting on.

If the blindfolded child makes a wrong guess, she must find another lap and try again. If she guesses correctly, then the child who squeaked is blindfolded and given the cushion. All the children in the circle change places and the game begins again.

STATUES

NUMBER OF PLAYERS: Any number

EQUIPMENT: None

DIFFICULTY: Ideal for children under 7

DURATION: About 15 to 20 minutes

Playing the Game

Any number can play this children's game, in which the idea is to sneak up on Grandmother, played by an adult or older child. Standing with her back to the players, who are lined up about 50 feet away, Grandmother says 'Go.' The children then start tiptoeing toward her. At intervals, Grandmother turns around suddenly. When the children see her start to turn, they must freeze in their tracks. If Grandmother sees a child move, the child is out of the game.

The first to touch Grandmother, or the last one left in the game, wins.

TELEPHONE

NUMBER OF PLAYERS: Any number

EQUIPMENT: None

DIFFICULTY: Ideal for children under 7

DURATION: About 15 to 20 minutes

Playing the Game

Children start by sitting in a circle. One child is chosen to start the game by whispering a short message to one of the children sitting next to her. The child whispers the message—or what she thinks is the message—to the child next to her, and so on until the message reaches the last child.

The last child announces the message to the group, and it is compared with the original message, which is announced by the child who started the game.

WHAT'S ON THE TRAY?

NUMBER OF PLAYERS: Any number

EQUIPMENT: Tray, a variety of objects, dish towel, pencils and paper

DIFFICULTY: Can be played by children of all ages

DURATION: About 5 minutes

Setup

Before the party, lay out a number of objects on a tray and cover them with a dish towel. Give each of the players a pencil and some paper.

Playing the Game

When you are ready to play, remove the dish towel and allow the children to study the objects for one minute, then remove the tray from sight.

Allow the children a few minutes to write down as many of the objects as they can remember. The winner is the child who can remember the most. For older children—or adults—simply add more objects to the tray and make them as varied as possible.

Family Party Games

Holiday times are often a reason for family get-togethers or for social gatherings. These lighthearted games will guarantee that the party gets off on the right foot.

BEETLE

NUMBER OF PLAYERS: Two to eight

EQUIPMENT: Paper and pencil, one die

DIFFICULTY: Suitable for children 5 and up

DURATION: About 30 minutes

The object of this game is to complete a drawing of a beetle, but it is not as easy as it sounds.

The beetle must be drawn bit by bit. The parts of
the beetle's body are numbered as follows to
correspond with the numbers on a die:

1 - Body   2 - Head   3 - Leg

4 - Eye   5 - Tail   6 - Feeler

Playing the Game

Each player has a large sheet of paper and a pencil. Players
take turns rolling the die and adding the corresponding part to
their beetles. The only rules are that the body must be drawn
first, and the head must be drawn before the eyes and feelers. A
completed beetle consists of 13 parts: a body, a head, a tail, two
eyes, two feelers, and six legs. If a player rolls a number that does
not allow him to add a part to his drawing, his turn is forfeited.

Winning the Game

The first player to complete a beetle shouts 'Beetle!' and wins.

BLOW BALL

NUMBER OF PLAYERS: Enough for a competition

EQUIPMENT: Ping-pong balls and straws

DIFFICULTY: Easy for all ages

DURATION: A few minutes per race

Playing the Game

The players line up on their hands and knees, and each child
is given a straw and a ping-pong ball. The aim of the game is

for each child to blow the ping-pong ball across the floor
from the start to the finish line.

If a child touches the ball with the straw or with any part of
his body, he is sent back to the starting line. The first child to
blow his ball over the finish line is the winner.

Variations

Nose Ball

Instead of using straws, the players have to push the ping-
pong balls with their noses—but no other part of the body.

DUMB CRAMBO

NUMBER OF PLAYERS: Six or more

EQUIPMENT: None

DIFFICULTY: Lots of noisy fun for adults and older children

DURATION: About 1 hour

*The forerunner to charades and The Game, Dumb Crambo
has the advantage of being simpler and noisier
than either of its successors.*

Setup

Start by dividing players into two teams.
One team leaves the room while the other
thinks of a word—usually a verb—and in any
case simple enough to have plenty of potential for rhyming.
When the first team returns, the members are told not the
word itself, but a word that rhymes with it. For instance, if the
word was 'stop,' they might be told 'mop.' Except for this one
word, the two teams are prohibited from speaking to each other.

Playing the Game

At this point, the first team leaves the room again to come up
with three guesses as to the identity of the secret word. Once
the team members have decided, they return to the room and
all proceed to mime the first of their guesses.

Audience response

For instance, in the previous example, a team member might mime 'drop' by pretending to drop something heavy on his feet. If this guess is correct, the team is cheered with boisterous applause. Otherwise, they are booed and hissed at in the loudest possible way.

The performing team only gets three tries, and regardless of success or failure, the teams switch roles at the end of the round and play progresses as before. Score can be kept if desired, but to experience the real fun of this game, the team members serving as the audience should focus on exaggerating their responses to the point of total absurdity, although these responses may on no account incorporate any form of speech.

THE GAME

NUMBER OF PLAYERS: Four or more

EQUIPMENT: Pencil and paper

DIFFICULTY: Easy for some, difficult for others

DURATION: From 30 minutes to several hours

In this high-spirited team game, opposing sides silently act out a phrase or movie title to their teammates, who try to guess it correctly. As its name implies, this game is a perennial classic, and it comes in two versions, the first being relatively subdued, and the second relatively chaotic. Both require a minimum of four players, as well as a good deal of skill and ingenuity.

Playing the Game

To begin, divide the players into two equal teams and follow the instructions for the version that appeals to you most.

Version 1

In this version, each team compiles a list of phrases—proverbs, movie titles, figures of speech, or anything that comes into their heads. The number of phrases should equal

Diagram 1: Holding three fingers in the air signifies that the phrase contains three words

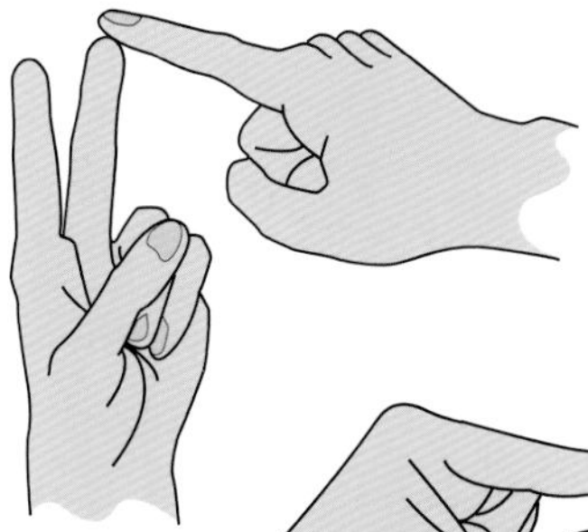

Diagram 2: Indicating the second finger means that you are acting the second word

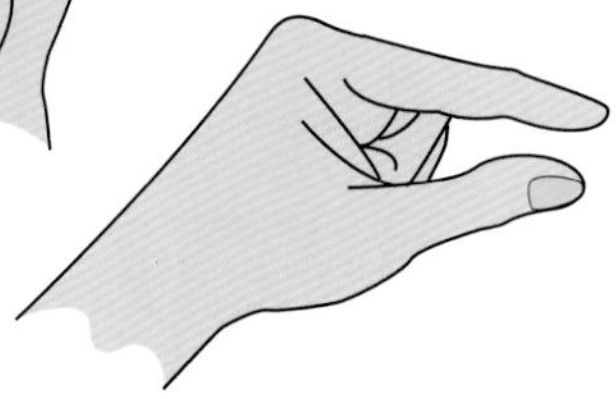

Diagram 3: Indicating a small word

the number of players in the opposing team. Next, a player needs to be chosen as the first actor—perhaps whoever seems most (or least) enthusiastic. This player will be given a single phrase from the opposing team's list, which he must act out to his teammates without using words. While the actor's team struggles to guess the phrase, the opposing team members sit back and enjoy the fruits of their hard work. The round is over when the actor's team either guesses the phrase or gives up, at which point teams switch roles, and a player from the opposing team takes the stage. Play continues until both lists are finished and everyone has had a turn as actor.

Version 2

This version is basically a race, mediated by a quiz leader who belongs to neither team. The quiz leader compiles the list of phrases and gives the first phrase out to one player from each team simultaneously. The players then return to their respective teams and act out the phrases as quickly as possible, in the same way as in Version 1. When a player guesses the phrase correctly, he quickly runs to the quiz leader to get the second phrase. This continues until the list is exhausted. The first team to work through all the phrases wins.

This version has greater potential for excitement and mayhem, but also greater potential for cheating, since players can watch actors from the other team or listen to their guesses. To minimize this risk, place the teams as far apart as possible within the room. The quiz leader should keep a careful eye on things to ensure that play is going fairly.

Playing conventions

Both versions of The Game use the same conventions, which take the form of a primitive sign language. At the beginning of the pantomime, it is helpful to use one of the following signs to indicate the genre of the phrase to be acted out:

- **Opening your palms:** Book
- **Drawing an arch:** Play
- **Pulling sound from your open mouth:** Song or opera
- **Quotation marks:** Proverb
- **Drawing a square:** TV show
- **Winding a movie camera:** Film title.

Next indicate how many words the phrase contains by holding up the corresponding number of fingers. To show which word is being acted out at a given time, simply point to the relevant finger. To indicate how many syllables there are in the word, lay the appropriate number of fingers across your forearm. In addition to these conventions, there are a few auxiliary symbols which may come in handy:

- **Pulling your earlobe:** Indicates that the word or syllable rhymes with what is being acted.
- **Holding your thumb and forefinger slightly apart:** Indicates a very small word, such as 'and' or 'of.'
- **Drawing a circle in the air with both hands:** Indicates an attempt to act out the entire phrase at once.

Teammates may ask questions, but your response cannot go beyond a nod or shake of the head. Talking, whispering, or any form of verbal communication on the part of the actor is strictly prohibited.

Variations

Charades

This is a popular variant of The Game, in which speech, clothes,

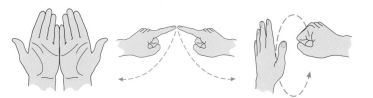

Diagram 4: It's a book... It's a play... It's a film...

and props can be used to help act out a word.

In charades, players are divided into two teams, and each chooses a word of two or more syllables to act out to the opposing team. As a group, the first team acts out its word, syllable by syllable, and finally acts out the entire concept. For instance, the word 'defendant' could be split into deaf, end, and ant.

Charades is not as strictly competitive as The Game, since the teams are essentially working together. Rather, the fun of it lies in each team coming up with the silliest and most outrageous ways to convey a word to the opponents. When acting out a word, players may use the same conventions as in The Game.

IN THE MANNER OF THE WORD

NUMBER OF PLAYERS: Four or more

EQUIPMENT: None

DIFFICULTY: Suitable for adults and older children

DURATION: A few hours

This game is similar to The Game and charades except that it is based entirely on adverbs. Like The Game, it comes in two distinct versions.

Playing the Game

In the first version, one player leaves the room and the others choose an adverb (a word used to describe a verb). When the player returns, he must attempt to discover the identify of the adverb, either by asking questions or by asking players to act out a situation. In both cases, players must speak or act 'in the manner of the word.'

For instance, if the word was 'giddily,' all questions would have to be answered in a state of flustered excitement. Or, if it was 'cruelly,' all situations, even the grooming of a kitten, would have to be acted with a heartless savagery. Play continues until the player guesses correctly or gives up.

In the second version, two players leave the room to think of an adverb, and upon their return must respond to the questions of the other players in the same manner as above.

MURDER IN THE DARK

NUMBER OF PLAYERS: Eight or more

EQUIPMENT: Pencil and paper

DIFFICULTY: Suitable for adults; too scary for young children

DURATION: About 1 hour

Setup

Tear some ordinary paper into slips—as many as there are players. Mark one slip with a black cross and another with a circle. Fold the slips in two, put them into a hat and have everyone draw one. Whoever draws the slip with the cross is the murderer, and whoever draws the slip with the circle is the detective. The murderer keeps his identity a secret, while the detective identifies himself to the group.

Playing the Game

After this announcement, switch off the lights. All the players but the detective then scatter in all directions. The murderer then proceeds to roam around the house and 'assassinate' his fellow players—either by whispering 'You're dead' or placing his hands around their necks. In either case, the victim lets out an agonized scream and slumps to the floor as the murderer slinks quietly away from the scene.

When the other players hear the scream, they must remain exactly where they are. The detective then rushes to the scene of the crime, turns on the lights and takes note of where everyone is standing. He then summons all the living players to the main room to be questioned about their movements. The murderer is allowed to lie to protect himself, but all the others must tell the truth.

Winning the Game

Once he is finished, the detective is allowed just two guesses as to the murderer's identity. The murderer must confess if officially accused. If the detective guesses correctly, he wins. Otherwise, the round goes to the murderer.

PICTIONARY®

NUMBER OF PLAYERS: At least three

EQUIPMENT: Game board and accessories (available in toy stores), including a one-minute timer, 500 word cards, a die, four markers, four category cards, four pads of paper, four pencils

DIFFICULTY: Suitable for 12 and up

DURATION: 30 minutes to about an hour, depending on the number of players

Pictionary is played by teams, and the object of the game is to identify words from pictures sketched by one of the team members. Team members take turns being the sketcher, and the number of team members does not have to be even.

The sketches cannot include numbers, letters, or the number symbol. The words are picked from five different categories: P: Person/Place/Animal; O: Object; A: Action; D: Difficult

Words; AP: All Play. Any word preceded by a triangle (>) is an All Play word, in which case all the teams tackle the word at the same time.

Playing the Game

Each team needs a pad, a pencil, a marker, and a category card. All the markers are placed on the game board's start square. The die is rolled and the highest roller goes first.

The starting team picks a card, and the sketcher has five seconds to study the word. Then the timer is set and the game begins. If the team members guess the word in one minute, they roll the die and move the marker accordingly. Then they pick a word from a category and the next team member sketches.

If the team members fail to identify the word, the die is passed to the team on their left. This team does not roll the die, but picks a card and chooses a word from the category that its marker is currently on. The opportunity to move forward only comes after correctly guessing a word.

If a word is in the All Play category, the card is shown to the sketchers from each of the teams and all the teams play at the same time. The first team to guess the All Play word correctly gains control of the die and immediately rolls and moves its marker. Members then choose a card and word from this category.

If no team guesses the All Play word correctly, the die is passed to the left.

To win, a team must enter the final All Play square after rolling the die, and then correctly guess the word that all the teams are trying to sketch. If another team guesses the word, it gains control of the die and play continues. If no one guesses the word, the die is passed to the left and play continues.

Winning the Game

In order to win, a team must be in control of the die when it correctly guesses the All Play word.

Variation

It is possible for only three players to play, but one person must elect to be the sketcher throughout the match. Also, there is a special version of the game available for children under 12.

SARDINES

Number of players: Four or more

Equipment: None

Difficulty: Easy for all ages

Duration: About half an hour on average; less if very young children

A variant of the familiar party game known as hide-and-seek, Sardines is best played with several players in a fairly large house.

First, one person is selected to go off and hide while the others remain behind. After a reasonable interval, the players split up and search for him. The first one to discover the hiding place of his companion waits until no one is looking and then ducks into the hiding place as well—easier, of course, if it is relatively spacious.

This process is then repeated until all the players but one are packed into the hiding place like sardines into a tin. The last player to find his giggling comrades is the loser and must be the first to hide in the next round.

TWISTER®

Number of players: Up to three, plus referee

Equipment: Twister mat plus spinner, available at most toy stores

Difficulty: Great fun for older children and adults

Duration: About 5 to 10 minutes

Setup

Twister is a potentially hilarious game that involves players moving their hands and feet onto different coloured circles on a mat. The winner is the person who avoids falling over. For this game, one person must take the role of referee.

Playing the Game

Spread the plastic mat on a flat surface and play without shoes on. Two players face each other from opposite ends of the mat, near the word Twister, with one foot on a yellow circle and the other foot on a blue circle. If there is a third player he stands, facing the middle from the red-circle side of the mat, with one foot on each of the two middle red circles.

The referee spins the spinner and calls out the body part and colour circle that it stops at. All the players, at the same time, must then try to move the body part onto a vacant circle of the correct colour—for example, a right foot onto a blue circle.

If one of the players already has a foot on a blue circle, he must try to move to another circle of the same colour. Only one body part can be on a circle at any one time—if two players land on the same circle, the referee decides who got there first. The other player must then try to find another circle to move to. If all the circles of that colour are in use, the referee must spin again.

Rules

A player must not remove a body part from a circle except to make a move, unless he lifts his hand or foot to allow another player to move underneath—in which case he must tell the referee first.

Winning the Game

If a player falls, or touches the ground with an elbow or knee, he is out of the game. If three people are playing, the remaining two continue until another player falls. The last player to remain standing is the winner.

WINKING

NUMBER OF PLAYERS: Four or more

EQUIPMENT: A deck of playing cards

DIFFICULTY: Suitable for children 7 and up

DURATION: About 1 hour

Despite its simplicity, Winking can be a game of real strategy and intrigue. Half the fun is watching the other players to see who can keep the straightest face.

Setup

Start by drawing as many cards from a deck as there are players—one of these cards must be the ace of spades, but the others are random selections. Lay the cards facedown on a table and have each player pick a card, showing it to no one. Whoever picks the ace of spades then takes on the role of the murderer, a fiendish individual whose identity remains unknown to the players at large.

Playing the Game

The murderer commits his crime by discreetly making eye contact with another player and shooting a deadly wink in her direction. When a player is hit by such a wink, she must wait a few seconds so as not to give the game away, then slump over dead. The object of the game—for everyone but the murderer—is to spot one of these winks in action from outside the line of fire, to witness a wink, in other words, without getting winked at. This is surprisingly difficult when everyone but the murderer is avoiding eye contact for fear of being murdered.

Winning the Game

If successful, a player may reveal the murderer's identity and be declared the winner. On the other hand, if the number of living players ever falls below three, it is no longer possible to witness a murder. In this case, it is the murderer who has won.

Old-Fashioned Parlor Games

In the late 1800s the parlor was a family room or a simple drawing room for entertaining, where people got together to play these informal games.

DO YOU LOVE YOUR NEIGHBOR?

NUMBER OF PLAYERS: Five or more

EQUIPMENT: As many chairs as there are players, less one

DIFFICULTY: Easy

DURATION: A few minutes

Playing the Game

Line up the chairs. One person remains standing and all the other players must sit down. The person standing asks one of the other players, 'Do you love your neighbor?' If this player says no, the players on both sides of him must change seats quickly. Or, he may reply, 'Yes, except for those wearing black' or '…except for those with blue eyes.' Then all those players fitting the description must get up and change seats.

While players are standing to change seats, the player who asked the question can try to sit down. If she succeeds, the player left standing is the new question master and asks another player, 'Do you love your neighbor?'

FEATHER

NUMBER OF PLAYERS: Five or more

EQUIPMENT: A feather

DIFFICULTY: Easy

DURATION: A few minutes

Playing the Game

Players sit together in a tight circle, either on chairs or on the floor. One player throws a feather into the air. Then, as the feather descends, the player it comes closest to must blow it to keep it in the air. If the feather falls to the ground, the closest player throws the feather back in the air. If a player is touched by the feather he is out. He must leave, and the others close the circle. (A balloon can be used instead of a feather.)

The winner is the last person not to be touched by the feather.

FOLLOW THE LEADER

NUMBER OF PLAYERS: Four or more

EQUIPMENT: None

DIFFICULTY: Easy

DURATION: A few minutes

Playing the Game

One player leaves the room. The other players elect a leader who initiates an action, which all the other players must copy, such as scratching his head, tapping his foot, or clapping his hands.

The player outside the room is invited back in. The object of the game is for the leader to change the action at frequent intervals and for all the other players to follow his lead while the outsider tries to spot who the leader is. Each player takes a turn at going out of the room.

HOT AND COLD

NUMBER OF PLAYERS: At least three

EQUIPMENT: Any object that is easy to conceal

DIFFICULTY: Easy

DURATION: Up to 10 minutes

Playing the Game

One person leaves the room, and those remaining hide an object, such as a hat, a ball, a clock, or even an egg, somewhere in the room. The location is known only to those remaining. The person returns to the room and starts to look for the hidden object. As he searches the others cry out 'hot,' 'very hot,' or 'scorching,' when he gets close to finding the object or 'cold,' 'very cold,' or 'freezing' as he gets farther away. When the person searching finds the object, another person is chosen to go out of the room, and the object is hidden in another place.

LOOKABOUT

NUMBER OF PLAYERS: Four or more

EQUIPMENT: Any object that is easy to conceal

DIFFICULTY: Easy

DURATION: About 10 minutes

Playing the Game

Players are shown an object—a pen, a thimble, a teaspoon, anything small will do—then asked to leave the room. One of the players remains in the room and hides the object. Then the other players return to the room and search for it. As each player finds the object, he leaves it where it is, says nothing, and sits down. The last person standing is the loser. It is better to wander somewhere else in the room before sitting down, unless you want to reveal to everyone where the object is hidden.

MUMMIES

NUMBER OF PLAYERS: Six or more

EQUIPMENT: Several rolls of toilet tissue—at least half as many as there are players

DIFFICULTY: Easy and fun for children of all ages

DURATION: 3 minutes

Playing the Game

Players divide into pairs and one person in each pair is given a roll of toilet tissue. At the signal, this person must try to wrap up his partner like an Egyptian mummy, using the tissue and completing the job within three minutes. The two judged to have created the best mummy are the winners.

PASS THE SLIPPER

NUMBER OF PLAYERS: Six or more

EQUIPMENT: Traditionally a slipper, but any similarly-sized object will do

DIFFICULTY: Easy

DURATION: About 10 minutes

Playing the Game

One player stands in the middle and the other players form a circle around him, either sitting on chairs or on the floor. The player in the middle of the circle closes his eyes and the other players pass an object behind their backs around the circle. When the player in the middle opens his eyes, the passing stops, and he must guess who is holding the object.

If he guesses correctly, then he sits down and the player holding the object stands in the middle of the circle.

Victorian and pioneer parlor games

The golden age of games was undoubtedly during the Victorian era in Britain and the pioneer days of America in the late 1800s—although many games date back much earlier than this. Before electricity or television, long evenings were passed playing a variety of games, designed then for adults, but played today by both adults and children.

People gathered together at house parties in Victorian country mansions, where the many rooms were put to good use. Parlor games could be played in one room, card games in another, and word games in yet another.

Racing Games

You'll need plenty of room to enjoy these traditional children's games. If you don't have a big yard, you can play these at the park, at the beach, or in a community hall.

BACK-TO-BACK RACE

NUMBER OF PLAYERS: At least four

EQUIPMENT: None

DIFFICULTY: Suitable for all ages, though young children may fall over easily

DURATION: A few minutes per race

This fun race may seem like a simple idea, but it is a true test of cooperation and coordination.

Playing the Game

Players divide into pairs. Each pair stands back to back and links arms at the elbows. They line up at the start, then at the signal they race to the finish line. The first pair to cross the line is the winner.

BALLOON RACE

NUMBER OF PLAYERS: Enough for a competition

EQUIPMENT: Balloons

DIFFICULTY: Easy for all ages

DURATION: A minute or two per race

The aim of this game is to move a balloon along without holding it.

Playing the Game

In this race, each child is given a balloon. She can punch or kick the balloon with her hands, elbows, head, feet, or any other part of the body, but the balloon must not be held.

Children line up, and at the signal race to the finish line.

The first one over the finish line is the winner.

Left: Balloon Race
Right: Egg and Spoon Race

EGG AND SPOON RACE

NUMBER OF PLAYERS: Four minimum, but larger numbers are most fun

EQUIPMENT: Spoons, hard-boiled eggs, or ping-pong balls

DIFFICULTY: Not so easy for tiny children

DURATION: A minute or two per race

This game can also be played with a feather and paper plate.

Setup

Give each child a spoon and an egg or a ping-pong ball. He must hold the spoon with the egg or ball on it with one hand only, without using the other hand to steady it.

Playing the Game

The contestants line up at the start and on the signal they race toward the finish line. If the egg or ball drops they can only use the hand holding the spoon to scoop the object back into the spoon. The first person to cross the line with the egg or ping-pong ball in the spoon is the winner.

Variations

Team Egg and Spoon Race

This game is played as a relay race between teams.

The first child on a team races to a marker with his egg or ping-pong ball and spoon, then returns to pass the egg from his spoon to the spoon of the next child on his team.

The first team to have all its players carry the egg to the marker and back is the winner.

No-hands Egg and Spoon Race

In this game for older children, the contestants are divided into two teams and line up one behind the other. Each child has a spoon he holds in his mouth. An egg or ping-pong ball is put into the spoon of the child at the front of each team. He then turns and tries to transfer the egg or ball into the spoon of the child behind him, and so on down the line. Hands cannot be used at any time; if the egg or ball drops a child must try to scoop it up with the spoon still in the mouth. The winner is the first team to transfer the egg down the line to the last child.

PIGGYBACK RACE

NUMBER OF PLAYERS: At least four

EQUIPMENT: None

DIFFICULTY: Suitable for older children

DURATION: A few minutes per race

Playing the Game

The players divide into pairs. Each child climbs onto his partner's back, then all the players line up at the start. At the signal they race to the finish line. The first pair to cross the line is the winner.

Variation

Trading places

At the finish line the rider and carrier swap, and they race back to the start. The first pair to cross the starting line wins.

POTATO RACE

NUMBER OF PLAYERS: At least three

EQUIPMENT: Potatoes, cardboard boxes or wastepaper baskets

DIFFICULTY: Fun for all ages

DURATION: A few minutes

Playing the Game

The children line up at the start, each one in front of a cardboard box or wastepaper basket. In front of each child, at

5 ft. (1.5 m) intervals, are three potatoes. At the signal each child races to collect the first potato, then runs back and drops it into the box or basket. He then returns to collect the second potato, which he puts in the box or basket, and finally he collects the third potato. The winner is the first child to drop his third potato in the box or basket.

Variation

Potato Tag

Divide the contestants into two teams of equal numbers, each with a box or basket. Arrange as many potatoes as you have children in the teams at 5 ft. (1.5 m) intervals. The first child races forward and collects the first potato, then returns and drops it in the box or basket before tagging the second child in his team, who collects the second potato and so on.

The winner is the first team to collect and drop all its potatoes into the box or basket.

RELAY RACES

NUMBER OF PLAYERS: Enough to make two teams

EQUIPMENT: Balls or beanbags

DIFFICULTY: Suitable for older children

DURATION: A few minutes per race

Playing the Game

Divide the players into two teams. Both teams line up, one behind the other, at the starting line. The first player carries the ball. On the signal the first player runs to a marker—which may be something she has to touch or a line she has to cross or stand on—then races back and hands the ball to the next child in her team. This child races to the marker, goes back, and hands the ball to the next child. All the team members must carry the ball to the marker and back, and the first team to do this is the winner.

Variations

More relays

Many races can be played as a relay, such as the Egg and Spoon Race or Potato Race, listed earlier. To make it more interesting, each player can perform a forfeit at the marker, such as taking off and putting on an old sweater, turning in a circle, or doing a somersault.

Or each team can sit in a circle, with one child chosen to go first. On the signal the child jumps up and runs around the circle before returning to sit in his place. The child on his right then jumps up and runs around, and so on until all the children in the circle have run.

The team that finishes first is the winner.

Above: Children enjoying a sack race

SACK RACE

NUMBER OF PLAYERS: At least four, but larger numbers are most fun

EQUIPMENT: Potato sacks, old pillowcases, or burlap sacks

DIFFICULTY: Easy for all ages

DURATION: A minute or two per race

Playing the Game

Give each child a sack, which she must step into and hold up around her waist. The contestants line up at the start, and on the signal they race toward the finish line, hopping with both feet together while holding the sack up.

The first person to cross the line is the winner.

THREE-LEGGED RACE

NUMBER OF PLAYERS: At least four

EQUIPMENT: A selection of scarves, large handkerchiefs, or old ties

DIFFICULTY: Easy for all ages

DURATION: Only about one minute per race

Playing the Game

The players organize themselves into pairs then stand next to each other. The right leg of one child is tied with a scarf to the left leg of his partner. All the pairs line up at the start, and on the signal they race toward the finish line. The first pair to cross the line is the winner.

WHEELBARROW RACE

NUMBER OF PLAYERS: Enough for a race

EQUIPMENT: None

DIFFICULTY: Probably too difficult for very young children

DURATION: A minute or two per race

Make sure that the play area is soft—a yard, park, beach, or a large carpeted room.

Playing the Game

Divide the players into pairs. One child gets down on all fours and the second player lifts her up by the ankles so that she is moving on her hands only and is steered by her partner just like a wheelbarrow. All the pairs race from the start to the finish line. The first pair over the line is the winner.

Variation

Trading places

When they reach the finish line, the two change places so that the second child is now the front of the wheelbarrow and the first child holds her ankles and does the steering. They race back to the starting line, and the first pair over this line is the winner.

Super Party Games

These games will spice up any social event. Give the occasion a murder mystery theme, or try an after-dinner revelation game and find out if you know your guests as well as you think.

BUZZ & BUZZ-FIZZ

NUMBER OF PLAYERS: At least three

EQUIPMENT: None

DIFFICULTY: Easy for adults and older children

DURATION: About 5 to 10 minutes per game

A game that requires quick thinking, it seems easy at first glance but often proves to be frustratingly difficult. The key is to play as fast as possible so players do not have time to think for long about what they are saying.

Playing the Game

Players sit in a circle and take turns shouting out numbers: The first shouts 'one,' the next 'two,' and so on. The only twist is any number that is a multiple of five must be replaced with the word 'buzz.' Thus, one encounters sequences such as 'four,' 'buzz,' 'six,' and 'nine,' 'buzz,' '11.' Furthermore, if a number contains a five but is not a multiple of it, only the five is replaced by 'buzz.' Fifty-seven, for example, would become 'buzz-seven.'

Winning the Game

If a player hesitates too long, forgets to say 'buzz,' or says it at an inappropriate time, he is out of the round. The last person left in the round is declared the winner.

Variations

To make the game more challenging, try adding a stipulation that a player must stand up and sit back down again when saying 'buzz.' With this rule, anyone successfully reaching the number 55 ('buzz-buzz') would have to stand up and sit down twice. Or, if players are dropping out of the game too quickly, try granting them three strikes each before ejecting them from the round.

Another version of this game is known as Fizz and involves replacing multiples of seven with the word 'fizz.' If players are feeling particularly brave, they can play a hybrid game called

Buzz-fizz, which incorporates the rules of both games, leading to such headache-inducing sequences as: 'buzz,' 'six,' 'fizz,' 'eight,' 'nine,' 'buzz,' '11,' '12,' '13,' 'fizz,' 'buzz,' '16,' 'one-fizz,' and so on. In this version, the numbers 35 and 57 would both, for their own reasons, be represented by the expression 'buzz-fizz,' whereas the number 75, if anyone managed to hold out long enough to reach it, could only accurately be expressed as 'fizz-buzz.'

DINNER PARTY MURDER MYSTERY

NUMBER OF PLAYERS: Eight or more

EQUIPMENT: Crime and character descriptions, suspect statements, clue cards, a scene-of-the-crime description, name tags, additional evidence

DIFFICULTY: Suitable for adults

DURATION: Several hours

Setup

Dinner party murder mystery games can be bought from game shops, mail order, or via the Internet—or, with a little ingenuity you can create your own. Eight or more players is best and, if you are using your own resources, you will need to assemble a few easily obtainable items as noted above.

As the host you are responsible for creating a menu and surroundings that match the theme of the murder mystery. Everyone invited to the dinner party is given a character to play, and it is fun if people can be persuaded to dress up appropriately. People may choose to stay in character throughout the course of the event—but that is not necessary.

Playing the Game

A description of the crime should be included on the invitation as well as a list of the other suspects—the guest list for the dinner party. The crime might be the murder of a glamorous movie star who lived nearby, for example, or a local politician who had a murky background. You can come

up with all sorts of imaginative ideas, inspired perhaps by detective novels or TV crime series.

As the evening progresses the main suspects (known only to the hosts until they are revealed at the party) are asked to read out statements or act out scenes. Clues are revealed throughout the course of the party and any additional evidence, such as letters, documents, or crime weapons, shown to the guests. You can create a scene of the crime for the guests to examine, or you can simply provide a written description.

At the end of the party each of your guests writes down who they believe to be the guilty person. If you buy a commercial version of the game, the solution is sealed and it is possible for the hosts to play the game as well.

A dinner party murder mystery can be as complex or as simple as you like, which may also depend on how flamboyant your guest list is. It can be as straightforward as a few clues and statements read out between courses. If nothing else it will help the conversation flow as your guests discuss 'whodunit.'

Above: *Dig in at a dinner party murder mystery.*

GOOD MORNING, MADAM

NUMBER OF PLAYERS: Four or more

EQUIPMENT: One or two decks of cards

DIFFICULTY: For adults and children; concentration is required

DURATION: About 30 minutes

A silly, noisy game that requires players to pay close attention to the cards as they are dealt.

Playing the Game

Deal out one deck of cards for four players, two decks for six or more. Without looking at what they have been dealt, players take turns placing a card faceup on a pile in the middle of the table. If a card between 2 and 10 appears, play passes to the next player, but if an ace, king, queen, or jack is played, certain responses are in order, as follows:

- **Ace:** Slap your palm down on top of it.
- **King:** Perform a military salute.
- **Queen:** Shout 'Good morning, Madam!'
- **Jack:** Shout 'Boo!'

Winning the Game

The first person to perform the correct response when one of these cards shows up takes possession of the entire pile of cards and adds them to his hand. The winner is the first person to collect all the cards that have been dealt.

I HAVE NEVER

NUMBER OF PLAYERS: Three or more

EQUIPMENT: None

DIFFICULTY: Suitable for adults; more difficult than it seems

DURATION: About 15 minutes per round

Playing the Game

Players sit in a circle, and each takes a turn declaring something he has never done. A point is scored if, and only if, this 'I have never...' turns out to be unique—that is, if everyone else in the group has done it. Thus, players should do their best to think of common activities which they have, for some reason, never participated in: 'I have never left the country,' 'I have never eaten tuna fish,' 'I have never seen any movie in the *Star Wars* series,' or something similar.

Winning the Game

Honesty is crucial for the game to work, since it is unlikely that the players will have any way of confirming one another's claims. The first player to get three points wins.

LIKES & DISLIKES

NUMBER OF PLAYERS: Six or more

EQUIPMENT: Pencil and paper

DIFFICULTY: A challenging game for adults

DURATION: About 30 minutes

This game has no real winners or losers, but can be lots of fun all the same.

Playing the Game

Each player uses a pen and paper to compose a list of five things he likes and five things he dislikes, drawing from any aspect of his experience. The lists are then folded up and collected into a pile.

Whichever player feels up to the task then proceeds to read the lists aloud, one by one, and the others have to guess the author of each.

Depending on how well the players know one another, this game can be an enjoyable means of gaining insight into the personalities of others.

Above: *If you're the first to spot one of these cards, you win the pile in Good Morning, Madam.*

GAMES TO PLAY ANYWHERE

Games on the Go 158

Ten-Minute Games 164

Games on the Go

A long car journey—or even a short one—can be boring, especially for children. Here are some ways you can make the time go quickly while you sharpen your word and puzzle skills.

ASSOCIATION

NUMBER OF PLAYERS: Three or more

EQUIPMENT: None

DIFFICULTY: Quick thinking is required, so this game is not suitable for young children or a group of children of very mixed ability

DURATION: 5 minutes for each round

In this simple game, players must in turn come up with words associated with the last word spoken—at lightning speed.

Playing the Game

First, one player says a word; then the second player says a word that is somehow associated with it; then the third player says a word that is somehow associated with the second word, and so on. The game must be played fast and furiously for it to remain challenging.

Scoring

Players each start with three lives. Any player who hesitates before saying a word loses a life. If there is some ambiguity, the question of whether or not a player hesitated can be put to a vote. If anyone feels that a word called by a player has no legitimate association with the previous word, he can challenge that player to explain the association. If no convincing explanation is provided, the challenged player loses a life; otherwise, the challenger loses a life.

Winning the Game

Any player who loses three lives is out of the round, and the last player left in the round is the winner.

BOTTICELLI

NUMBER OF PLAYERS: Three or more

EQUIPMENT: None

DIFFICULTY: Suitable for adults and teens

DURATION: About 15 minutes per game, but it can be played for hours

This challenging game of guessing a celebrity's identity requires plenty of cunning questioning and lateral thinking. A game for a group of three or more adults, Botticelli was once known as 'The Box,' since playing it can make you feel as if you are standing in a courtroom witness box. The origin of the new name remains obscure.

Playing the Game

The game begins with one player secretly adopting the identity of any famous character, real or fictional, from any era. Keeping his identity to himself, the mystery person then announces only his first initial to the group. The other players then take turns questioning the mystery person, but they must do so in a very roundabout way, by thinking of a famous person whose name begins with the letter given and asking the mystery person indirectly if that is his identity. For instance, if the mystery person's name begins with S, a player may ask, 'Are you a character from *Star Wars?*' but not 'Are you Luke Skywalker?'

The mystery person, in turn, must reply by saying, 'I am not...' followed by the name of a famous person whose name fits the criteria, although his answer is not required to be identical to the person that the questioner was thinking of. Thus, in the previous example, the mystery person could answer either 'I am not Luke Skywalker' or 'I am not Han Solo' without fear of being penalized. It is important to note here that the same indirect question can be asked three times within the game, and that the mystery person must deny a different identity every time. Another interesting rule is that the mystery person can answer in this way even if the questioner has successfully guessed his identity. In other words, even if the mystery person *is* Luke Skywalker, if asked indirectly he is allowed to claim that he is not.

Strategy

Real opportunity arises when the mystery person cannot think of an appropriate identity to deny. If, for example, a player asks him, 'Are you the actor who played Kojak?' and he replies with something like, 'Um…who?' then the player gets to ask him a direct question about his identity, which must be answered truthfully with a 'yes' or 'no.' Examples of good questions are: 'Are you alive?' 'Are you fictional?' or 'Are you an artist of any kind?' If the mystery person feels that he has been set up—in other words, that there is no celebrity meeting the criteria—he can challenge the questioner to provide an acceptable example—in this case, Telly Savalas.

If the questioner cannot do so, or if the question is deemed to be unreasonably obscure by a consensus of the players, the direct question is disallowed. Note also that if a player asks the same question multiple times, he must actually have multiple identities in mind. Thus, a questioner cannot force the mystery person into a direct question by asking, 'Were you the 27th president of the United States?' twice in a row or other such tactics.

Winning the Game

The game continues in this way until one of the players reveals the identity of the mystery person by using one of his direct questions to challenge him: 'Are you Luke Skywalker?' A player who thus wins the game has the privilege of becoming the next mystery person. On the other hand, if 15 minutes go by and no one has guessed correctly, then the mystery person announces his secret identity and proceeds to adopt another.

DEFINITIONS

NUMBER OF PLAYERS: Three or more

EQUIPMENT: None

DIFFICULTY: For adults and older children

DURATION: A couple of minutes per game, but it can be played for hours

Playing the Game

The first player chooses a word, such as 'apple,' and the next player has to define the word as accurately as possible. For example: 'red/yellow fruit' or 'round fruit for eating' or 'fruit found in an orchard.' If she defines the word correctly she names a word for the next player to define. If she gets it wrong she misses her turn in that round.

It can help to have a dictionary handy to settle disputes if adults are playing. However, if children are playing in the car an adult can be chosen to act as the judge.

EARTH, WATER, AIR

NUMBER OF PLAYERS: Three or more

EQUIPMENT: None

DIFFICULTY: For adults and children

DURATION: About half an hour

Playing the Game

The first player calls out Earth, Water, or Air. The next player has to name an animal, bird, fish, or insect that lives in the element that has been called out. If he does this correctly he names an element for the next player; if he cannot name a creature he misses his turn until the next round. The winner is the first person to name 10 creatures.

FIVE OF A KIND

NUMBER OF PLAYERS: Two or more

EQUIPMENT: None

DIFFICULTY: Fun for young children

DURATION: Up to an hour during a car journey

Playing the Game

Players take turns naming something that may occasionally be seen from the car, such as a mailbox, a church, or a house. All the players then look out for the thing that has been named, calling out as soon as they see it. The player who is the first to call out gets one point. The winner is the first player to collect five points.

HOW MANY WORDS?

NUMBER OF PLAYERS: Two or three

EQUIPMENT: None

DIFFICULTY: For adults and older children

DURATION: About 10 minutes

Playing the Game

One player chooses a letter. The next player has to name as many words as she can think of beginning with this letter while the player who chose the letter counts to 60—or times one minute on a watch. A third player—or the player naming the words—must keep count of the number of words.

Each player has a turn at choosing a letter and naming the words. The player who names the most words is the winner.

I SPY

NUMBER OF PLAYERS: Three or more

EQUIPMENT: None

DIFFICULTY: Fun for young children

DURATION: Up to an hour—until interest is lost

This game was created primarily for bored children, who insist that it is lots of fun.

Playing the Game

One player selects an object visible from the play area and declares, 'I spy with my little eye something that begins with...' followed by the first letter of the object in question. The other players then take turns guessing the identity of the object. The first person to guess correctly is the winner and takes a turn at spying.

To make the game slightly more interesting, you can allow each person ten yes-or-no questions about the spied object: 'Is it green?' 'Could I fit it in my pocket?' or 'Does it make a loud noise?'

LICENSE PLATES

NUMBER OF PLAYERS: Two or more

EQUIPMENT: Pencil and paper

DIFFICULTY: Children 7 and up

DURATION: Up to half an hour

This is a simple game designed to keep small children from annoying one another on long car trips.

Playing the Game

An adult starts by specifying a certain number, based on how restless the children are, and the children each write down a word with that number of letters. The players then keep a close watch on the rear ends of passing vehicles, crossing off letters from their word as they appear on the car license plates.

Winning the Game

The first player to cross off all the letters is the winner.

Variations

Many variations on this theme are possible. Children can write down the entire alphabet or the numbers 0 to 100 and play in the same way as above. Additionally, the scope of the game can be widened to include not only license plates but street signs, storefronts, and billboards. In fact, to make the game really challenging, license plates can be banned altogether.

RUBIK'S CUBE ®

NUMBER OF PLAYERS: One

EQUIPMENT: Rubik's cube

DIFFICULTY: Challenging for older children and adults

DURATION: Several hours

This ingenious puzzle, invented in 1974 by Enro Rubik, enjoyed immense popularity in the early 1980s and can still be found in toy stores.

Playing the Game

The puzzle consists of a bright, multicoloured plastic cube composed of 26 smaller cubes, each of which displays a different colour on each of its visible sides. The device is

To cheat or not to cheat?

In some ways, Rubik's Cube is a double conundrum: To solve it unassisted seems almost impossible, yet to follow a set of instructions hardly seems satisfying. In the 1980s, as Rubik's-mania swept the globe, many books were published demonstrating how to solve the cube. Today, most of these are probably gathering dust in attics or on the bargain rack at secondhand bookstores. In their place, however, are a wealth of Internet websites offering not only step-by-step instructions for cube-solving but also a collection of complex mathematical algorithms relating to the treacherous permutations of the cube.

Ultimately, the question of how much outside assistance is really advisable is still one that each cube owner must answer for himself. While purists might insist that even a single hint is too many, most will find that, without the help of fairly detailed instructions, their cube will meet one of two fates, all too common during the '80s: Either it will lie forgotten and perpetually unsolved in the bottom of a closet, or it will be disassembled in a fit of frustrated rage.

constructed in such a way that each face of the larger cube can be independently rotated, thus changing the orientation and positions of the smaller cubes. The object of the puzzle is simple: to manipulate the larger cube in such a way that each of its six sides displays a single, solid colour.

This sounds easy enough in theory, but as anyone who has ever tried to get the better of one of these puzzles can tell you, it is maddeningly difficult in practice, since every move of the cube disrupts the colour arrangements on several different faces at once.

TWENTY QUESTIONS

NUMBER OF PLAYERS: Four or more

EQUIPMENT: None

DIFFICULTY: For grown-ups; children would find it too demanding

DURATION: About 10 minutes per round; about 1 hour for a game

A team effort, this is the classic guessing game, also known as Animal, Vegetable, Mineral.

Playing the Game

One player thinks of a person, place, thing or idea—any noun—and tells the others whether it is animal, vegetable, mineral, abstract, or mixture, although in some versions the last two categories are omitted. These classifications, though usually self-evident, may be defined as follows:

- **Animal:** Any person, animal, or animal product, including cheese, leather, wool, and so on.
- **Vegetable:** Any plant, fungus, or other nonanimal form of life, as well as products made from them, such as wood, macaroni, and cotton.
- **Mineral:** Anything not recently derived from a living thing, such as rocks or power-steering fluid. Materials such as plastic and gasoline, which are technically produced from ancient organic material, also fall safely into this category.
- **Abstract:** Anything you cannot touch with your hands, such as democracy or spiritual enlightenment.
- **Mixture:** Something containing more than one of the above; it must include a general description of which elements are in the mixture.

The other players are then allowed 20 yes-or-no questions to find out what the word is: 'Is it alive?' 'Do most people have one in their homes?' 'Is it bigger than a breadbox?'

Winning the Game

Direct guesses count as questions but, if they prove incorrect, the guesser is out of the round. If someone guesses correctly before the 20 questions are up, that player wins and can choose the next word. Otherwise, the player who chose the word is the winner. Naturally, a player shown to have provided misleading answers is automatically disqualified.

Variations

One variation of Twenty Questions switches things around by having a player leave the room while the others collectively come up with an object, which must then be guessed by the player after returning. This version can be played as a competition, in which players take turns being the guesser but are knocked out of the game after a single failure. In this case, the last player left is the winner.

Ten-Minute Games

Sometimes a quick and easy game is just what is needed to keep kids entertained at a party, while in the car, or even on the beach. These games can be played almost anywhere.

FINGERS

NUMBER OF PLAYERS: Two

EQUIPMENT: None

DIFFICULTY: Easy for adults and children

DURATION: About 5 minutes

Playing the Game

Each player holds one hand behind his back and decides how many fingers he wants to hold out on that hand (thumbs count as a finger and a clenched fist counts as zero).

On the signal, each player brings his hand to the front. At the same time he calls out the number that he thinks the fingers held out on the hands of both players will add up to. The winner is the first player to make three correct guesses.

HANGMAN

NUMBER OF PLAYERS: Two and up

EQUIPMENT: Pencil and paper

DIFFICULTY: Depends on the level of vocabulary of players

DURATION: About 10 minutes per game, but longer if there are many players

Playing the Game

One player thinks of a word or phrase and writes down as many dashes as it has letters. Next to these dashes is drawn the base of a gallows. The other player then has to name different letters of which the word might be composed.

If a letter appears in the word, each dash where the letter appears is filled in with that letter. Otherwise, the incorrect guess is written down as a reminder and one segment of a hanged man is drawn suspended from the gallows. The hanged man usually consists of six segments—a head, a body, two arms and two legs—but his structure can be more elaborate if agreed upon beforehand.

Winning the Game

Play continues until the second player guesses the word or phrase correctly before the entire hanged man can be drawn.

Variation

In another version, a quiz leader is appointed and players are divided into two teams. The quiz leader then thinks of a word or phrase and writes out the appropriate number of dashes. The first team must then try to guess the word as above, while its hanged man is drawn to the side.

If the team guesses the word correctly, it wins points based on how many segments remain to be drawn on the hanged man. For example, if only the head and body have been drawn, the team wins 4 points because the hanged man has six segments. If team members fail to guess correctly, they are awarded nothing.

The quiz leader then thinks of a new word and play passes to the opposing team. Play can continue indefinitely, or until some predetermined goal is reached.

OUTLINES

NUMBER OF PLAYERS: Two

EQUIPMENT: Paper and coloured pens or crayons

DIFFICULTY: For children 7 and up

DURATION: About 5 minutes

Playing the Game

The first player draws a squiggle on the paper using one of the pens or crayons. The second player starts drawing from one end of the squiggle, using the second coloured pen or crayon, and attempts to make a recognizable picture without lifting his pen or crayon from the paper. Players take turns starting with the squiggle and completing the picture.

ROCK, PAPER, SCISSORS (SCISSORS, PAPER, STONE)

NUMBER OF PLAYERS: Two

EQUIPMENT: None

DIFFICULTY: Adults and children 7 and up

DURATION: About 15 minutes for a few rounds

This is a simple game that can be played almost anywhere.

Playing the Game

To begin, both players put one hand behind their backs and, at the count of three, bring it out again in the form of either scissors (two fingers extended in a V), paper (hand held horizontally), or a rock (hand clenched into a fist).

Each of these formations beats one of its opponents and is beat by the other. Specifically, scissors cut paper, paper covers rock, and rock crushes scissors. If both players use the same formation, the round is a draw.

Although based fundamentally on chance, this game can evolve over several rounds into one of judgment and strategy. If the players are feeling particularly competitive, it can become a real battle of wills.

SPOOF

NUMBER OF PLAYERS: Two and up

EQUIPMENT: Small objects such as coins or buttons

DIFFICULTY: For adults and older children

DURATION: As long as the fun lasts

Playing the Game

Give three small objects to each participant. Players then conceal anywhere between zero and three of these objects in their fists, and hold their clenched fists out in front of them.

In turn, going around clockwise, each player much guess the total number of objects concealed in all the players' fists. Although the first player can guess any number, each subsequent guess must be different.

Once the guessing is over, the objects are counted and the player whose guess was closest to the actual number is declared the winner.

TIC-TAC-TOE (NOUGHTS AND CROSSES)

NUMBER OF PLAYERS: Two

EQUIPMENT: Paper and pencils

DIFFICULTY: Easy to play, not so easy to win

DURATION: A few minutes per game

This simple paper-and-pencil game can be played anywhere.

Playing the Game

Draw a nine-square grid. Flip a coin to decide who starts. If the winner chooses to be *crosses,* she writes an X in one of the nine boxes. The other player has to be *noughts* and writes an O in another box.

The aim of the game is to draw three X's or O's in a line, horizontally, vertically, or diagonally. Players take turns, and the winner is the first person to make a complete line. It is easy to prevent a winning line from being drawn, but not so easy to win the game outright, and games often end in a draw. Usually the person who begins has a slight advantage. After the first game, players take turns to begin.

Variation

Number Tic-Tac-Toe

Using pencil and paper, make a nine-square grid. One player uses the odd numbers between one and nine and the other player uses the even numbers between two and eight. The odd number player has one extra number and goes first, putting an odd number anywhere on the grid. The winner is the player who completes a row of three numbers—either vertically, horizontally or diagonally—that add up to 15. Players take turns using odd and even numbers.

INDOOR GAMES

Games of Skill 168

Pencil and Paper Games 182

Word and Spoken Games 193

Games of Skill

The games of skill we tackle as children can become the games that we continue to enjoy all our lives. Some are lighthearted while others are fiercely competitive.

CAROM BILLIARDS

NUMBER OF PLAYERS: Two, or four in pairs

EQUIPMENT: Table, standard snooker or billiards cues and three balls

DIFFICULTY: The game can be enjoyed at widely varying skill levels

DURATION: There is no standard time limit

In this game individual players or a pair aim to gain an agreed number of points. It is played on a smaller table than ordinary billiards; there are no pockets and the markings are different.

Setup

The table is a 10 x 5 ft. (3.04 x 1.52 m) rectangle with no pockets. It is divided into fourths along its short dimension by three lines, or *strings,* called the *head, center,* and *foot* strings; each has a spot in the middle that is named for its

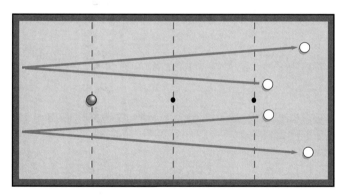

Diagram 1: Lagging decides who goes first

Diagram 2: Safety shot in carom billiards

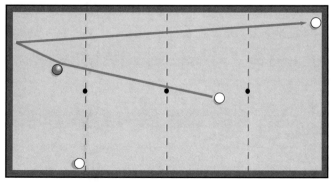

string (*head, middle,* and *foot spots*). The head string is the one nearest to and parallel with the head cushion, and the foot string is the one nearest the opposite foot cushion. Standard billiards cues are used, along with three billiard balls: one plain white cue ball, one white cue ball with a spot, and one red ball. Each player or team is assigned one of the cue balls for the entire game.

Order of play

The person or team to go first is decided by a procedure called *lagging* (diagram 1). The red ball is placed on the foot spot, and opponents place their cue balls on the head string on either side of, and within 6 in. (15 cm) of, the head spot. They each take a turn banking their cue balls off the foot cushion, attempting to return them as close as possible to the head cushion. The cue ball must not move the red ball nor cross to the other side of the table, where it might interfere with the other player's line. The player whose ball ends up nearest the head cushion starts the game.

Playing the Game

The basic game, called *straight rail carom,* begins with a *break shot.* The red ball is placed on the foot spot and the *object ball,* the opponent's cue ball, on the head spot. One's own cue ball is placed as for lagging. The player attempts to strike the cue ball so that it first makes contact with the red ball, and then hits the object ball (a carom shot). A successful carom shot scores 1 point and permits the player to continue his turn.

After the break, striking both balls in any order may score a carom shot, so long as the two are hit in succession. A player who fails to make a carom shot loses 1 point and ends his turn. Once per session, a player can end his turn without having a point deducted by making a *safety shot* (diagram 2). This requires that the cue ball hit another ball, and that the cue ball itself or the ball that was hit then comes to rest in contact with a cushion. To attempt a second safety shot results in a 1-point deduction and the end of the turn. The game ends when the agreed number of points is reached.

Generally, the normal restrictions of snooker and billiards apply with respect to fouls and point deductions. For example, it is a foul to shoot while a ball is still moving, or to shove the cue ball rather than hitting it cleanly.

Special circumstances

Ball off the table: Causing the cue ball to fly off the table results in the deduction of 1 point and the end of the turn. (The ball is replaced on the head spot, if available, the foot spot if the head spot is not available, or the center spot if neither is open.) Causing the other balls to leave the table is not a foul—balls are replaced on the head spot (white ball) or foot spot (red ball), respectively. If all three balls fly off the table at once, the balls are repositioned as for a break shot.

Balls touching and against a cushion: If one ball is the cue ball, it must either be played away from the ball it is touching, or all the balls must be repositioned as for a break shot.

Crotch shots: The red and object balls (that is, the opponents' cue balls) are *crotched* when they are both in a corner—that is, within an imaginary triangle consisting of the corner and a line drawn 4½ in. (12 cm) from the apex of the corner. Only three successive scoring shots can be made; trying to make a fourth results in the end of the turn.

Variations

In the *one-cushion variation,* a point is awarded only when the cue ball hits a cushion before striking the other two balls, or when, before hitting a cushion, the cue ball strikes one object ball, and then hits a cushion before striking the other ball. In the *three-cushion variant,* a point is scored only when the cue ball:

- Hits at least three cushions before striking both balls;
- Hits at least three cushions after striking the first ball but before striking the second; or
- Hits exactly three cushions, one or two before striking the first ball and the remainder before hitting the second ball.

String weaving

String weaving is a pastime that evolved in many cultures around the world. It was played in Britain in 1782 when Charles Lamb, the children's author, recorded weaving a cat's cradle with his school friends.

Many cultures still practice string weaving. One of the most complex string designs originates from the Navajo Indians of the southwestern United States and is a zigzag pattern called Navajo lightning. The Inuit people of the Arctic create caribou, bears, and sleds out of string. At one time, only the girls were allowed to weave string figures. This was because it was feared that the boys would become entangled in their harpoon lines if they became too dexterous.

CAT'S CRADLE

NUMBER OF PLAYERS: One

EQUIPMENT: A piece of string about 3 ft. (1m) long, tied in a circle

DIFFICULTY: Age 7 and up

DURATION: No time limit

String weaving is a skill learned by children around the world, and the cat's cradle is common to many cultures.

Following are three steps to show how it is done:

Loop the string around both hands (diagram 3) so that the

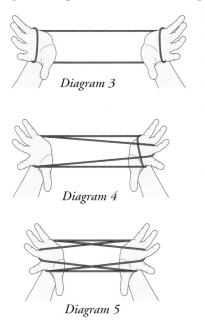

Diagram 3

Diagram 4

Diagram 5

string passes around the little finger and thumb and across the palm of each hand. Then pick up the string lying across the left palm with the index finger of the right hand (diagram 4).

Next, pick up the string lying across the right palm with the index finger of the left hand (diagram 5). This is the cat's cradle. Its name is a corruption of *cratch cradle*, an archaic term for a cattle feed rack or manger, which the strings are meant to resemble.

DARTS

NUMBER OF PLAYERS: Either two people or teams

EQUIPMENT: Dartboard and darts

DIFFICULTY: A game for both amateurs and professionals, but not suitable for children

DURATION: Around 10 to 15 minutes per game

Players take turns throwing pointed missiles at a circular board made of sisal wedges held together by a steel band. A dart consists of a point affixed to a barrel by which the dart is gripped, and at the other end is a shaft with feathers attached that make the dart fly. Players should take care—darts are sharp. The game should be located so as to minimize danger from flying missiles, and shoes should be worn.

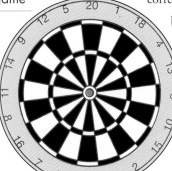

Setup

The standard board is 18 in. (46 cm) in diameter, divided into 20 wedges, each worth from 1 to 20 points, laid out as in diagram 6. The target area includes three narrow concentric rings. The outer, or *doubles* ring, doubles the wedge's points; the middle, or *triples* ring, triples the points. The small ring surrounding the middle, the *outer bull*, scores 25, and the middle circle, the *inner bull* (also called the bull or bull's-eye) scores 50 points.

The board is hung with the number 20 wedge at the top and the inner bull 5 ft. 8 in. (1.6 m) from the ground. Players throw from behind one of two throwing lines, or *oches:* One is 7 ft. 9 in. (2.3 m) away from the dartboard and the other is 9 ft. 7 in. (3 m) away. Choice depends on a player's skill.

Playing the Game

Players begin by *corking up,* each throwing a dart at the board. The player whose dart lands closest to the bull starts the game. A turn consists of three throws, feet behind the throwing line, after which the darts are retrieved. No second tries are allowed. A dart on the board may not be touched during a turn.

Scoring

Scoring depends upon the game, of which there are two main kinds. In 301 and 501, each competitor starts with the score corresponding to the name of the game. Players try to be the first to reduce their scores to exactly zero. The last dart before zero must be in the doubles ring. If a dart reduces the score to less than zero—or busts—the round does not count.

Variations

Darts Cricket

This is the other main darts game, played mainly in

Diagram 6: A dartboard and darts

Britain. Only the six scoring wedges numbered from 15 to 20 and the bull are used. Each individual or team tries to make three hits on each of the wedges and two hits on the bull. The winner is the player with the most points when the first player completes the required hits. A double counts as two hits, and a triple as three. Once a target has been hit three times by one player or side, it is open, meaning that either team can continue to score points on it. When both sides have made their three hits, the target is closed and no more points can be made on it.

FIVESTONES

NUMBER OF PLAYERS: Two or more

EQUIPMENT: Five small stones

DIFFICULTY: Practice is needed to improve skills

DURATION: There is no standard time limit

In this older version of jacks, players toss and catch five small, cube-shaped stones. Try to find pebbles that are squarish rather than flat. In the basic throw, the jockey, all the stones are placed in the palm of the hand, tossed in the air and caught on the back of the hand. They are tossed again, using the back of the hand, and caught in the palm.

Playing the Game

A player first makes a basic throw and must catch at least one stone in the palm to continue. If successful, play continues with *one-er's*. One stone is kept in the throwing hand; any other stones caught in the basic throw are transferred to the nonthrowing hand. (If all were caught on the basic throw, four are deliberately dropped to continue the game.) In one-er's, the stone in the throwing hand is tossed, and the player attempts with the same hand to pick up one of the previously

dropped stones before catching the tossed stone. A player continues to retrieve stones one by one until none is left, then moves on to perform *two-er's, three-er's* and *four-er's*. At each level, four stones are deliberately dropped and are retrieved two, three, and four at a time, respectively, before catching the fifth stone. After any miss the turn is over and resumes at the missed level on the next turn.

Variations

There are many variations of Fivestones. The following are some examples:

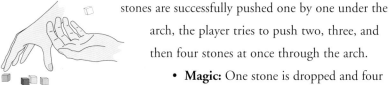

- **Arches:** Four stones are thrown close together and an arch formed behind them as shown in diagram 7. A stone is thrown in the air with the other hand, and the player must push a stone through the arch (diagram 8) before catching the thrown stone (diagram 9). Once all four stones are successfully pushed one by one under the arch, the player tries to push two, three, and then four stones at once through the arch.

Diagram 7: The hand position for Arches

- **Magic:** One stone is dropped and four are thrown in the air. All four must be caught after picking up the dropped stone.

- **Magic Flycatchers:** This is the same as Magic, except that the stones in the air must be caught with an overhand snatch.

Diagram 8: Flicking a stone through the arch

Diagram 9: Catching the stone

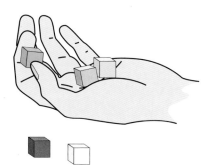

Diagram 10: Holding a stone in Pecks

Diagram 11:

Picking up a stone in Pecks

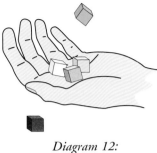

Diagram 12:

Catching a stone in Pecks

• **Pecks, Bushels, and Claws:** The game begins with the basic throw. If all stones are caught, the player skips the first stage, *Pecks.* Otherwise, one of the caught stones must be held between the thumb and forefinger, as shown in diagram 10. This stone is then thrown in the air and a dropped stone is picked up, as in diagram 11, before the thrown stone is caught (diagram 12). When all the dropped stones have been picked up one at a time, the player moves on to *Bushels.* Again there is a basic throw, and if all the stones are caught, the player goes on to *Claws.* Otherwise, all the stones that have been caught are thrown into the air, a dropped stone picked up, and the thrown stones caught.

When all the dropped stones have been retrieved in this way, the player moves to Claws. There is a basic throw; if no stones

are dropped, the player stops. Otherwise, the caught stones are placed on the back of the hand, and dropped stones are picked up between each successive pair of fingers on the throwing hand without dropping any off the back of the hand. Once all the stones are retrieved, the stones on the back of the hand are thrown up and must be caught in the palm. Finally, stones are placed between the fingers and must be worked into the palm without using the other hand.

FOOSBALL® (TABLE FOOTBALL)

NUMBER OF PLAYERS: Two to four, plus a referee if required

EQUIPMENT: Specially designed table and ball

DIFFICULTY: Suitable for age 12 and up

DURATION: About 5 minutes per match

Setup

A Foosball table is loosely marked like a soccer field and figures are attached to eight rods that are spun by handles, four on each side of the table (see photograph at left). The figures rotate to kick a ball, and the object of the game is to score points by kicking the ball into the opponent's goal. A point is scored when the ball enters the goal—even if it then comes out again.

In a team game each player plays with only two rods, although team members can change rods between points, games, or if the game is stopped for another reason. At the end of the game the players change sides.

Competition matches are organized through the United States Table Soccer Association (USTSA) and the American Table Soccer Federation (ATSF), both affiliated with table football manufacturers, and for these games there is a complex set of rules. In friendly matches the players can decide the rules.

Above: *A game of Foosball, also known as table football.*

Playing the Game

The ball enters the table through a serving hole, and the server for the start of the match is decided by a flip of the coin; subsequent serves are taken by the team or player who has just been scored against. The team or player who wins the flip decides if he wants to serve or choose the side of the table to play on; the loser takes second choice.

The server can spin the ball to try to influence the serve, but no goal is allowed unless the ball is first touched by one of the server's figures. If the ball leaves the table at any time during play it is served again by the player or team who originally served the ball. The exception is when the ball is kicked out by a clearing shot from the server's two-rod (the rod with two players, in defense), in which case the ball is returned to this team's two-rod to restart the game.

Game rules

The ball must be kept in play and can only be kept by a figure for 10 to 15 seconds between shots. If the ball comes to a complete stop out of reach of any of the figures it is declared a dead ball. If the ball is dead anywhere between the two opposing two-rods, the ball is served again by the team that originally served the ball. If the ball comes to a stop between the two-rod and the goal, then the ball is put back in play by the figure nearest to the dead ball, who must pass the ball to another figure before the ball is fully back in play.

Spinning the rods more than 360 degrees either before or after kicking the ball is not allowed. A goal scored from a spinning rod is disallowed and the ball put back into play by the goalie. If a rod is spun during play the opposing team can decide either to continue play or to serve the ball again. Jarring the table or touching your opponent's rods, either accidentally or on purpose, is also an infringement. For the first two offenses the opposing team can decide to continue play or re-serve the ball; the third offense is considered a technical foul.

The roots of the game

The game of table soccer, or table football as it is known in Britain, probably originated in Germany in the 1920s or '30s. The German word for soccer (football) is *fußball*—the 'ß' is pronounced as a double 'S'—and hence as the game was introduced to the United States it became known as 'foosball' or sometimes 'fusball.'

The original tables were created as a game for local German football teams to play in the clubhouse or bar after a weekend game. They were simple wooden affairs made by local carpenters or even a member of the team. American soldiers posted in Europe after World War II became familiar with the new coin-operated machines and as they returned home a market for table soccer opened up.

At the end of the 1960s the game took off in the United States, and today there is a United States Table Soccer Association that issues official rules. Many local leagues and championships are now played across the country. It remains a popular pastime in Europe.

When a technical foul is called, play stops and the opposing team takes a shot from the three-rod (the rod with three players, the offense). One shot is taken and whether or not a goal is scored play is then stopped. The ball is put back into play at the spot at which the foul was called.

A ball pinned to the wall or to the playing field on the five-rod cannot be passed directly to the three-rod, but must touch at least two figures as it is put into play. Before attempting a pass from the five-rod, the ball may hit the side of the table twice. At the third hit the pass will be declared illegal.

If a pass is stopped by trapping it against the side of the table this does not count as one of the two allowed hits. Changing the speed or direction of the ball from the front of a figure before passing is illegal in this situation, but it is legal to do this from the side of the figure. If any of these rules are broken the opposing team can decide to continue play or serve the ball.

Time-out

Each player or team is allowed two time-outs during the game lasting 30 seconds. An example would be to clear an obstacle from the table. Time-out can only be called when in possession of the ball or when the ball is not in play. The ball remains on the table and is put back into play from that position.

Variation
Goalie War

In this even faster and more exciting version of table football, the three- and five-rods are lifted up off the table, and the defenders play against each other. Four players can play, with one player per rod.

Two balls are served at the same time to play *two-ball rollerball*. If each team scores a goal no points are awarded and the balls are served again. When one team has scored it can stop the game any time it is in possession and claim the point. Then the two balls are served again. One team can score two goals and then the two balls are served again. If the ball goes in and comes out of the goal, no point is scored and play continues.

JACKS

NUMBER OF PLAYERS: Two or more, or singly

EQUIPMENT: A set of six to 15 jacks and a rubber ball

DIFFICULTY: Suitable for age 5 and up

DURATION: Games can be short or long

The present-day version of jacks evolved from the game of Fivestones (see page 172), which, confusingly, is itself sometimes called jacks.

Setup

Play requires a set of *jacks,* small cast-metal pieces consisting of six centrally joined spokes tipped with small spheres. The aim is to pick up or otherwise manipulate the jacks while simultaneously bouncing and catching a rubber ball. Any number can play.

Aim of the game

The play begins with *onesies*, picking up one jack at a time until all are picked up, then moves on to *twosies,* picking up two at a time, until finally all the jacks are picked up at once. When the number to be picked up does not go evenly into the total number of jacks, any leftover jacks are picked up on the last ball.

Playing the Game

To begin each level a player gathers all the jacks in one hand and gently throws them onto the ground. The ball is tossed into the air—it will be allowed to bounce once—and one or more jacks are picked up with the throwing hand before catching the ball using the same hand. A turn continues until the player misses, either by missing the ball, missing a jack, moving a jack that is not picked up, or dropping a jack from the hand. Picked up jacks can be transferred to the nonthrowing hand before the next throw. When a player misses, his turn is over; the next turn begins with the number previously missed.

Additional rounds

There are several additions and variations that can be joined to the basic game, including:

- **Eggs in the Basket:** Jacks must be transferred into the nonthrowing hand before the ball is caught.

Jacks popular worldwide

■ ■

Jacks in one form or another (also called Chuckstones, Dibs, Dabs, Fivestones, and Knucklebones) has been around for centuries; the earliest games used small bones from the ankles of sheep or similar animals. It was popular in ancient Greece and Rome—where wagers were often laid on the outcomes.

As a simple children's game, with many regional variations, distinctive features often survive: Jacks continues to be played with bones in Mongolia; Tally, still known in the north of England, has deep roots. Its name descends directly from the Latin *tali* (plural of *talus*, an anklebone), a word for a certain kind of Roman dice, and suggests a lineage that reaches back, howsoever crookedly, to Roman settlement in the region.

- **Pigs in the Pen:** The nonthrowing hand forms a flat pen on the ground with thumb and forefinger, leaving an opening between the ends of the fingers. The jacks must be pushed or flicked into the pen before the ball is caught. First one jack is pushed, then two, then three, and so on.

- **Pigs over the Fence:** The nonthrowing hand is grounded on its side to form a 'fence,' and the jacks must be placed on the other side of the fence—first one, then two, and so on— before the ball is caught.

MARBLES

NUMBER OF PLAYERS: Two to six

EQUIPMENT: Five marbles and a shooter per player, chalk

DIFFICULTY: Some skill required

DURATION: About 15 minutes

The game of marbles appears in many variations; the two below are mainstays. Marbles are hard spheres of plastic or glass about ½ in. (15 mm) across. Many games also require a shooter or taw, a marble about ¾ in. (20 mm) in diameter.

Setup

Players mark out a chalk circle about 8 ft. (2.5 m) in diameter. Each one places a marble on the ring so that the marbles are an equal distance apart. Then they draw a line about 4 ft. (1.3 m) away from the circle to serve as a shooting line.

To decide the order of play, each player rolls his shooter toward the middle of the circle. The closest goes first, and the others go in the order of their closeness to the middle.

Playing the Game

In turn, each player kneels behind the shooting line and attempts to hit one of the marbles on the ring with his shooter hard enough so that both marbles end up outside the circle (diagram 13). The player must keep his knees outside the circle but can lean inward with his arms and torso. He places his first two knuckles of his forefinger on the ground so that the finger is at a right angle, supports the marble on the crook of his finger, then flicks it with his thumb. If a player is successful, he captures the marble and takes another turn. If he is not, either

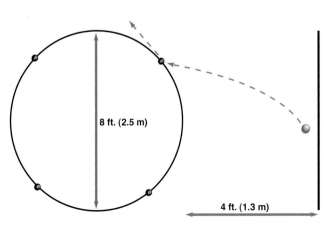

8 ft. (2.5 m)

4 ft. (1.3 m)

Diagram 13: Shooting the ring with marbles

because he misses or because the marble does not go far enough, his turn is over, and he must place another one of his own marbles on the ring.

Winning the Game

The game ends when there are no more marbles on the ring. The player with the most marbles wins.

Variations

Ring Taw

In this game, a circle about 1 ft. (30 cm) across is inscribed inside an 8 ft. (2.5 m) diameter circle, as shown in diagram 14. Order of play is determined as described above. First, each player puts two marbles inside the inner circle. Shooting from outside the outer circle, the first player tries to knock a marble out of the inner circle. If he is successful, he captures the marble and takes another shot, playing his shooter from wherever it lies. If not, his turn ends, but the shooter remains where it is. Subsequent players follow the same procedure, except that they can either try to dislodge a marble from the inner circle or to hit another player's shooter. When a shooter is hit, it must stay where it lands and its owner must pay the hitter one marble.

The winner is the player with the most marbles at the time the last marble is knocked out of the inner circle, ending the game.

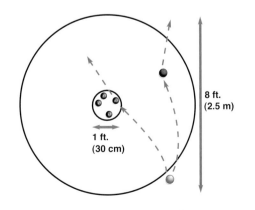

Diagram 14: Marbles Ring Taw

NOK HOCKEY®

NUMBER OF PLAYERS: Two

EQUIPMENT: A playing board, two wooden goal blocks, two wooden pucks, two plastic hockey sticks

DIFFICULTY: Suitable for age 5 and up

DURATION: As agreed by the players

This game was invented and launched in New York in the 1940s and is still very popular across the United States today.

Playing the Game

The object of the game is to score points by knocking the puck into the goals using the hockey sticks. The players must sit or stand directly behind their goal nets to play—shots are not allowed to be taken from the sides of the board.

The puck is put into play as one player drops it in the face-off central circle on the board. A player can only hit the puck when it is in her defense area or when it is in the central free play area.

If the puck is knocked off the board, the player who knocked it out puts it back into play from the defense area. The player to score the most goals during an agreed time period is the winner.

PICKUP STICKS

NUMBER OF PLAYERS: Two to four

EQUIPMENT: Set of pickup sticks

DIFFICULTY: Suitable for age 5 and up

DURATION: About 10 minutes

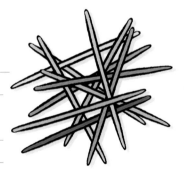

Setup

Sets of pickup sticks contain about 50 thin sticks, 6 in. (15 cm) long, often marked with coloured rings denoting different values, usually from 1 to 5. They are available in toy shops and novelty stores, but are sometimes called by different names.

Playing the Game

One player drops all the sticks on the floor. Players then take turns trying to remove one stick at a time from the pile without disturbing any of the others. Once a stick is touched, it must be successfully extracted before another stick may be touched or moved. A player can continue to remove sticks, using only fingers, so long as no other stick moves in the process. When the pile is disturbed, the turn is over.

Winning the Game

The winner is the player with the most, or the highest scoring, sticks at the end of the game.

TABLE FOOTBALL see FOOSBALL®

TABLE TENNIS (PING-PONG®)

NUMBER OF PLAYERS: Two for singles, four for doubles

EQUIPMENT: Table, net, bats, balls

DIFFICULTY: Great fun for all ages and levels

DURATION: About 15 minutes per game

Table tennis is a professional sport that is also enjoyed by millions of amateurs.

Setup

The sport is played, using special paddles and small plastic balls, on a table resembling a miniature tennis court and net. Like tennis, it has a singles and a doubles version, and the playing surface is divided into four *courts,* a right- and left-hand court on each side of the net.

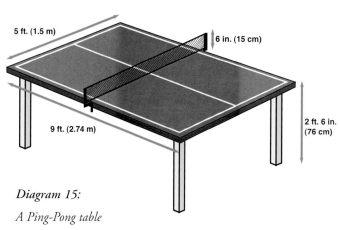

Diagram 16: The pencil grip in table tennis

Regulation equipment

The professional game sets standards for all the equipment. The dimensions of the table should be 9 x 5 ft. (2.7 x 1.5 m), standing 2 ft. 6 in. (76 cm) tall. Lines at the edges of the table are ¾ in. (1.9 cm) wide, and the vertical line in the middle is ⅛ in. (3 mm) wide. The net should be 6 in. (15 cm) high. Paddles must also conform to certain dimensions and must use only allowed adhesives to fasten the rubber hitting surface onto the sides of the paddle. Balls must be of a standard size and bounciness.

Playing the Game

Play begins when the ball is served: A player stands anywhere behind his end of the table, throws the ball, palm upward, at least 6 in. (15 cm) into the air, and strikes it with the flat of the paddle. The serve must bounce once on the server's side and cross the net without touching. A serve that touches the net is a *let,* and is re-served (touching the net does not matter except on the serve). A serve that fails to make it over the net, or which bounces more or less than once beforehand, gives the point to the receiver.

Scoring

After a good serve, the receiver must return the ball, allowing no more than one bounce on his side of the net, or the server wins the point. If the ball is successfully returned, the server must send it back across the net, and so on, until the point is won.

A ball hit so that it sails over the opponent's side of the table without bouncing at all is out-of-bounds, and a point is awarded to the

5 ft. (1.5 m)

6 in. (15 cm)

9 ft. (2.74 m)

2 ft. 6 in. (76 cm)

Diagram 15:
A Ping-Pong table

Chinese table tennis

▪ ▪

Table tennis is China's most popular sport; it has an estimated 4 million tournament players, compared to about 4,000 in the United States. The Chinese were the first to use the pencil grip, or pen-holder grip (diagram 16), and they overwhelmed opponents from other countries throughout the 1970s and beyond. They still dominate the sport, although many have switched to the more traditional handshake grip. During the '70s, when China was still isolated from the rest of the world, international table tennis matches were among the first contacts between the Chinese and Westerners and were credited in part with the ultimate easing of diplomatic relations.

opponent. The following moves also earn points for the opponent: Striking the ball twice, or before it has bounced (volleying); hitting with the paddle's edge; touching the table or net; or ricocheting the ball from some other surface (wall, ceiling) onto the table.

Winning the Game

Each player gets five consecutive serves, then service goes over to the other side. The first player to reach 21 with at least a 2-point lead is the winner. If the players tie at 20, service alternates between them until one accumulates the necessary 2-point lead. Players switch ends of the table to begin each new game.

The expedite rule

In serious play, unless both players have at least 19 points by 15 minutes into the game, the expedite rule goes into effect: To prevent extended rallies, which prolong the game, the strokes of the receiving player are counted, with the point awarded at the 13th good return. After this, with the rule still in force, serve

alternates between players until there is a winner. (Precise terms of the rule differ among various officiating organizations.)

Variation

Doubles

The first server stands behind the right-hand court and must serve with one bounce in that court into the diagonally opposite court. The return must be made by the opponent at the diagonally opposite corner, and must then be played by the server's partner. Alternation of strokes between the partners continues throughout the play of every point. Should the wrong player take a shot, the other team gains the point.

Service changes at the same intervals as in the basic game but remains always in the right-hand court, so that partners swap positions left for right each time their side is to serve. Serve passes from the original server to the original receiver, then to the original server's partner, and finally to the original receiver's partner.

TIDDLYWINKS

NUMBER OF PLAYERS: Two, using two sets of counters, or four, playing in pairs

EQUIPMENT: Counters, felt mat, a cup

DIFFICULTY: A certain amount of skill is needed, so it's better for older children

DURATION: 20 minutes for singles; 25 minutes for pairs

The object in tiddlywinks is to propel small plastic discs into a faraway cup. Generally, two players or two teams participate. Though originally a children's game, it has been played competitively over the last 50 years by adults; standardized rules and equipment have evolved—and a memorable vocabulary, as well.

Setup

The game is played with small plastic discs called *winks*, of four

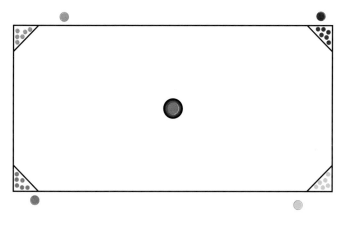

Diagram 17: The start of a game of tiddlywinks

colours; six winks are provided in each colour: two larger ones, measuring 1 in. (2.2 cm), and four smaller, a little over half an inch (1.6 cm). In team play, blue and red are partners as are green and yellow. In singles play, each player takes two colours.

Winks are squeezed into the air by means of a larger disc called a *squidger*, which can be up to 0.2 in. (5 mm) thick and from 1 to 2 in. (2.1 to 5 cm) in diameter. Serious players use different squidgers for different shots. The playing surface is a felt mat, 72 x 55 in. (182 x 139 cm) in size. Winks are propelled into a cup (the *pot*), 1.5 in. (3.8 cm) high, 1.5 in. (3.8 cm) at the base, and 2 in. (4.8 cm) at the top.

The pot is placed in the middle of the mat. At the mat's four corners are diagonal baselines, 55 in. (139 cm) from the middle. Winks are placed behind the baselines, one colour in each corner, arranged alphabetically in clockwise order: The mat surface within the baselines comprises the field of play.

Deciding who goes first

Before play begins, one wink of each colour is flipped, or *squidged*, toward the pot. Winner of the *squidge-off*, closest to the pot, goes first. All winks are then put back behind the baselines before the game begins.

Playing the Game

The first player shoots a wink from behind his baseline. Then the others play in turn, going clockwise around the mat. Players get one shot per turn—unless they get one of their

winks in the pot, in which case they get an extra turn. Every shot must be made within 30 seconds of the last.

If a player sends one of his winks off the playing surface, he loses his next turn. There is no penalty, however, for sending another player's wink off. In either case, the wink is replaced ¾ in. (2.2 cm) from the edge of the mat, as near as possible to where it went off. A player can elect to pass his turn.

A wink that is *squopped*, or covered—however slightly—by another wink may not be played until it is *unsquopped*, or uncovered. Players often squop deliberately as a matter of

Tiddlywink words

This game has spawned a large number of specialized terms, of which these are only a sampling—mostly of things that have gone wrong:

- **Cuddle:** To shoot a wink close to a pile
- **Drunken wink:** A wink that wanders and rolls around the mat
- **Gromp:** A shot that moves a pile of winks to squop another wink
- **Nurdle:** To shoot a wink so that it ends up too close to the pot to be potted
- **Perversion:** Any game played with winks besides the standard game
- **Piddle:** (U.S.) A delicate shot in which a squopped wink is nudged free
- **Poss:** (U.K.) To send a wink a much shorter distance than intended
- **Rabbit-bashing:** Piling up a high score against an inferior opponent
- **Submarine:** To shoot a wink that ends up squopped under another wink
- **Visine:** (U.S.) A shot in which a red wink is squopped.

Above: Tiddlywinks come in many colours.

strategy, and piles of several winks may develop. A player whose winks are all squopped cannot play.

A game can last a maximum of 20 minutes for teams, or 25 minutes for two players, plus five extra rounds following the timed period, after which play ends and point scores are calculated. When time elapses, the round in progress is completed, so that the original starting player begins in the extra rounds. If a player gets all his winks in the pot, or *pots*

out (which rarely happens), the time limit no longer applies; remaining players simply go for the pot in turn until two more players pot out.

Shooting

Although a good tiddlywinks player must be able to *pot,* or shoot winks into the pot, much of the skill of the game involves shooting to squop or unsquop a wink. The squidger may only touch initially the surface of an unsquopped wink, and a shot may begin no further above the winks' surface than 2 in. (5 cm). But within these constraints many technical refinements are possible, as shown in the accompanying diagrams.

Scoring

Seven overall game points are awarded, after a computation based on points called *tiddlies.* (If a player pots out, tiddlies do not need to be counted because, as noted above, players simply continue shooting for the pot until second and third place are decided.) In the usual case, each wink that is potted counts 3

Diagram 18:
The potting shot

Diagram 19:
A Bristol—used to move both your wink and one that you have squopped onto an opponent's wink

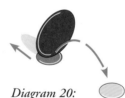

Diagram 20:
A squopping shot

tiddlies, and each unsquopped wink counts 1 tiddly. The player with the highest tiddly total gets 4 game points, second highest gets 2 points, and third highest gets 1.

Diagram 21: *A boondock— used to send a squopped wink away from the pot*

Diagram 22: *A crud shot – shooting your wink as hard as you can at a pile to cause disruption*

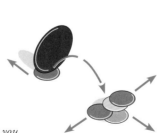

Diagram 23: *A bomb shot*

If more than one player gets the same number of tiddlies, game points for the tied place and the one below it are added together and divided among the players. For example, if Yellow wins first place with 7 tiddlies, and Green and Red both have 5 tiddlies, tying for second, the game points for second and third are added (2 + 1) and divided between the Green and Red players (1.5 each).

Pencil and Paper Games

Pencil and paper games are ideal for passing the time on long trips. These activities with words, numbers, or figures can provide a welcome break from reading or traditional crosswords.

ALPHABET RACE

NUMBER OF PLAYERS: Two or more

EQUIPMENT: Pencil and paper

DIFFICULTY: Both adults and children can play, though the game is not suitable for very small children

DURATION: 15 to 30 minutes

This primitive version of Scrabble® needs no board or tiles, and each player uses only 26 letters. Although it requires less time and equipment than its commercial cousin, it can also be much more frustrating.

Setup

Each player begins by writing out the alphabet on a piece of paper. Use a separate piece of paper as the board.

Playing the Game

The first player then writes down a word on the board (without duplication letters), spacing the letters out carefully, and crossing each one off of his alphabet list. The second player then adds a word to the board, which connects at right angles to the first, and crosses the new letters off his own list. Play continues in this way, with each player adding a word using only the letters that remain on their lists. If a player cannot form a word, he may pass and miss a turn.

Strategy

In the example below, the first player has written MOTHER, the second has added an O and a P to

m	o	t	h	e	r
	o				
z	i	p			
	n				

Diagram 1:
Alphabet Race

create TOP, and the third has used his Z and his I by creating ZIP. The first player has then added an N to the I to form IN. With only 26 letters each, forming words can quickly become

difficult. For this reason, you may wish to alter the rules somewhat, perhaps by doubling or tripling the number of vowels or even doubling the entire alphabet.

Winning the Game

If a player manages to finish off all 26 letters in his list, he is declared the winner. Otherwise, play continues until everyone is stuck and the player who has used the most letters wins.

ANAGRAMS

NUMBER OF PLAYERS: Two, but more if playing the team variation

EQUIPMENT: Pencil and paper

DIFFICULTY: Too difficult for young children; best for adults and teens

DURATION: About 30 minutes for preparation and 30 minutes for play

FILMS

Dogger Flin — Goldfinger

Hubren — Ben Hur

Primo Snappy — Mary Poppins

POP STARS

Dan O Man — Madonna

Rum Chap Roul — Procul Harum

Teeth Bales — The Beatles

BIRDS

Pigame — Magpie

Niff Up — Puffin

But Lite — Blue Tit

FIVE-LETTER WORDS

Retbe — Beret

Bmthu — Thumb

Steap — Paste

Players agree on several categories and then work out anagrams to fit them. An anagram is a word or phrase formed from the rearranged letters of another. For instance, an anagram for the name Clint Eastwood is Old West Action, although such thematic correlation is not required.

Playing the Game

In this game, two players think up a list of five

Diagram 2: Sample anagrams

categories, and each spends about half an hour coming up with three anagrams whose solutions fit into each of the categories. The two players then trade lists and compete to see who can solve more of the other's anagrams in a set amount of time—seven minutes is good for beginners.

Variations

Altering the game

For longer or shorter play, the number of anagrams or categories may be altered. The winning player then devises the list of categories for the next round. A team version of this game can also be played in which a quiz leader comes up with the anagrams and distributes the same list to both teams.

BATTLESHIP

NUMBER OF PLAYERS: Two

EQUIPMENT: Pencil and paper

DIFFICULTY: Fairly easy; suitable for adults and older children

DURATION: Around 15 minutes per game

Players try to guess the positions of their opponent's fleet on a paper grid, and whoever is first to locate the most vessels 'destroys' the fleet and wins the game. Although available in a commercial version, this game can easily be played with just a pencil and paper.

Setup

Each of the two players begins by drawing two 10 x 10 grids, marking out the rows with the numbers 1 through 10 and the columns with the letters A through J. One grid is for the home fleet and the other for the enemy fleet. Without letting his opponent catch a glimpse, each player marks his home grid with a fleet of ships, comprised as follows: one battleship (made up of four squares), two cruisers (three squares each), three destroyers (two squares each) and four submarines (single squares).

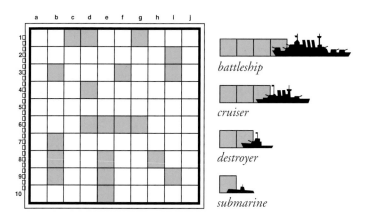

Diagram 3: Battleship

If a starship battle is desired, these names can be modernized without harm to the game. Ships are marked using the first letters of their names and can be arranged however the player chooses—horizontally, vertically, or diagonally—so long as they do not touch each other, even by so much as a corner. Once all ships have been drawn, toss a coin to see who will go first.

Playing the Game

The players then take turns calling out reference numbers in an attempt to hit each other's ships, with three attempts allowed on each turn. If a square called by a player is occupied on his opponent's home fleet grid by any part of a ship, said opponent must honestly report what kind of vessel has been hit. For instance, based on diagram 3, if your opponent called B7, you would respond by saying, 'You hit my cruiser.'

Winning the Game

Players record their attacks on the enemy fleet grid, marking misses with X's and hits with O's. Once all squares of a particular ship have been hit, the ship is considered sunk, and must be reported as such. The first player to sink all the ships in the enemy fleet is the winner.

Variations

Salvo

This game is more complex and is suitable for older players. The game uses the same basic grids, but the fleets are composed only of one battleship (five squares), one cruiser (two squares) and two destroyers (two squares each).

Instead of firing three shots at a time, players fire a salvo of seven shots at once.

At first, a salvo consists of seven shots, but as the ships in a player's home fleet are sunk, his salvo is diminished as follows: subtract three shots for a sunken battleship, two for a cruiser, and one for a destroyer. After a player fires a salvo, his opponent does not report which individual shots were successful, but only the number of hits made on each ship. For example: 'One hit on a destroyer and two on a battleship.' Play then moves to the second player, while the first devises a new salvo that will help determine which of his original shots were successful—a task requiring significant skills of analysis.

As in the first version, the winner is the first player to sink the enemy fleet.

BOXES

NUMBER OF PLAYERS: Two

EQUIPMENT: Pencil and paper

DIFFICULTY: Best for adults and children over 10

DURATION: About 30 minutes (10 minutes per game)

A deceptively simple game in which players compete to complete the most squares on a grid.

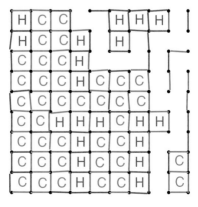

Diagram 4: Boxes

Setup

Start by making a 10 x 10 grid of dots on a piece of paper. Using pens of different colours, the two players take turns drawing a line between any two dots. If a line forms the final side of a box, the player marks the box with his initial and takes another turn (diagram 4). If this line encloses another box, he can initial that one too and take another turn. The game continues until all possible lines have been drawn, at which point the player with the most boxes is declared the winner.

Strategy

This game involves a good deal of strategy, since, as the game progresses, it becomes increasingly difficult to draw a line without leaving a box that your opponent can finish. If variation is desired, new rules can be added to the game: For instance, you could reverse the game by declaring that the player with the fewest boxes is the winner. For longer game play, simply make a larger grid.

BRIDGE THE WORD

NUMBER OF PLAYERS: Three or more

EQUIPMENT: Pencil and paper

DIFFICULTY: Suitable for older children and adults

DURATION: About 10 to 20 minutes

This stimulating word game requires players to think hard and come up with a variety of words that start and end with specific letters.

Setup

First, each player draws six horizontal lines on a piece of paper.

Playing the Game

Players agree on a six-letter word and write it once down the left-hand side of the paper and once, backward, down the right-hand side of the paper, so that each line is bracketed by a different pair of letters. Then, players try to fill in all six lines with words that begin and end with the appropriate letters—the longer the words are the better.

Winning the Game

Once everyone has finished, players each count the total number of letters in their new words. Whoever has used the most letters is the winner.

CATEGORIES

NUMBER OF PLAYERS: Three or more

EQUIPMENT: Pencil and paper

DIFFICULTY: Best for adults and older children

DURATION: About 15 minutes

This game is similar to both Guggenheim (page 188) and Legs (page189) and incorporates much of the excitement of each.

Setup

To begin with, players must agree on eight or nine categories, which should be as varied as possible—anything from seven-letter words to parts of the body.

Playing the Game

Choosing a letter at random from a book or dictionary, players have ten minutes to write down as many words as possible in each category, starting with the appropriate letter (see diagram 5).

CATEGORIES	D	B
five-letter nouns	dunce, duvet, diver	bidet, bench, belfry
cities	Dover, Denver, Detroit	
breeds of dog	Doberman, Dachshund	
novelists	Dickens, Dostoyevsky	
composers	Debussy	
countries	Denmark	
poets	Donne	
parts of the body	duodenum, diaphragm, disc	

Diagram 5: Categories in progress

Scoring

When the time is up, work out scores as follows: one point for every word that appears on another player's list, and two points for every word that does not. Agree on rules for the eligibility of words beforehand and put disputed words to a vote.

Winning the Game

The player with the most points is the winner.

Variation

Alphabet Version

A more challenging form of the game involves choosing a single category and writing the letters A through Z down the left-hand side of a sheet of paper. Players then spend two minutes trying to fill in appropriate words for every letter of the alphabet. Any player who manages to come up with a word for all 26 letters within the time limit wins automatically. Otherwise, scores are calculated as above.

CENTURY GAME

NUMBER OF PLAYERS: Two or more

EQUIPMENT: Pencils and paper

DIFFICULTY: Suitable for children age 8 and up

DURATION: About 5 minutes per round

Playing the Game

This is an addition game that uses numbers between one and ten. The first player writes down any number between one and ten. The next player writes down another number between one and ten, adds the two numbers together and writes down the total. The object of the game is to be the player who makes the sum add up to exactly 100.

Variations

Subtraction Game

Starting with 100, and using numbers between one and ten, the object of the game is to be the player who makes the calculation equal exactly one.

For older players you can make the sum more complicated by choosing a total larger than 100 and using numbers no greater than 25, for example, and no less than 10.

CONSEQUENCES

NUMBER OF PLAYERS: Two or more

EQUIPMENT: Pencil and paper

DIFFICULTY: Best for adults and older children

DURATION: About 20 minutes per game

Playing the Game

Each player writes one line of a story on a piece of paper, folds the paper over so as to conceal the line, and passes the paper to the right. Since the players have no idea what has been written beforehand, the following pattern is used to create an 11-line story with some semblance of coherency:

- The (one or two adjectives)
- (male character) met the
- (one or two adjectives)
- (female character) at
- (location).
- He (action).
- She (action).

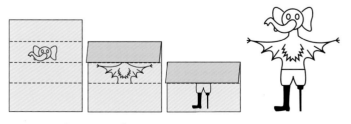

Diagram 6: A game of Picture Consequences

The Exquisite Corpse

In the 1920s, the Parisian surrealists, led by writer André Breton, played a version of Consequences called *The Exquisite Corpse*. Named after one of its early results—'The exquisite corpse shall drink the new wine'—the game followed the same basic rules as described here, except that writings were composed word by word rather than line by line, following a pre-determined pattern such as *adjective, noun, transitive-verb, adjective, noun.*

The surrealists believed that the game's collaborative nature helped to tap into realms of the unconscious not accessible through more rational means. Many visual Exquisite Corpses were also produced during this period, sensual line drawings with contributors such as Joan Miro and Man Ray, and the results now hang in art galleries.

- He said (statement).
- She said (statement).
- The consequence was (consequence).
- And the world said (statement).

Silliness is naturally of the utmost importance when filling in the details. A typical result might run as follows:

The godlike, unpretentious Woody Allen met the traitorous and salivating Sylvia Plath at the Gateway to Eternity. He spared no expense in creating an ignominious spectacle. She sat in a pile of mulberries. He said, 'What a delightful patch of roses we've got this time of year.' She said, 'It is a far, far greater thing I do now than I have ever done before.' The consequence was an entire generation of psychological cripples. And the world said, 'You call this customer service?'

If desired, multiple stories can be passed around at once.

Variation

Picture Consequences

A variation on this game that children particularly enjoy involves creating a picture rather than a story. The first player draws a head, folds the paper over so as to conceal all but the very bottom lines, and passes the paper to the next player, who draws a neck. By stages, a torso, legs, and feet are added to the picture, after which the paper is unfolded and the fearsome creature revealed (diagram 6, previous page).

	T	**R**	**A**	**I**	**N**
food	toast	radish	apple	ice cream	noodles
pleasures	talking	reading	art	ice skating	necking
foreign towns	Tours	Rampur	Athens	Islamabad	Naples
boys' names	Thomas	Ralph	Archibald	Ian	Nathan
bad habits	twitching	ranting	anticipating	imbibing	nibbling

Diagram 8: Guggenheim in progress

CROSSWORD

NUMBER OF PLAYERS: Two; can also be played in teams

EQUIPMENT: Pencil and paper

DIFFICULTY: For adults and older children

DURATION: About 10 minutes (for a two-player game)

Setup

Two players each draw a 5 x 5 grid on a piece of paper.

Playing the Game

Players then take turns calling out letters of the alphabet. After each turn, both players must write the letter in a square of their grid, aiming to form words reading either down or across.

Although it is easy to form words with your own letters, making good use of letters called by your opponent is much more difficult. In any case, words must be at least two letters each, cannot be abbreviations or proper nouns, and must be separated from each other by at least one letter. Additional rules should be agreed upon beforehand.

E	P	A	N	E	1
C	B	D	E	T	0
L	Y	O	X	R	1
O	R	O	T	S	1
Q	U	I	E	T	2
0	0	1	1	0	7

Diagram 7: Crossword in progress

Winning the Game

Once all the squares are filled in, players tally up their scores, with one point given for each completed word and a bonus point given for any word of five letters. The player with the highest score wins.

This game can be played by three or more players without altering the rules, but it does become more difficult. If desired, a larger grid can be used.

GUGGENHEIM (SCATTERGORIES®)

NUMBER OF PLAYERS: Two or more

EQUIPMENT: Pencil and paper

DIFFICULTY: For adults and older children

DURATION: About 10 minutes per game

This classic game was allegedly invented by the aristocratic family of the same name. In the United States it is also known as the commercial game Scattergories.

Setup

To begin, players choose five different categories. These can be anything: food, phobias, historical figures, or whatever the players can manage to agree on. Next, one player selects a five-letter word at random from a book or dictionary, and each player draws a 5 x 5 grid, marking the rows with

the names of the categories, and the columns with the letters of the word, as shown in diagram 8.

Playing the Game

Set a timer for approximately two minutes: Players must race to fill in all the boxes of their grids with words that fit into the appropriate categories and start with the appropriate letters.

Scoring

Unique words, which no other players have thought of, are worth two points, while others are worth only one. Thus, if the category is food and the letter is i, it would be advantageous to stretch your imagination past the realm of ice cream, since it would probably be taken by one of your competitors.

Winning the Game

The player with the most points wins.

HEADLINES

NUMBER OF PLAYERS: Three or more

EQUIPMENT: Pencil and paper

DIFFICULTY: For adults

DURATION: About 5 minutes per round; half an hour for a game

This is a simple, cooperative game with no winners or losers.

Playing the Game

The object is to create imitation newspaper headlines in the following way: First, one player writes down a word. Then, the second player adds a word either before or after it. A phrase

grows thus, player by player, with the intent of constructing a satisfyingly lurid and sensational headline. Much of the fun lies in the fact that a single word can completely redirect the headline's meaning.

For example, consider the probable evolution of the following headline:

FEDERAL RABBIT KILLER STRIKES GOLD-PLATED GRANDMOTHER REPEATEDLY

The game continues until players decide the headline conveys all that it should.

cat	cockroach
clergyman	chandler
cupboard	chimneysweep
caterpillar	chair
cheetah	cabdriver
cheater	camel
clown	canine
closet	chinchilla
carpenter	cobbler
carpetbagger	cockerel
chicken	consumer
cashier	charmer
citizen	captive
chiropodist	chauffeur

Diagram 9: A list of words with legs

LEGS

NUMBER OF PLAYERS: Three to 12

EQUIPMENT: Pencil and paper

DIFFICULTY: More suitable for adults

DURATION: About 5 minutes per round

Legs is an ideal after-dinner game, played with just pencil and paper. It may at first seem simple, but the fun starts when players find they have to rack their brains.

Playing the Game

One person chooses a letter at random, and players have two minutes to compile lists of things beginning with that letter that can have legs: People, animals, furniture—anything at all—the more obscure the better.

Winning the Game

When the time is up, each person takes turns reading off his list and crossing off any word that was chosen by more than one player. Then the players all count how many words are left on their lists. Whoever has the most words is the winner.

As in Guggenheim and Categories, the point of this game is to avoid the obvious words, such as dog and dancer, and strive toward more unusual ones, such as diplodocus, draftsman, and davenport.

LOTTO

NUMBER OF PLAYERS: Four or more

EQUIPMENT: Lotto cards and numbered discs

DIFFICULTY: Easy for all ages

DURATION: 20 minutes on average

The forerunner to bingo, this game is also known as Housey-Housey. It can be played by as many players as can fit in the room. It is simple to play, since the outcome is based entirely on chance, but it requires a great deal of preparation unless prefabricated materials are purchased.

Setup

To begin with, construct as many lotto cards as there are players (see diagram 10). Each card must have three rows and nine columns. Each row contains four blank spaces and five numbers, in any arrangement, so that each card carries 15 numbers in all. Furthermore, the numbers must be divided up by columns, so that the first column contains only numbers from 1 to 10; the second, numbers from 11 to 20, and so on, until the last column contains numbers from 81 to 90. The numbers chosen should be random and unique to each card. Finally, 90 discs must be created bearing the numbers from 1 to 90.

		23	33		56	62		80
1	12			47		67	78	
	16		34	49			79	81

Diagram 10: A lotto card

Playing the Game

As the game begins each player is issued a card, and the discs are placed in a bag and handed to the designated caller. The caller then takes one disc at a time out of the bag and calls the number out to the players. Any time a player has the number on his card called, he can mark it off.

Winning the Game

The first player to mark off all the numbers on his card shouts 'lotto' and wins the game.

PICTURES

NUMBER OF PLAYERS: Minimum three

EQUIPMENT: A large blackboard and chalk (or whiteboard and markers)

DIFFICULTY: Can be adapted for all ages

DURATION: About 30 minutes

This is basically a written version of The Game (see page 141), and therefore is suitable for playing in confined spaces, such as in a car.

Setup

Preparation is the same as in The Game: Players divide into two teams, each of which comes up with a list of phrases.

The first player from the first team is then given a phrase by the opposing team, which he must communicate to his teammates only by drawing. Once they have either guessed or given up, the teams switch roles, and play continues in this way until everyone has had a turn at drawing.

Playing the Game

The signs used for Pictures are similar to those used in The Game: An arch means a play; a camera means a movie; a musical note means a song; a book means exactly what you think it would mean, and a pair of quotation marks means a saying. Each letter is represented by a dash, with syllables being broken up by dots and words being broken up by spaces.

You may choose to illustrate either a word or a syllable by drawing a picture over the appropriate range of dashes. 'Sounds like' can be indicated by drawing an ear. Of course, no actual letters or numbers can be used in a drawing, since doing so would defeat the entire purpose of the game.

The team with the most correct guesses wins.

POETRY GAME

NUMBER OF PLAYERS: Three is the minimum

EQUIPMENT: Pencil and paper

DIFFICULTY: A game for adults and older children

DURATION: About 15 minutes

Each player adds a line to a poem that he is not allowed to read. The final nonsensical poem is read out to gales of laughter. There are no winners or losers—just a lot of silliness.

Playing the Game

The first player starts off by writing two lines of poetry on a piece of paper. In composing the verse, seriousness is technically allowed, but it is generally better to err on the side of nonsense. The paper is then folded so as to cover up the first line and passed to the second player, who adds two more lines of poetry, one of which should probably rhyme with the second line or at least have the same rhythm. The paper then continues on its journey, each player taking care to cover up all but the last line of verse before passing it onward.

Once the poem reaches a predetermined length or everyone's poetic inspiration has been exhausted, the paper is unfolded and read with great enthusiasm to the crowd. If increased output is desired, multiple pieces of paper can be circulated at once.

QUIZZES

NUMBER OF PLAYERS: Three or more

EQUIPMENT: Pencil and paper

DIFFICULTY: Can be adapted for any age group

DURATION: About 1 hour for preparation and another hour for play

These days, most people associate quiz games with either TV shows or prepackaged board games such as Trivial Pursuit®. However, many are surprised by how easy it is to arrange a perfectly enjoyable quiz game with nothing more than a pencil and paper. The only problem is finding a quizmaster knowledgeable enough to compose a list of challenging questions on relatively short notice. For this reason, it is usually advisable to have some sort of encyclopedia or fact book on hand to hurry things up.

Playing the Game

Once the questions are compiled, game play is easy. The quizmaster simply reads off the questions one by one, and the players have a certain amount of time in which to record their answers.

Winning the Game

At the end of the round, the player with the most correct answers is the winner. If there are more than four or five players in a game, it can also be enjoyable to divide players into teams.

SHORT STORIES

NUMBER OF PLAYERS: Two or more

EQUIPMENT: Pencil and paper

DIFFICULTY: Best for adults and older children

DURATION: About 2 minutes per game

Like so many others, this game is simple in theory but difficult in practice.

Playing the Game

Players each take up a pencil and paper and are given two minutes to write the longest sentence they can come up with using only words of three letters or less. For example:

'The man and his cat saw a big red dog and had a fit, so the cat is now my pet, and the man is in a hut for mad men, and the dog is in a big box so no one can see him or his red fur, and he is sad too.'

If you wish to make the game more difficult, you can do so by reducing the time limit, restricting players to words of exactly three letters or both. Whoever composes the longest sentence is the winner.

SPROUTS

NUMBER OF PLAYERS: Two

EQUIPMENT: Pencil and paper

DIFFICULTY: Easy but challenging

DURATION: About 10 minutes per session

Similar to Boxes, this game starts with the drawing of eight dots, spaced well apart from each other, on a piece of paper.

Playing the Game

Two players take turns drawing lines connecting any two dots or connecting a dot to itself. When a line is finished, a new dot is added somewhere along its length. Three rules come into play: First, a line cannot cross itself or any other line; second, a line cannot be drawn through a dot, and third, a dot cannot have more than three lines leaving it.

The player who draws the last permissible line is declared the winner. For longer game play, start with more dots.

STAIRWAY

NUMBER OF PLAYERS: Two or more

EQUIPMENT: Pencil and paper

DIFFICULTY: Fun for older children

DURATION: As long as the players wish

For this game, it is useful to have a large vocabulary.

Playing the Game

First, choose a letter at random. Then, give players a set amount of time to build a 'stairway' of words, in which each word is exactly one letter longer than the one above it. Only the first letters of the words must be the same. With some letters, such as Z, it will be necessary to start the stairway with a three-letter word, but most have a two-letter possibility. When time is called, the winner is the player with the longest list. Any spelling errors result in immediate disqualification, even if the error does not affect the length of the word.

TRANSFORMATION

NUMBER OF PLAYERS: Three or more

EQUIPMENT: Pencil and paper

DIFFICULTY: Mostly easy, if the words are fairly short

DURATION: About 15 to 20 minutes

Playing the Game

In this game, the same pair of words is given to all the players, who must then try to convert one word into the other by changing one letter at a time. The only restriction is that each intermediary step must also be a valid English word. Thus, a transformation from 'TASK' into 'WILL' might go as follows:

TASK, TALK, WALK, WALL, WILL

The winner can be either the player who completes the transformation the fastest or the one who does so in the fewest number of steps.

Word and Spoken Games

These games are the most fun when played with a large group of people at parties or in the classroom. While some are simple, others demand strategy, verbal dexterity, and a sharp mind!

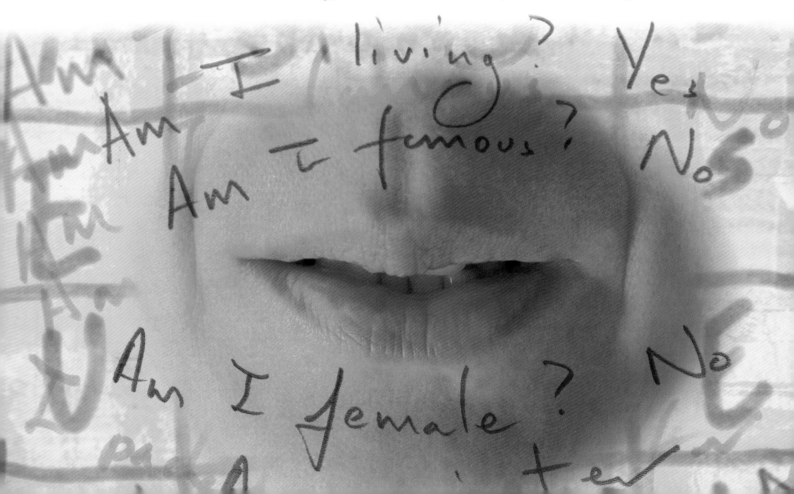

ANALOGIES

NUMBER OF PLAYER: Four minimum

EQUIPMENT: None

DIFFICULTY: Suitable for adults; too sophisticated for children

DURATION: About an hour

This sociable game is simple and fun but can lead to insults—intended or otherwise.

Playing the Game

To begin, one player thinks of someone whose qualities are fairly well known to everyone in attendance—this could be a celebrity, an absent friend, or even one of the players themselves. The player tells the others which of these general categories the person falls into, but not his or her actual identity, which the players must try to guess by using analogies. For example, one of the players might ask, 'What sort of building would the person be?' and the first player would have to answer as accurately as possible. If the person in question were a hard-nosed employer, the answer might be 'a maximum security prison camp,' whereas a slapstick comedian might be described as 'an amusement park.'

Winning the Game

The game continues until somebody wins by guessing the identity of the person.

COFFEE POT

NUMBER OF PLAYERS: Four to eight

EQUIPMENT: None

DIFFICULTY: Best for adults

DURATION: About 30 minutes

Playing the Game

One player thinks of a word and proceeds to spout off two or three sentences in which this word is replaced by the phrase 'coffee pot.' Players then get to ask one question each, to which the first player must respond with an answer incorporating 'coffee pot,' with 'coffee pot' continuing to stand for the same secret word. For example, if the secret word is 'shoes,' the first player might say, 'I bought some new coffee pots yesterday,' The second player, thinking the word is 'potatoes,' might then ask, 'Do you eat them with butter?' The first player might respond, 'No, you can't eat coffee pots!'

In some versions, the interrogators can use 'coffee pot' in their questions, even though they do not yet know what it means. For example, 'Where did you buy your new coffee pots?'

Winning the Game

The first player who correctly guesses the identity of the secret word gets a point. If no one has guessed after everyone has asked a question, the point goes to the first player.

This game is generally more fun if a word is chosen which has multiple meanings, such as 'strike' or 'bill.' Alternatively, two or more words which sound the same, such as 'knight' and 'night'—can be considered as one word for the purposes of the game and replaced concurrently with 'coffee pot.'

Each player gets one turn at making up a 'coffee pot' word, after which the points are added up and the player with the most points is the winner.

THE DICTIONARY GAME

NUMBER OF PLAYERS: Four to six

EQUIPMENT: Dictionary, pencils, and paper

DIFFICULTY: A good vocabulary is an asset

DURATION: About 30 minutes

A lively team word game in which one side tries to guess the other side's chosen word from facts offered that may be true or false. Versions of this game have appeared in several different incarnations on television, radio, or as commercial board games. All that is really required for an enjoyable round, however, is a good dictionary, preferably one offering plenty of obscure words, and four or more clever participants.

Playing the Game

Players start by dividing into two teams. Each team chooses an obscure word from the dictionary. One player on each side writes down an actual definition for his team's word, while the others make up false but believable definitions. Each team then announces the word and team members take turns presenting its definitions to the opposition. The other team must then do its best to identity the true definition of the word.

If team members guess correctly, they win a point; otherwise, the point goes to their opponents. The fun of the game lies in the embellishment of the definitions, both true and false, by the players presenting them. It is perfectly acceptable, for instance, to garnish a valid definition with an erroneous explanation of the word's origins, as long as the core of the word's meaning remains intact.

FORBIDDEN WORDS

NUMBER OF PLAYERS: Two or more

EQUIPMENT: Pencil and paper to keep score

DIFFICULTY: Suitable for children age 7 and up

DURATION: 5 minutes per round

Playing the Game

One player goes out of the room. The other players decide on a word. The first player comes back into the room and the other players engage her in conversation for five minutes, or

another time agreed upon by the players.

The object of the game is to make the player who was out of the room use the chosen word as many times as possible. Each time she uses it she is penalized aloud with one point (a player should be allocated to keep count).

However, if she guesses the word and names it correctly before her time is up, her points are wiped out and she returns to zero. It is best not to pick very common words such as 'a' or 'the' because the player will guess them very quickly.

Each player takes a turn at going out of the room. At the end of the round the winner is the player with the least number of points or with zero. If there is more than one player with zero points another game should be played to decide the winner.

GHOSTS

NUMBER OF PLAYERS: Six or more

EQUIPMENT: Pencil and paper

DIFFICULTY: Best for adults

DURATION: About 30 minutes

This is a highly challenging word game that continues to be fun even if you lose.

Setup

Players sit in a circle and take turns calling out letters, which are written down in sequence on a piece of paper.

Playing the Game

The only requirement is that the sequence of letters, as called so far, must potentially be the beginning of an English word.

Additionally, each player is issued three lives, which may be lost in several ways. First, any player who completes an English word of four or more letters loses a life. For this reason, players may be tempted to add letters to the sequence which do not actually lead in the direction of any word whatsoever.

For example, if the sequence so far is ILLUSTRAT, you would want at all costs to avoid calling the letter E, for in that case you would lose a life. In your

panic, you might call out the letter U. However, if the next player in line chooses, he may challenge you and demand to know what word you were thinking of whose beginning was ILLUSTRATU. Since there is no such word, you would then lose a life. On the other hand, if you were challenged after calling an I, you could present the word ILLUSTRATIVE to your challenger, who would then lose a life himself. In any of these cases, a new round would begin with a new sequence of letters.

Ghosts can cause a commotion

A player who has lost all three lives becomes a ghost and is not allowed to participate further in the game. If you are a ghost, you can still have fun, though, by haunting the living players loudly and abrasively in an attempt to get them to talk to you. Any who do so are immediately turned into ghosts themselves, regardless of how many lives they had left. Thus, the game gradually becomes a double challenge: calling out crafty sequences of letters while ignoring the constant shriekings of the undead.

Winning the Game

The last player left alive at the end of the game is the winner.

Variation
Superghost or Fore-and-Aft

This version allows players to add letters either to the end or the beginning of the sequence. Thus, if you are stuck with

INFOR and wish to avoid spelling INFORM, you can add an S to the beginning of the sequence, moving in the direction of MISINFORM.

I LOVE MY LOVE

NUMBER OF PLAYERS: Three or more

EQUIPMENT: None

DIFFICULTY: Suitable for adults, not children

DURATION: About 1 hour

Playing the Game

In this game, which dates back at least to the 17th century, players take turns completing the sentence 'I love my love because he/she is...' with an adjective, going in alphabetical order, from A to Z. For example:

I love my love because he is Artistic.

I love my love because she is Belligerent.

I love my love because he is Crazy.

Any player who cannot think of an adjective starting with the appropriate letter is out of the game, and the last player left is the winner.

The game isn't really about winning or losing, however, but about silliness, creativity and, if you are in the mood to be truthful, the surprising insights into your romantic relationships. It is especially enjoyable if there is a couple among the players.

Variation
Adding Names

A more complicated version of I Love My Love adds names and places to the game, according to the following format:

I love my love because she is Killer-Diller and her name is Kate and she comes from Kuala Lumpur.

If the game still proves too simple, new elements such as adverbs can be added at the players' discretion.

I PACKED MY BAG

NUMBER OF PLAYERS: Two or more

EQUIPMENT: None

DIFFICULTY: Suitable for adults and children

DURATION: About 15 minutes per round

This is a simple game of memory.

Playing the Game

One player starts the round by saying, 'I packed my bag.' The next player repeats this statement and names an item put in the bag. For instance, 'I packed my bag and put in a box fan.' The play then moves from player to player, with each one listing all the previous items and then adding a new one. After a few turns, the list might look something like this:

'I packed my bag and put in a box fan, a mix tape, a snowboard, a bottle of Scotch, two moon-shaped pillows, a large truck, a 19th-century decadent novel, and a portrait of Prince Charles.'

Winning the Game

If players are having trouble memorizing items, you can help them out by requiring all items to be listed alphabetically.

Any player who omits an item from the list or places it in the wrong order is out of the round. The last player left in the round is the winner.

SPELLING ROUND

NUMBER OF PLAYERS: Six or more

EQUIPMENT: A dictionary

DIFFICULTY: Players set their own level

DURATION: 5 minutes per round

This simple game may have the side effect of enhancing spelling skills.

Divide players into two teams and a quizmaster. The quizmaster calls out a word from the dictionary, and the first player in the first team attempts to spell it. If the player spells the word correctly, the first team gets a point; otherwise, the first player on the second team gets a chance at spelling the word and gaining a bonus point.

Either way, the quizmaster then asks the first player on the second team to spell a new word, and play progresses in this way until all players have taken a turn, at which point the team with the most points is declared the winner.

Variations

There are several variations on the basic game, two of which are described here:

- Stand the teams in two lines, facing each other. The quiz leader should then ask each player to spell a word, alternating from team to team. Once a player has finished spelling, the player directly across from him must call out either 'Right' or 'Wrong', depending on whether the word has been spelled correctly or not.

Any player who calls out incorrectly must leave the game, and the team with the last player left is the winner. Actually spelling a word incorrectly thus incurs no penalty. Should they wish, players can be particularly sneaky, purposely misspelling words in order to trick the members of the opposing team.

- Abandon the use of teams and have players score points for themselves. The quiz leader should ask the first player to spell a word. If the word is spelled correctly, the player is given another word to spell. Otherwise, the quizmaster moves on to the next person.

Each player gets to keep spelling words until a mistake is made, and whoever correctly spells the most words wins. Any of these versions can be made considerably more difficult by forcing players to spell words backward.

TABOO

NUMBER OF PLAYERS: Three or more

EQUIPMENT: None

DIFFICULTY: Great fun for children and adults

DURATION: Around 20 minutes

A simple but entertaining word game in which players answer the quiz leader's questions while trying not to say the forbidden word. This party game is reminiscent of the famous scene in the movie Monty Python and the Holy Grail, *in which a group of knights are prohibited from using the word 'it.'*

Playing the Game

Players choose a common word such as 'and,' 'the,' or even 'it,' and declare it to be taboo. Next they choose a quiz leader who proceeds to question the players about anything at all, attempting to provoke use of the forbidden word. Any player who utters the taboo word or hesitates too long trying to find a way around it is out of the round. The last player left in the game is the winner.

Variation

Taboo Letter

In another version, an individual letter is designated taboo and any word containing that letter is prohibited. This is usually extremely difficult and makes for a shorter game, since players generally drop out of the round much faster.

WHO AM I?

NUMBER OF PLAYERS: Four or more

EQUIPMENT: Paper and pencil

DIFFICULTY: Easy for all ages

DURATION: A game can last for 5 minutes or 1 hour, depending on the players

This is a simple game for a large group of people who know each other fairly well.

Playing the Game

Each player starts by writing his name on a slip of paper, folding the slip in half, and putting it into a container. Players then all draw a slip at random from the container and discreetly read the name. If any player turns out to have drawn his own name, the process should probably be repeated. Otherwise, the players each proceed to adopt the character and mannerisms of the person whose name they have drawn, while the others try and guess who is being imitated.

The more organized way to do this is to have players take turns adopting their assumed identities—walking, talking, and moving about while everyone else watches.

Another way, which is probably more fun, is to have each person start his imitation at once, interacting as usual, except that everyone has now become somebody else. This game is not really about winning or losing and is rarely very hard, but it does occasionally give you surprising insight into how other people perceive you.

6

OUTDOOR GAMES

Active Games

Most of these activities are playground games that have been enjoyed by generations of children. A few are worthy of being revisited as adult party games. Some require a great deal of skill.

CAT AND MOUSE

NUMBER OF PLAYERS: 12 or more

EQUIPMENT: None

DIFFICULTY: Suitable for children age 5 and up

DURATION: About 5 minutes per game

Playing the Game

All but two of the players stand in a circle. One of the remaining players is the 'cat' and stands inside the circle; the other is the 'mouse' and stays on the outside of the circle.

The object of the game is for the cat to break out of the circle and catch the mouse. The players in the circle cannot hold hands, but they must try to stop the cat from breaking through.

The game is over if the cat catches the mouse, or if the cat is unable to break out of the circle within five minutes. If the cat catches the mouse, another two players take the roles of cat and mouse.

CLAPPING GAMES

NUMBER OF PLAYERS: Two

EQUIPMENT: None

DIFFICULTY: Easy once rhymes have been learned

DURATION: A few minutes per rhyme

The basis of the game is simply clapping hands with your partner; however, there are many variations.

Playing the Game

Pairs can clap one hand at a time, palms or backs of hands, double claps, hands up or hands down, and touching thighs, shoulders, or hands between claps.

There are many rhymes to go with the clapping games. The following rhyme has been around for some time and is popular in many countries:

Miss Mary Mack, Mack, Mack
All dressed in black, black, black

With silver buttons, buttons, buttons
All down her back, back, back
She asked her mother, mother, mother
For fifty cents (pence), cents (pence), cents (pence)
To see the elephants, elephants, elephants
Jump over the fence, fence, fence
They went so high, high, high
They reached the sky, sky, sky
They never came back, back, back
Till (mid) the fourth of July, July, July.

DODGE BALL

NUMBER OF PLAYERS: Eight to 20

EQUIPMENT: A soft rubber ball, about 8 in. (20 cm) in diameter

DIFFICULTY: Energy and agility are needed. Suitable for children age 8 to 10

DURATION: About 10 minutes per game

In this fast-moving game participants try to hit an opponent below the waist with a large, soft rubber ball.

Setup

This game, known as Free Zone dodge ball, needs rectangular boundary lines about 46 ft. (14 m) x 26 ft. (8 m) and a line across the middle. Draw the lines with chalk or, if possible, use a basketball court.

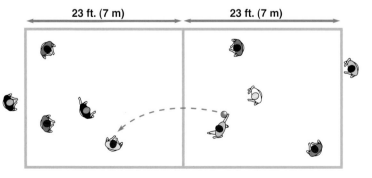

Diagram 1: Free Zone dodge ball

Playing the Game

Players divide into two teams, one on each side of the middle line. The game begins when one player throws the ball at someone on the opposite team. If the player is hit by the ball below the waist, he is out of the game and the ball is returned to the thrower's team. If the ball is caught before it bounces, the original thrower is out. If it bounces without hitting a player, any member of the opposing team can pick up the ball and try to hit someone on the original thrower's team.

Those who are out continue to play, but from behind the opponent's end of the court. They may receive passes from teammates not yet out or retrieve balls that escape across the free zone's back line.

Winning the Game

The out players can also try to throw at opponents. The game ends when all the players on one team are out. Or, the team with the most remaining players at the end of 10 minutes can be declared the winner.

Variation

Train Dodge Ball

A variation suitable for young children, this game needs 12 or more players. Four children stand inside a circle about 23 ft. (7 m) in diameter, formed by the other players. The children in the middle form a *train*, putting their hands around the waist of the child in front. The first child in line is the *engine* and the last is the *caboose.* The two in the middle are the *carriages.* Players in the circle try to hit the caboose below the waist with the ball. The engine tries to fend off the ball by kicking or throwing it. The carriages are not allowed to help.

If the caboose is hit, the player who did the hitting becomes the engine and the second carriage player becomes the caboose. The first caboose leaves the train and joins the circle. The game continues until each player has been the engine.

The winner is the engine who keeps the caboose safe for the longest time.

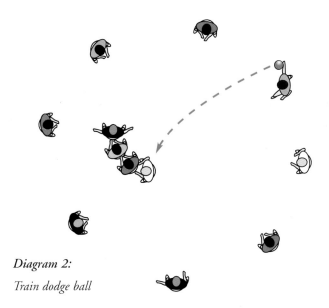

Diagram 2:

Train dodge ball

EXCHANGE TAG

NUMBER OF PLAYERS: Six to 20

EQUIPMENT: None

DIFFICULTY: Suitable for 5- to 10-year-olds

DURATION: 15 to 20 minutes

This is a great party game because children can let off steam and make lots of noise. At least ten children are needed for a formal game of tag. There are many ways to play, but here are two good ones.

Playing the Game

Ten or more children form a circle about 8 yd. (7 m) across, and sit on the ground. The child who is 'it,' the chaser, stands in the middle of the circle and calls the names of two children. They then have to run around the circle and sit down in one another's places without being tagged by the chaser. If a child is tagged, he becomes the new chaser.

Variations

Bulldog

Two boundary lines about 50 ft. (15 m) apart are selected. One person, the catcher, stands between the boundaries, while the other children stand behind one of the boundaries.

On an agreed signal, the children behind the boundary line run across the field to get behind the other boundary. While they are in transit, they can be tagged by the catcher. All the children who are tagged become catchers. The free children, at the next signal, must run back to the original boundary, and again, any who are tagged become catchers. The game continues until only one child is left free. She is the winner, or bulldog, and becomes the first catcher for the next round.

FOLLOW THE LEADER

NUMBER OF PLAYERS: Six to 20

EQUIPMENT: None

DIFFICULTY: Suitable for 5- to 10-year-olds

DURATION: About 10 minutes

Playing the Game

A leader is chosen and the other players line up behind him. They must all follow the leader and do exactly as he does— hopping, skipping, jumping, or any other action. Any player who fails to do as the leader does is out.

Each player takes a turn at being the leader.

FOX AND RABBIT

NUMBER OF PLAYERS: 10 or more

EQUIPMENT: None

DIFFICULTY: Suitable for 5- to 10-year-olds

DURATION: About 15 minutes

Playing the Game

Players divide into groups of four, plus one rabbit and one fox. Three of each group of four make a circle, standing with their hands on each other's shoulders. The fourth player is a rabbit crouching in the middle of the *warren*.

The object of the game is for the fox to catch a rabbit, but the rabbit cannot be caught once it is inside a warren. When the game starts, the fox chases the spare rabbit that is outside of a warren. This rabbit can run into a warren at any time, but the rabbit inside must then leave. This rabbit cannot return to the warren it has just left but must go to another warren.

When the fox catches a rabbit the two change roles and this rabbit becomes the next fox.

HARE AND HOUNDS

NUMBER OF PLAYERS: 5 or more

EQUIPMENT: Coloured paper or chalk

DIFFICULTY: Suitable for children age 9 and up

DURATION: About half an hour

Playing the Game

One person is chosen to be the hare and the rest of the players are hounds. The game needs to be played in a large area such as a park, and the aim is for one of the hounds to catch the hare.

The hare is given the coloured paper or chalk and has a five minute start. She must leave a trail by dropping a piece of coloured paper or making a mark with the chalk every 100 paces. She can take as complicated a route as she likes, but she must leave the marks in easy-to-see places. She then hides from the hounds.

The hound who tags the hare is the winner. When the game is finished, the children can race to be the first to pick up any coloured paper that has been left on the ground.

HIDE AND SEEK

NUMBER OF PLAYERS: Six or more

EQUIPMENT: None

DIFFICULTY: Suitable for children age 5 and up

DURATION: About 5 minutes for a round

Playing the Game

In this venerable game, one child is 'it,' also known as the *seeker*. He stands at a *base*, hides his eyes, and counts to 20 while the other children run off to hide.

When the count is over, the seeker shouts, 'Ready or not, here I come,' and begins looking for the other children. The first one he finds and tags is 'it' for the next round, which does not start until all the children are accounted for.

Variation

Liberation

In a common variation, while the seeker is out looking, a hider may attempt to sneak back to the base. If he touches the base without being seen and tagged, he shouts, 'Ollie, ollie, oxen free,' to let the seeker know he has liberated himself and cannot become 'it' in this round.

HOPSCOTCH

NUMBER OF PLAYERS: Two to 10

EQUIPMENT: Chalk, a small stone

DIFFICULTY: Needs practice at first; suitable for children age 6 to 10

DURATION: About 20 minutes, depending on number of players

The site of a hopscotch game should be level and paved.

Setup

One of the players draws in chalk a 10 ft. (3 m) x 4 ft. (1.2 m) grid. The grid in diagram 3 is just an example; there are many variations in layout and rules.

Playing the Game

The first player throws a small rock called a *puck* into the rectangle marked '1' and hops into it on one foot. Staying on one foot, she picks up the puck and hops back to the starting line without landing on a line.

Having retrieved the puck from area '1,' she throws it into the part of the grid marked '2,' hops in and retrieves it, again turning and hopping back to the starting line. Her turn continues unless she commits an error—either by throwing to the wrong area, hopping onto a line, or allowing both feet to touch the ground at once.

After a mistake, the turn passes to the next player. When it is the first player's turn again, she starts with the area where she left off on her last attempt. The first to reach 'out' and hop back successfully wins.

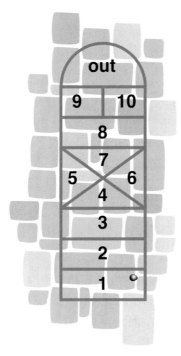

Diagram 3: Hopscotch

JUMP ROPE (SKIPPING)

NUMBER OF PLAYERS: One to several

EQUIPMENT: Short rope 7 ft. (2 m) long, or long rope 14 ft. (4 m) long

DIFFICULTY: Suitable for children age 7 and up

DURATION: A few minutes per rhyme

Jump rope, as it is known in the United States, or skipping, as it is known in Britain, is a game played the world over in school playgrounds—but it is also a great way for anyone to keep fit.

Playing the Game

Jump rope can be a game for one player using a short rope, which she turns and then jumps over, or it can be a game for three or more players with two people holding a longer rope, one at each end turning the rope for the other players to jump in and over.

There are many tricks and rhymes that add to the fun of the game. One sequence for the single skipper gets increasingly difficult. It starts with a *sideswing*. The skipper does a normal jump then puts her hands together and swings the rope to one side of her body. When she is ready she opens her hands, swings the rope down, and jumps.

Next she introduces a *front cross* by doing a regular jump then crossing her arms in front of her body and jumping through the loop she has made with the rope.

Next she does a *cross-cross,* which involves crossing the rope in front of her body then quickly uncrossing her arms and crossing them again to make the loop that she jumps through.

Finally she introduces a *front back cross:* She does a single bounce then a sideswing. Keeping one arm crossing the front of her body and one arm crossing behind her back, she jumps through the rope then goes back into a sideswing.

Children particularly enjoy playing jump rope in a group. There are many rhymes that they can sing as they jump in and out of the swinging rope. Two people turn and one person jumps, chanting:

> *I like coffee, I like tea*
> *I like* (the person's name that you want to jump in) *to jump with me*
> *One, two, three—change places* (the two jumpers change places)
> *Four, five, six—change places…'*

Above: *Jump rope or skipping has been popular since the 1800s.*

The two keep jumping and changing places until they miss or get tangled in the rope. In a group of children, the winners are the pair who make the most changes.

Variations

Chinese Jump Rope ((Elastics or French Skipping)

Three or more children age 7 and up can play; they need a 10 ft. (3 m) length of elastic joined to make a loop. Two players stand with the elastic pulled tight around their ankles. The third player jumps the elastic using a variety of movements. This is a rhyme that uses specific movements:

> *Chocolate cake, when you bake*
> *How many minutes will you take?*
> *One, two, three, four*

The player jumps in so that the left foot is outside and the right foot inside the elastic. She waits until she hears the number one, then jumps up and lands with the right foot outside and the left foot inside the elastic.

On two, the player jumps up and lands with both feet inside the elastic; on three, the player jumps up and lands with both feet outside the elastic, and on four, the player jumps up and lands with her feet holding down both sides of the elastic.

The player could also land with both feet on one side of the elastic, or take the elastic with each foot and cross her legs so that she is standing inside an X, then jump out again landing with both feet outside the elastic.

When the jumper completes the set sequence successfully, another player takes a turn.

Double Dutch

Double Dutch is played with two long ropes, about 14 ft. (4 m) long, turned by two players in an eggbeater motion. Three or more children age 7 and up can play. The ropes are turned in opposite directions circling toward the middle. Each player on the jumping line has to move in and jump over both ropes.

More tricks and rhymes

Birthday Girl

In this group skipping game, two rope turners speed up the rope as they recite the months of the year.

The rhyme goes like this:

All in together girls
It's fine weather girls
When is your birthday?
Please jump in.

Each jumper then listens out for her birthday month, then jumps in at the right moment.

All out together girls
It's fine weather girls
When is your birthday?
Please jump out.

The turners count from 1 to 31, and the jumper jumps out on her birthday.

Helicopter, Helicopter

One person turns the rope above her head and slowly starts to lower it down. The other players recite:

Helicopter, helicopter, please come down,
If you don't I'll shoot you down
To the witches' town,
Bang, bang, bang.

When the rope is 'shot down,' it is swung on the ground by one handle like the blades of a helicopter and all the players jump it as it goes around.

The jumper with the highest number of jumps is the winner.

Rhymes and fancy footwork are added for the skilled Double Dutcher:

I'm a little Dutch girl dressed in blue,
Here are the things I like to do.
Salute the Captain,
Curtsy to the queen,
Turn my back on a big submarine.
I can do a tap dance,
I can do the splits,
I can do the polka just like this!

JUGGLING

NUMBER OF PLAYERS: One

EQUIPMENT: Three juggling balls, tennis balls, or similar

DIFFICULTY: Suitable for children age 12 and up

DURATION: As long as desired

Playing the Game

To learn simple juggling, a player starts with just one ball and stands with feet slightly apart, elbows bent, and hands parallel to the ground. Practice throwing the ball from one hand to the other, then back again. Throw the ball up with the right hand so that when the ball reaches its peak, it is above the left hand. From the left hand it can be thrown to reach its peak just above the right hand.

When this is mastered, you can move on to two balls, one held in each hand. Throw the ball from the right hand, then when it reaches its peak just above the left hand, throw the ball from the left hand. There should be a slight delay between first catching the ball in the left hand and then in the right hand.

Then introduce the third ball. Hold two balls in the right hand and one in the left. First throw the ball at the front of the right hand. Then when it reaches its peak above the left hand, throw the ball from the left hand. As you catch the first ball in the left hand, and the second ball reaches its peak,

A history of juggling

A tomb painting of jugglers from ancient Egyptian times is evidence that this skill has been around for thousands of years. In the Middle Ages the court jester to the king was also the juggler, and jugglers traveled from town to town to entertain the people and pass on news they had learned on the road. Vaudeville entertainers of the early 1900s in the United States and Europe often included jugglers.

Street performers keep the art of juggling alive—juggling balls, hoops, clubs, or more unusual household objects. The world's best jugglers can briefly keep up to ten balls in the air at one time—with fewer balls they can juggle for long periods of time and perform stunning tricks.

both hands together on his back and doing the splits as he leaps over his partner.

When playing with more than two players, all the players but one bend down in an evenly spaced row. The remaining player jumps over all of his companions, then bends down at the end of the row. The first player bent over straightens up and jumps, then bends down again at the end of the row, and so on until everyone has jumped.

Above: Children playing leapfrog

throw the other ball from the right hand. Catch the second ball in the right hand and throw the next ball from the left hand, leaving that hand clear to catch a ball as it descends. Finally, catch the last ball in the right hand.

Practice this sequence until you can juggle three balls in a flowing, continuous motion.

LEAPFROG

NUMBER OF PLAYERS: Two or more

EQUIPMENT: None

DIFFICULTY: Suitable for children age 6 and up

DURATION: A few minutes

Playing the Game

The first player bends down with his hands on his knees for a high jump, or his elbows on his knees for a lower jump, and with his back parallel to the ground.

The second player then leaps over the first player by placing

SEVENS

NUMBER OF PLAYERS: One or more

EQUIPMENT: Tennis ball or similar

DIFFICULTY: Suitable for children age 12 and up

DURATION: As long as desired

Playing the Game

The object of this game is to catch and throw a ball in seven different ways without dropping it. Each player keeps a count of his own number of successful throws, and the winner is the player with the highest score.

Following is the order of the throws:

- **One:** The player throws the ball against a wall and catches it.
- **Two:** The player throws the ball into the air and claps three times before catching it.
- **Three:** The player throws the ball into the air and claps his hands behind his back before catching it.
- **Four:** The player throws the ball into the air, claps his

hands, and touches his shoulders before catching it.

- **Five:** The player bounces the ball and turns around completely before catching it.
- **Six:** The player beats the ball on the ground three times with one hand before catching it.
- **Seven:** The player throws the ball up with one hand and catches it with the other.

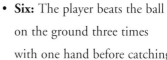

Variations

Using two balls

One player uses two balls and throws them against a wall in various ways. The balls are thrown underhand in a fluid motion that is usually accompanied by a rhyme or chant. This is almost like juggling against a wall, and the skilled player can include challenges such as clapping between throws, throwing one ball under a leg, or bouncing the balls from the ground up to the wall before catching them.

TREASURE HUNT

NUMBER OF PLAYERS: Four or more

EQUIPMENT: Pencil and paper, envelopes, prize

DIFFICULTY: Suitable for adults and children age 7 and up

DURATION: About an hour

The object of the game is to follow a set of clues from hiding place to hiding place until the treasure is found.

Playing the Game

The person setting up the treasure hunt must work in advance, hiding the treasure and the clues. For younger children this game is best played in a yard or garden; a park is fine for older children, while a much wider setting, such as an area of town, could be the game zone for adults.

It is most fun for players to work in pairs or teams. The first clue is given to each team and subsequent clues are left at each hiding place in envelopes marked for each team. If this is a game for children organized in a small space, then give them different starting clues so that they do not just follow each other from clue to clue.

TUG-OF-WAR

NUMBER OF PLAYERS: Eight or more

EQUIPMENT: Strong rope, chalk, or piece of string

DIFFICULTY: Suitable for children age 6 and up

DURATION: About an hour

Playing the Game

Mark a line using the chalk or string. Two teams line up, at least 3 ft. (1 m) behind the line, one behind the other on either side of this mark, each person holding onto the rope.

The object of the game is to pull the other team over the mark. As soon as the front player touches or is pulled over the mark, the other team has won.

It is best to play this game on a soft surface, such as grass, as the winning team tends to collapse when the other team gives way.

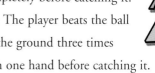

Above: A tug-of-war

Sports Games

Playing sports is an excellent way to keep physically and mentally fit—whether you are 5 or 75. Children who enjoy playing sports are more likely to keep fit and active as adults.

BADMINTON

NUMBER OF PLAYERS: Two; four for doubles

EQUIPMENT: Net, shuttlecocks, rackets

DIFFICULTY: Good coordination and athletic skills are required

DURATION: 20 minutes

This game is played by two individuals or doubles teams, who use light rackets (racquets) to serve and return a shuttlecock over a central net across a large court. Although badminton resembles tennis, it actually derives from a game that originated in India centuries ago. A shuttlecock, weighing 0.17 oz. (4.7 g) to 0.19 oz. (5.5 g), consists of a weighted base topped by 14 to 16 natural or synthetic feathers. Because the shuttlecock is so light, it is easily affected by wind. Serious players usually play inside, and outdoor players would be well advised to use one of the heavier shuttlecocks.

Setup

Diagram 1 shows a badminton court. The line nearest the net is the short service line. At the back of the court are the long service lines (the furthest line for singles, the inner line for doubles). The long middle lines divide the court into the left

Above: A badminton game in progress

and right service courts. Side boundaries for singles are marked by the dotted lines, and for doubles by the solid lines. The net hangs from posts 5 ft. 1 in. (1.55 m) high, 1 in. (2.5 cm) below the top of the posts. It is 2 ft. 6 in. (76 cm) in breadth.

Scoring

As in tennis, only the server can score. If a receiver fails to make a legal return or commits a fault, the server gets one point and serves again. If the server misses or commits a fault, service passes to the receiver. A fault occurs if:

- A player hits the shuttlecock while it is on the opponent's side of the court (although follow-through that goes over the net is permitted)
- A player touches the shuttlecock (except with the racket)
- A player or racket touches the net

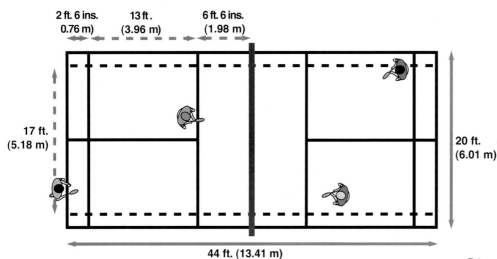

Diagram 1: A badminton court

2 ft. 6 ins. (0.76 m)   13 ft. (3.96 m)   6 ft. 6 ins. (1.98 m)

17 ft. (5.18 m)

20 ft. (6.01 m)

44 ft. (13.41 m)

- The racket or any part of the player's body goes into the opponent's court.

Side changes

In official competition, men's and doubles games are played to 15 points, and women's singles to 11. Players change sides after 8 points in a 15-point game and after 6 points in an 11-point game. If the score becomes tied 1 or 2 points below the winning level, the player or side that was ahead before the tie has the option to 'set' the game. This must be done before the next serve following the tie. If the game is set, all previous points are ignored, and the sides start with love-all (zero points each). The first side to reach three points wins the game.

Playing the Game

Singles play

The winner of an initial coin toss may choose either to serve first or to take the side of the court that seems most advantageous. The first server stands in her right-hand service court and delivers the shuttlecock diagonally across the net to the receiver's right-hand court. In order for the serve to be legal, the shuttlecock needs to drop from above waist height onto the racket, which must be below the waist and pointing toward the ground when contact is made. The serve has to cross the net and fall between the service lines of the correct court. If any of the above requirements is not met, service goes over to the opponent.

Until the serve is hit, a receiver is required to remain still with both feet in the service court. She must return the shuttlecock with no more than one stroke. The return has to remain within bounds and go over the net, but need not be within a particular service court.

Doubles

There are a few special rules for doubles play. The court's dimensions are somewhat different: The outer side boundaries and the inner long service line are used. On a serve, only the player in the service court diagonally opposite the server can strike the shuttlecock. (After the serve, either of the partners may play a stroke.) Players on a team take turns serving, and the original receiver is the first to serve for her team.

BASEBALL

NUMBER OF PLAYERS:	Two teams of 9 players each
EQUIPMENT:	Bat, ball, fielding gloves
DIFFICULTY:	Athletically demanding
DURATION:	2 to 3 hours (or less, by agreement)

Although it can no longer accurately be called America's national pastime, having been eclipsed in popularity by professional football as a spectator sport and basketball as a participatory activity, baseball remains a major summertime presence in nearly every corner of North America—as well as in Japan, the Caribbean, and parts of Central and South America.

Some sports historians say that Civil War General Abner Doubleday invented the game in the sleepy hamlet of Cooperstown, New York, in 1839. Yet there is evidence of games very much like present-day baseball having been played in the American Northeast in the early 1800s. In all likelihood, baseball evolved from a British game called rounders (see page 236); the rules were standardized by Alexander Cartwright in 1845, and the first professional leagues organized in the early 1870s.

Setup

The dimensions (and geometry) of the game have remained largely unchanged for a century and a half. The playing field (called a *baseball diamond,* although it better resembles an isosceles triangle whose bottom has bulged into an arc) is divided into two sections: *infield* and *outfield.* The infield

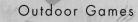

contains four bases, which are in fact arranged as a diamond, and the *pitcher's mound.* The bases are 90 ft. (27 m) apart, and the middle of the pitcher's mound (called the *rubber*) is 60 ft. 6 in. (18.4 m) from home base, which has come to be called *home plate.*

The area surrounding home plate, the base paths between home and first base and home and third base, as well as the pitcher's mound and the wide area between first and third base, are surfaced with finely treated dirt. The remainder of the infield and the entire outfield (except for a strip near the

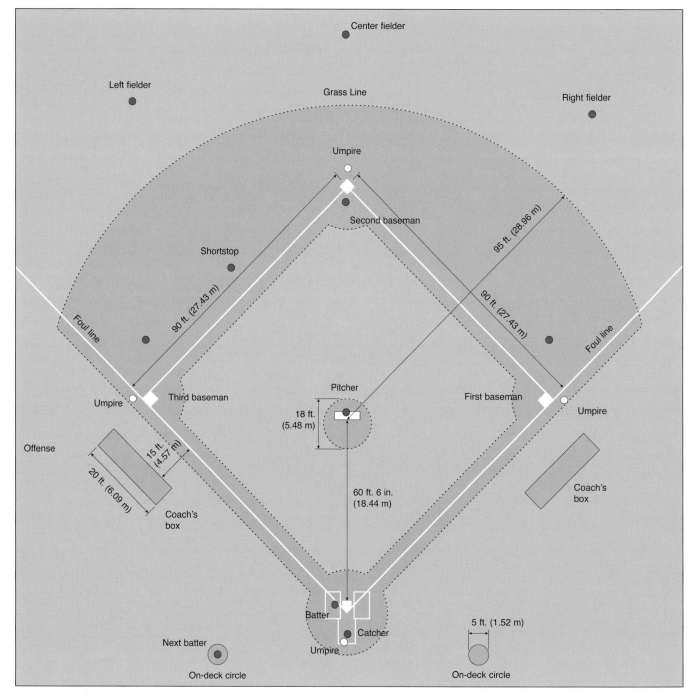

Diagram 2: A standard baseball field with positions and measurements

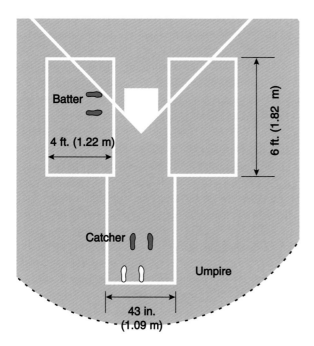

Diagram 3: Detail of the home plate in baseball

outfield wall called the *warning track*) are covered with extremely lush grass. In the late 1960s and early 1970s there was a trend toward redoing the grass portions of ballparks in artificial turf. Astroturf® was born of necessity when grass failed to grow in the first indoor baseball stadium—the Houston Astrodome. In a short space of time other teams, impressed by Astroturf's cheap maintenance, installed it in their outdoor stadiums, and by the mid-1970s nearly half the major league teams had gone over to fake grass. Today, many knee injuries and rugburns later, grass has returned to all but a few stadiums.

Teams

There are nine players on a team. The *catcher* squats behind home plate; the *pitcher* stands on the pitcher's mound (which is 10 in. [25 cm] high); the *first* and *second basemen* are positioned between first and second base—their precise stations determined by the nature of the particular batter—the *shortstop* and *third baseman* likewise stand between second and third base; the three outfield positions are quite logically designated as *left fielder, center fielder,* and *right fielder.* The infielders and outfielders shift around in their positions according to game situations, and depending on whether the batter is right-handed or left-handed, in their ongoing attempt to keep the batter from hitting safely.

Playing the Game

The visiting team always bats first; the home team takes up positions on the field. Batters come to the plate in turns until

The state of the game

Baseball has had a difficult time adjusting to modern economics. Until the 1970s, players belonged unconditionally to the teams that originally signed them. A series of lawsuits ended that system; team owners resisted change, and the antagonistic relationship that developed between players and management caused several work stoppages, including the cancellation of several months' play at the end of the 1994 season and the beginning of the 1995 season. In 1994, the much-venerated World Series went unplayed for the first time since 1904, to the considerable dismay of devoted fans. But the 2002 labor agreement provided a huge step in the direction of stability.

The game has succeeded in winning back much of its following thanks to a bevy of new, retro-designed stadiums, the seemingly annual assault on home run records, and to uncommonly exciting postseason games and series.

Until World War II, when baseball was exclusively a game for white Americans, the term World Series had a fairly ironic ring. Now, when the Major Leagues comprise players from 15 countries (by unofficial count) on four continents, the term has more validity.

three are out. Here are some ways to be called out once a ball is hit:

- A ball—fair or foul—is caught before it hits the ground.
- A ball touches the ground, but a fielder gets the ball to first base faster than the batter can run there.
- A batter is tagged with the ball by a fielder, pitcher, or catcher before he reaches a base.

Three outs of any variety mean a team's turn at bat, or *inning*, is over, and so the teams change places. A game consists of nine such innings. (If the home team is leading after the first half of the ninth inning, it does not bat in the latter half. If the game is tied after nine innings, play continues until a winner is determined. Games have lasted as long as 26 innings.)

A batter who has reached a base becomes a *runner*. Runners attempt to advance around the bases to home plate, thus scoring a *run*. Hits by teammates afford the best opportunity, but a runner may advance at any time, taking advantage of a fielding error, for example, or stealing a base if the pitcher is not paying close enough attention. When the ball is hit into the air, a runner must *tag up* (touch the base he occupies after the ball is caught) before trying to run. Running is not mandatory: If the chances of safe advance are not good, a runner need not move—except when there is no empty base for a hitter to occupy. In the most common case, with a runner on first and a ground ball hit toward an infielder, the runner must vacate first base and make a run for second, where in all probability he will be

Above: *A safely organized game of baseball can be a fun and exhilarating activity for children.*

forced out. With agile fielding there is time also to throw the hitter out at first, making a *double play*. A runner is out when:

- **Forced out:** The ball arrives first at the only base open to the runner; the fielder need only catch the ball and touch the base to make the out.
- **Tagged out:** The runner, while off base, is touched with the ball or a glove holding the ball.

Batting

The odds would seem to be very much against the batter. In addition to all those men in the outfield and infield prepared to catch any ball he hits, the pitcher (who is often capable of throwing the ball at 95 to 100 mph (152 to 160 km/h) can strike him out. A *strike* occurs when the batter swings and misses a pitch, or when he elects not to swing and the umpire judges the pitch as having been over the plate and neither high nor low, or when the batter hits a *foul ball* (makes contact with the ball but fails to hit it into fair territory— within the baselines). Any combination of three strikes and the batter has *struck out*—although he cannot strike out on a foul ball.

If the umpire judges a pitch not to have been a strike—to have missed high or low, inside or outside—it is called a *ball*. Four bad pitches and the batter receives a base on balls, more commonly known as a *walk*. If a pitch hits the batter, then

Right: The pitcher in action

he is awarded first base. Otherwise, a batter may reach base only by a fielder's error or by hitting safely, which is to say by hitting the ball where no fielder is present. This is most commonly done by hitting the ball hard—on the ground between infielders, on a low line into the outfield, on a soaring drive beyond the outfielders' reach, or entirely out of the ballpark. It can also be done by hitting the ball softly— which is sometimes done intentionally, but more often not— so that no fielder can reach it in time to throw the runner out at first base. A safe hit is known as a *base hit*, or simply as a hit. A batter reaches first base on a *single*, second on a *double*, third on a *triple*, and rounds the bases on a *home run*.

Pitching

While the *fastball* remains the principal weapon of most pitchers' arsenals, and while pitchers, like hitters, have become bigger and stronger with passing generations, even the fastest of fastballers must augment his regular pitch with a *breaking ball*.

Until well into the 20th century a school of thought held that the *curveball* was an optical illusion. Not until a series of stop-motion photographs showed a baseball winding between two posts approximately 55 and 60 ft. (17 and 18 m) away were cynics convinced that the ball was capable of lateral movement. The standard curveball is thrown with a rapid, clockwise (for a right-hander) break of the wrist just as the ball is released. The pitcher hides his grip from the batter until the last instant, so the batter must discern from the ball's rotation and speed whether it is a fastball or a slower, more crooked delivery. The average fastball zooms toward

Of home runs, now and then

Until the 1920s and the era of the legendary Babe Ruth (below, center), the home run was something of a rarity, as few players had the power to hit the ball out of the park.

Ruth did so with regularity, and to such great acclaim, that eventually the composition of the ball itself was covertly altered. The new 'live' ball led to a frenzy of home runs and extra-base hits in general, peaking in 1930 and 1931, when various Herculean batting records were set—many of which have not been challenged since.

In recent years there have been renewed charges of 'juiced' or altered baseballs because of an unprecedented home run glut. Ruth hit 60 homers in 1927, and that figure was equalled only once in the next 70 years, when Roger Maris hit 61 in 1961. But in the late 1990s and early 2000s, three players have combined to surpass the 60 figure six times.

the batter at about 90 mph (144 km/h); the curve will travel plateward at 70 to 75 mph (112 to 120 km/h), so the batter must deal with being caught off-balance as well as with the change of direction.

In addition to the curve, breaking pitches include the *slider*, thrown nearly as hard as the fastball, but with a slight break at the end; the *screwball*, thrown with a counterclockwise break of the wrist, so it bends toward the right-handed batter instead of away from him; and the misnamed knuckleball, thrown off the fingertips without any spin at all, so it floats and dips in an erratic and completely unpredictable trajectory. The *knuckleball* tends to be the dominant pitch of those who use it, as it is considerably slower, 50 to 60 mph (80 to 96 km/h), than the others, and allows its users to turn convention on its head and employ the fastball as a change of pace.

The *split-fingered fastball,* or *splitter,* meanwhile, is a devastating pitch that was almost unknown 20 years ago. The splitter is perhaps a product of the evolution of the modern ballplayer, as it requires extremely long fingers. The index and middle fingers squeeze the ball at its middle; the ball is thrown with the same motion and mechanics as a standard fastball, but the unique grip causes the ball to react like a tennis ball with extreme topspin, so it dives precipitously just as it reaches home plate. Many power pitchers have shunned the slider or the curve and instead use the splitter as their primary breaking ball.

Strategy

With no runners on base, the pitcher is free to pitch from a *windup*, in which he customarily raises both arms well above his head while lifting his left leg (if he is right-handed) in a sort of hyperbolic demonstration of the mechanics of throwing a ball. But when runners are on—especially when there is a man on first base—the pitcher must behave more economically, and employ the stretch. He stands straight up, the hand holding the ball enclosed in the gloved hand, and slowly lifts the hands to his chest while peering over his shoulder at the runner on first. A left-hander stares directly at the runner.

The runner is free to advance at any point to steal a base, and can do so at will if the pitcher throws from his windup. The purpose of the stretch is to keep the runner close to the base, or even to trick him into running prematurely and then throw behind him to the first baseman, after which (barring a bad throw) he will be tagged out at second base. Speedy runners wait for the instant the pitcher commits himself; if he is throwing to first, they dive back to the base; if he is throwing to the batter, they take off for second, whereupon the catcher must make a perfect throw or the base is stolen.

An example: The suicide squeeze play

Assume there are runners on first and third, nobody out. Let us say it's a tie game, eighth inning, and the worst two hitters in the lineup are about to bat. At such a point all the batting team needs is a long *fly ball* to take the lead. The runner on third must stay glued to the base until the ball is caught; then he can race for the plate. But the pitcher is known for throwing an excellent *sinker*, meaning it is likely the ball will be hit on the ground and the non-speedy runner on third will be thrown out at home. The manager calls for the *squeeze bunt*.

It is a do-or-die play, and only makes sense with fewer than two out, and further only makes sense if the pitcher tends to throw strikes. The pitcher goes into his stretch. The batter, instead of preparing to swing at the ball, faces the pitcher and drops the bat to waist level. The runner on third, once it is clear that the pitcher is throwing home, begins dashing for the plate. It remains now for the batter to make contact with the ball. If he does not, the runner is a sure out. If he does, if he bunts the ball on the ground—even if directly back to the pitcher—there will be insufficient time to field the ball and get it back to the catcher. The run will score.

CRICKET

NUMBER OF PLAYERS: 22; 11 players on each side

EQUIPMENT: Ball, bats, wickets

DIFFICULTY: Coordination skills are required, plus lots of energy for runs

DURATION: About two hours for a friendly game between friends, or a whole afternoon if breaks and rest periods are included; professional games last up to five days

In broad outline, a bat-wielding (a long bat made of willow wood, flat on one side) player tries to hit a ball—leather-covered, very solid, and about the size of a large orange—thrown without bending the elbow in a vigorous overhand style by a member of the opposing team, called the bowler. *If the player hits the ball he then runs back and forth within a narrow scoring zone, the pitch, thus chalking up runs for his own team. Cricket may seem like a very strange sport to the uninitiated: For one thing, an international match (or test) may go on for days, with players and spectators taking lunch and tea breaks. For another, everyone may seem eerily well behaved as sporting crowds go—cricket's tradition and rules are deeply imbued with a sense of fair play and good sportsmanship.*

Right: *This batsman is well-protected with helmet, pads, and gloves.*

Setup

A cricket field is usually an oval shape, not more than 160 yd. (146 m) across, with boundaries clearly marked. In the middle of the field is the *pitch*, a hard-packed, closely cropped rectangular area in which the bowling and batting action takes place. At either end of the pitch is a curious arrangement of sticks called a *wicket*. Each wicket consists of three uprights, or *stumps*, driven into the ground and two short pieces, or *bails*, lying loosely in shallow grooves on top of them. Tops of the stumps are 28 in. (71 cm) high and 3 in. (7.5 cm) apart, making a total width of 9 in. (23 cm) for the wicket. The bowler aims to hit the wicket with the ball—which would mean that the player is out—and the player tries to score runs while defending his wicket.

Rules do govern the dimensions of the pitch and its play markings, called *creases*: wickets are set 66 ft. (20.12 m) apart and define end lines called *bowling creases*; 4 ft. (1.22 m) in front of each is a second line, the *popping crease,* which is where a batsman will stand to receive the ball.

Playing the Game

Each team consists of 11 players. The fielding team stations itself around the play area, except that two have special functions: the *bowler,* who delivers the ball, and the *wicket-keeper,* who gathers the ball after it has been bowled. The team at bat sends two batsmen to the pitch, one to each wicket. The bowler delivers to one wicket; the batsman standing at the receiving end is called the *striker.* At the other, inactive wicket the *nonstriker* merely stands behind the popping crease, out of the way of the bowler's run-up and delivery.

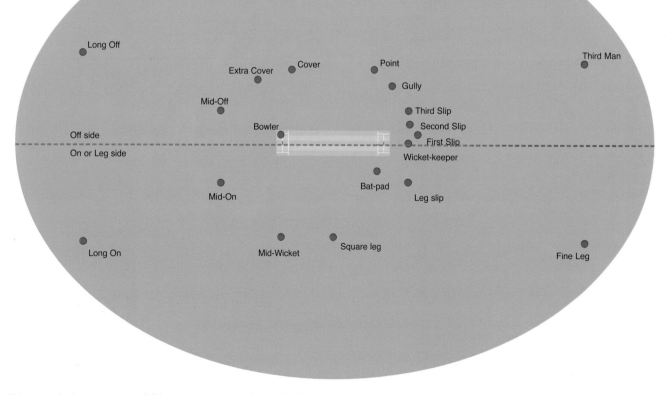

Diagram 4: Some common field positions on a cricket pitch (for a right-handed batsman)

A bowler bowls six balls, comprising an *over*, after which another fielder takes the ball and begins the next over, bowling from the pitch's other end. (The same fielder may bowl nonconsecutive overs, however, without restriction.) The striker, for his part, attempts to score runs by hitting the ball with his bat and running from end to end of the pitch—*grounding* his extended bat beyond the popping crease at each end—until no more runs may safely be taken. At the same time, the nonstriker must mirror his teammate's running, so that they swap ends in the course of each run. Thus, if only one run is taken, and the over has not yet concluded, striker and nonstriker reverse roles: The next ball will be delivered to the same wicket regardless of which batsman happens to be defending. A batsman may elect not to hit the ball, or not to attempt a run after hitting it.

The striker, depending on skill and speed, may try to play the ball into any part of the field, sending it into the air or along the ground. Indeed, he may even strike a ball that has come to rest, for whatever reason, in front of him. Many of his strokes, however, will be purely defensive, simply protecting his wicket.

When a batsman is declared *out* (see page 220), he is replaced by the next in his team's order until ten are out and no one remains to come in to bat—necessarily a lone batsman remains on the pitch, or *not out*. The team's *innings* is then over and it takes its turn at fielding. A complete match may consist of an agreed number of innings, usually two, or it may consist of a single innings for each team, with a specified number of overs in each innings. The first sort of match is apt to go on for days (or until an agreed time limit has been reached), while the second is suitable for one-day cricket.

Scoring

There are several other ways of scoring apart from actually hitting the ball and running. If a ball travels across the boundary line, or a fielder travels over the line with the ball, an automatic 4 runs are scored; the batsmen do not run. A ball that leaves the playing field *on the full* (without having touched the ground) is worth 6 runs.

Batsmen may benefit from erratic fielding: They may choose to continue running on an overthrow, scoring until it seems prudent to ground bats behind the popping crease. An overthrow that runs *out-of-bounds* scores an extra 4—added to the number of runs taken before the overthrow occurred.

And then there are extras. These runs are not the result of hitting a ball and are not credited to a batsman's total but to the team score. They are:

- **Bye:** If the striker misses and the wicket-keeper allows the ball to get away, batsmen may attempt to take runs.
- **Leg bye:** A striker may attempt runs, too, when he has deflected the ball with his body while trying to hit it.
- **No ball:** A bowler's infraction. Failure to deliver with some part of the front foot behind the popping crease or trailing the foot somewhere between the two creases

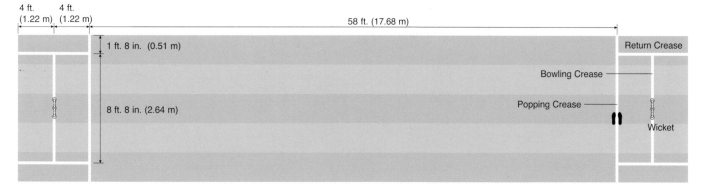

Diagram 5: The dimensions of a standard cricket pitch

More cricket lingo

More terms often encountered in a discussion of cricket include:

- **Block, drive, cut, hook, pull, sweep:** Descriptive of various batting strokes
- **Bouncer:** A ball striking the pitch well in front of the batsman; that is, bowled 'short'
- **Century:** The scoring of 100 runs, in a single innings, by a batsman
- **Duck:** Out without taking a run, as in 'out for a duck'
- **Hat trick:** A bowler's achievement, quite rare, taking three wickets on successive balls
- **Howzat?:** Called out to an umpire, an appeal for a ruling, usually concerning leg-before-wicket
- **Maiden:** An over in which no runs have been scored
- **Partnership:** Runs scored by two batsmen while paired on the pitch
- **Stumps:** Wicket uprights, but also the agreed-upon time for suspending a day's play
- **Swing:** Analagous to 'curve' in baseball; a ball's directional change while in the air
- **Yorker:** A ball that bounces at or near the popping crease; difficult to play.

is called 'no ball,' and 1 run awarded—unless the striker has hit the ball and attempts to score in the usual way. A no ball must be rebowled, just as with a wide.

- **Wide:** A delivery well off target, completely unplayable, will be judged a wide by the umpire, and 1 run awarded. A wide does not count as one of the over's six balls.

Getting out

If the ball, whether not hit or deflected by the bat or batsman, strikes the stumps and dislodges a bail, the batsman is bowled out, and must leave the field. Indeed, should a batsman inadvertently *break* his own wicket, perhaps with the bat or a fallen helmet, he is out *hit wicket*. Outs may be accomplished in other ways, as well:

- A striker may be caught out if a ball hit into the air is cleanly fielded, in bounds, before it reaches the ground.
- Either batsman may be run out when a fielder breaks his wicket while the batsman is outside the crease—usually running between wickets. Although the wicket can be broken by hand, actually holding the ball, it is also possible to throw at the wicket and break it in that way.
- A batsman is *stumped out* if the wicket-keeper, after catching the ball, breaks the wicket while the batsman's momentum, or perhaps indecision about running, has carried him outside the crease. A batsman must ground himself or his bat (that is, touch the ground) behind the popping crease after each delivery before the ball is 'dead'.
- If the striker defends his wicket by obstructing a ball with his leg, he may be called out *leg before wicket* (LBW) by the umpire (but only if the umpire believes the ball would have hit the stumps).
- Outs of a more technical nature include hitting the ball twice, handling the ball (except when hit on the hand by the delivery) or failure to appear on the field within two minutes of the previous out.

If a batsman has failed to ground his bat beyond the popping crease, usually in the course of taking several runs, the umpire signals one short, and a run is deducted from the score.

Fielding

Fielders use no special equipment, except for the wicket-keeper, who wears shin guards and gloves. (Fielders may, however, wear protective helmets.) They disperse themselves around the field

Above: *A batsman swings at a fast delivery during a cricket match in Van Cortlandt Park, New York City.*

to locations thought most strategic by the team captain.

The description of fielding positions imagines the field to be divided in certain ways relative to the pitch and to the striker. In the most usual case, with a right-handed striker taking up a batting stance, the half of the field in front of him is the *off side,* in back of him the *leg,* or *on,* area. If a line were drawn through the striker's wicket, perpendicular to the pitch, fielders taking up position near this axis are playing *square;* if close to an imaginary line along the pitch, they are playing *fine. Short* and *silly* signify, respectively, near to the batsman and closer still. *Deep* and *long* refer to fielders close to the boundary.

Clustered around the pitch, ranging from behind the striker's wicket to moving down the pitch and beyond, are *slip, gully, point,* and *mid* fielders. Thus, to take an example, silly mid-off describes a mid fielder, on the off side, playing close to the batsman.

One odd rule, arising from an unflattering passage in cricket's history, does restrict fielding placements: No more than two fielders (not counting the wicket-keeper) are permitted 'backward' of the striker's popping crease on the leg side, that is, occupying a quadrant originating approximately abreast of the batsman and sweeping out to the boundaries in

Above: *A wicket-keeper dives to make a difficult catch. Often the outcome of a cricket match depends on the split-second reflexes of a fielder.*

the backward direction, or behind the wicket. The events leading to the adoption of the rule, and to several others concerning dangerous bowling, took place during an English 1932–33 tour of Australia. English strategy relied in part on directing their bowling at the batsman's body and concentrating fielders in the area where desperately deflected balls were apt to be caught.

Bowling

The ball is delivered with a high overarm arc, never underarm, and never with a cocked-elbow throwing motion.

A bowler begins his run-up well back of the nonstriker's wicket and releases the ball (for a right-hander) as the left foot comes down on the popping crease. The bowler's approach can take him either to left or right of the wicket—most commonly a bowler passes the wicket on the side nearest his bowling arm, also known as 'over the wicket'; from the other side it is called 'around the wicket.' The umpire must be told if he chooses to switch sides.

Normally, a bowler intends the ball to bounce several feet in front of the batsman: Any spin he has imparted to the ball will cause an irregular rebound and make the striker's job a lot more difficult. The ball need not touch the ground, however; a full toss is perfectly legal, so long as it does not arrive above hip level to the striker.

The tradition of bowling is rich in technique and in the art of disguising the delivery—it greatly resembles in these respects baseball's specialty of pitching. As with baseball, there are two basic approaches to getting the batsman out: Speed and spin. A cricket ball bowled at near 90 mph (144 km/h), and perhaps bouncing a bit wildly on its seams, is a challenge to any batsman. Slower deliveries can be equally effective when a bowler uses wrist and finger action to spin the ball as it is released. *Off-spin* rotates clockwise (causing the ball to move inward to a right-handed batsman); *leg-spin*, counterclockwise, has an opposite expected action, bouncing outward and away from a right-handed batsman. The bowling lexicon records many variations and gradations: *arm-ball, cutter, flipper, top-spinner, googly* or *wrong'un*—and, for left-handers only, the general classifications *orthodox* (off-spinner) and *unorthodox* (leg-spinner).

CROQUET

NUMBER OF PLAYERS: Two to six

EQUIPMENT: Six croquet balls and wickets, mallets, nine hoops, two stakes

DIFFICULTY: A certain amount of skill is required

DURATION: 1½ hours is average

In croquet, a popular backyard game (as long as the backyard is large), players strike their balls with mallets and send them along a prescribed path through a series of

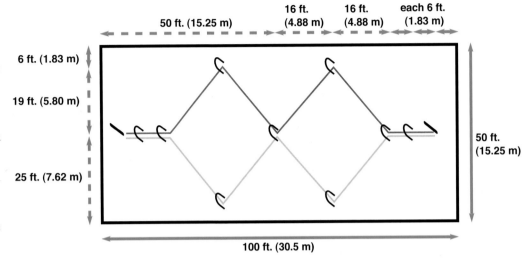

Diagram 6: A croquet court

hoops or wickets. *The first player or team to get all its balls through the course is the winner.*

Setup

Croquet is played on a rectangular grass area measuring about 100 ft. (30.5 m) x 50 ft. (15.25 m). Wickets are placed in the ground, as shown in diagram 6. Players start at one end of the court, pass their balls through the side and central wickets in the order shown in the diagram, and hit the stake at the other end of the court, the *turning stake*. They then change directions, go through the middle and the other side wickets by the prescribed route, finally hitting the stake at the origin, the *finishing stake*.

In a two- or three-player game, each person plays two balls. Teams play one ball per person, except that if an odd number wants to play teams, two members of the odd-numbered team alternate playing the same ball. The balls are grouped into 'hot' colours—red, yellow, and/or orange, and 'cool' colours—blue, black, and/or green. Opponents use balls from opposite colour groups.

Playing the Game

The order of play is decided by the flip of a coin or other random procedure. The winning player takes the blue ball,

A Victorian pastime

Although sometimes identified with the French ball-and-mallet game of Pall Mall (*Paille Maille*), which was popular in England in the early 17th century, croquet actually derives from an Irish game called Crooky. Probably a French import, it is thought to have been played in Ireland in the 1830s.

A croquet set was first marketed in England in about 1850 by Jacques and Co., who may be responsible for having Frenchified the spelling of Crooky. Croquet was an instant success and soon spread to the United States.

A genteel game that both men and women could play together, croquet lent itself to conversation and flirtation. Perhaps because of that reason, games of croquet were useful plot devices for many Victorian-era authors, including Lewis Carroll, Louisa May Alcott, Harriet Beecher Stowe, Benjamin Disraeli, Thomas Hardy, and Anthony Trollope. It was also the subject of many illustrations and paintings of the era, such as the example above.

which is always first, and the other players follow in the order their balls' colours are painted on the turning and finishing stakes. For each first shot, the ball is placed one mallet head's length behind the initial wicket. Most players grip the mallet in the same way they would grip a broom for sweeping, holding it to the left or right of the body—whichever feels more comfortable—or between the legs. Then the ball is gently tapped using only the face of the mallet; no backward swing is necessary. A turn consists of only one shot unless extra continuation shots are earned by:

- Passing through the correct wicket (one shot)
- Striking the turning stake (one shot)
- Passing through two wickets at once (two shots)
- Passing through a wicket and hitting the turning stake in one shot (two shots)
- Hitting an opposing player's ball, called *making a roquet* (two shots).

The same ball can only be roqueted once in a turn, except that a player who earns an extra shot by going through a wicket or hitting the stake may roquet the ball again.

Continuation shots cannot be held over from one turn to the next, or even accumulated during a turn: Earning a new continuation shot cancels out previously earned shots. For example, if a player strikes a second opponent's ball on his first extra shot after making a roquet, he only gets two more shots, not three.

Croquet shots and rovers

After making a roquet, the striker can use her first extra shot to make a *croquet* shot. The striker's ball is placed so that it touches the roqueted ball. Then the striker hits her ball while holding it still with her foot. Force is transferred to the roqueted ball, which is sent to another part of the court. (Balls that go out-of-bounds are placed inbounds at the point at which they went out.) The second continuation shot can then be used to further the player's own progress. A roqueted ball that passes through its next wicket as the result of a croquet shot is counted as fair, but no continuation shot is earned.

A *rover* is a ball that has passed through all the required wickets but has not yet hit the finishing stake. It remains in play and can be used to roquet the opponent's balls. Once a rover hits the finishing stake, it is out of the game, even if an opponent causes the hit.

Variations

Six-Wicket Croquet

In American Rules Six-Wicket Croquet, played in the United States, four balls (red, yellow, blue, and black) are used, so that a maximum of four players can play. If three play, two players form a team and the third player plays both the other two balls.

Courts are 105 ft. (32 m) x 84 ft. (25.6 m). The six wickets are laid out as shown in diagram 7, with only a single stake that is placed in the middle. The rules are similar to those of home croquet, but with some significant differences:

- The winner of the coin toss can decide whether to go first or second.
- The ball being struck during a croquet shot cannot be held in place.
- Only a *live ball* can be hit. A previously roqueted ball is *dead* for the striking player until her own ball has passed through a wicket, or until that opponent goes through the first repeated wicket

(that is, the seventh wicket). In the case of the latter, the striking player must announce that she is clearing the ball of its deadness—making it vulnerable once again to rocquet—at the beginning of her turn. A *deadness board*, updated after each turn, keeps track of which balls are dead to whom.

- A rover that roquets a ball can clear it of deadness only by roqueting another ball and then passing through a wicket.
- If a ball is roqueted out-of-bounds, or sent out-of-bounds with a croquet shot, the striker's turn ends, but the roqueted ball is not considered dead.

Association (International) Rules Croquet is played outside the United States. It uses the same layout as American Rules Croquet, but does not employ the concept of deadness. It also differs from backyard croquet in that:

- The wickets are called hoops and are run rather than passed through.

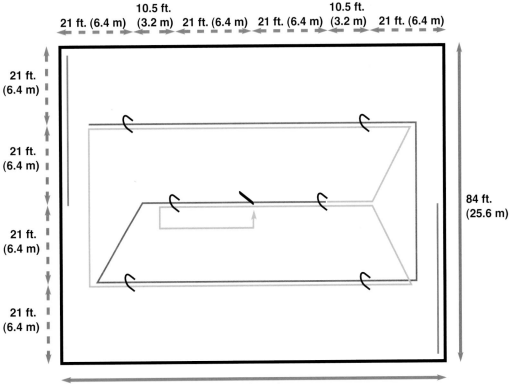

Diagram 7: Six-wicket croquet court

- The first shot of each ball must be taken from behind a balk line instead of a mallet-head's length from the first hoop (the two balk lines are included in diagram 7.)
- On a croquet shot, a striker may not put a hand or foot on her ball, and the roqueted ball must move or shake as a result of the shot; if it does not, both balls are placed where they were before the roquet, and the striker's turn ends.

FOOTBALL (AMERICAN)

NUMBER OF PLAYERS: 22, 11 on each team

EQUIPMENT: Football, protective pads, and helmets

DIFFICULTY: Physically punishing

DURATION: 1 hour of official time (usually 2 to 3 hours of real time), or shorter, by agreement

The game of football is probably the most complicated team sport in the world. Each play requires the drilled coordination of 11 team members, the oversight of up to seven refereeing officials, and compliance with the provisions of a very thick rule book. In the professional and college sport, player functions have become rather specialized, too; it is very rare, for example, that the same player would have a position on both the offensive and defensive team units, or that anyone but a full-time specialist would kick the ball for a field goal attempt.

Setup

Football is played on a rectangular field, 100 yd. (91.44 m) long, 53⅓ yd. (48.77 m) wide, with 10 yd. (9.14 m) extensions at both ends (these are the scoring areas, the *end zones*). The playing area is striped across its width every 5 yd. (4.57 m) by the *yard lines,* hence the familiar slang 'gridiron' for a football field. One-yard (0.914 m) intervals between yard lines are marked off by short graduations called *hash marks.* The two central rows of hash marks (there is also a row close to each sideline, or side boundary) define the limits within which the ball may be *spotted*, or put into play. Thus, although a play may finish close to a sideline, the ball will be moved toward the middle of the field, to a central hash mark on that side, so that the next play can start with some maneuvering room to both left and right. Hash marks create a centralized corridor of play about 6½ yd. (5.9 m) wide in professional football—somewhat wider in the collegiate version. At both ends of the field, 10 yd. (9.14 m) beyond each goal line, are H-shaped goalposts, used only for scoring field goals and touchdown conversions. (In both, the ball must pass between the uprights and above the crossbar to score.)

Position on the field is never stated in increments above 50 yd. (45.72 m); that is, the field is imagined to be divided into two halves, 50 yd. (45.72 m) 'belonging' to the team with the ball and the same amount to the team defending. If, for example, a team successfully passes the ball 20 yd. (18.28 m) starting from its 'own' 40 yd. (36.57 m) line and necessarily crossing the field's 50 yd. line, it has reached its opponents' 40 yd. line, not a 60 yd. line.

Left: Football players in action

Playing the Game

A coin toss determines who will kick off, giving initial possession to the team receiving the kick. The team with the ball tries to advance it, with running or passing plays, to the opponent's goal line and thus score a *touchdown* (6 points). After a touchdown an obligatory extra play from the 3 yd. (2.74 m) line allows the scoring team to convert (1 point) the touchdown by kicking the ball through the goalposts. In the modern game, a scoring team may opt to convert by passing or running the ball across the goal line, which scores 2 points instead of 1.

With possession of the ball a team is given four tries, or *downs*, to move the ball 10 yd. up the field. As soon as the ball is advanced at least 10 yd. (9.14 m), the count begins again, with a first down from the spot reached with the successful play. In practice, teams try to advance the ball in three downs. Because failure to move 10 yd. (9.14 m) would mean turning over possession to the other team, fourth down is routinely reserved for *punting*—kicking the ball as far as possible up the field, so the opponents will have the greatest possible distance to cover as they try, in turn, to score. In pressing circumstances, behind in score and time running out, a team may actually play the fourth down, courting the risk of turning over possession on disadvantageous terms.

Another common fourth-down situation, when a team is close to the goal line but can make no further progress, may call for a *field goal* (3 points) attempt, rather than a punt. Precisely how close depends on the judgment of the team coach and the skill of its kicker; attempts from 20 yd. (18.28 m)

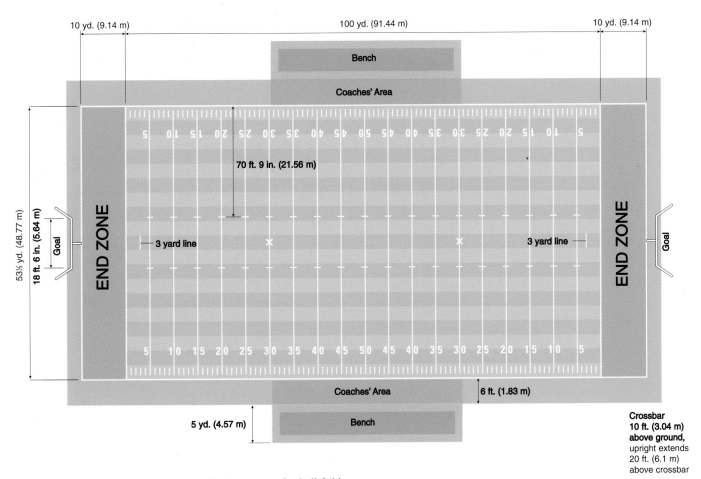

Diagram 8: The dimensions of a standard American football field

or closer are thought reasonable risks, from 30 yd. (27.43 m) or further, quite difficult. (Remember, the goalposts lie 10 yd. (9.14 m) beyond the goal lines, and the ball is hiked about 7 yd. (6.4 m) back to be set for the kicker. This makes 17 yd. (15.54 m) that must be added to the nominal 1 yd. (0.91 m) line distance of any attempt.)

If an offensive player with the ball is brought down in his own end zone, a *safety* (2 points) is awarded to the defensive team.

The team that scores must then relinquish possession, kicking off to the other team. Kickoff receivers have several options: If caught back in the end zone the ball is usually *grounded*, called a *touchback*, and brought forward automatically to the 20 yd (18.28 m) line. A receiver may

instead elect to run with the ball or to signal *fair catch*, indicating that he will not try to advance the ball and must not be tackled after making the catch. In dire straits, needing to regain possession and score, the kicking team may attempt an *onside kick*: like a normal kickoff, except the ball is deliberately sent slantwise and short, often bouncing erratically on the ground, with the hope of recovering it in the resulting scramble for possession. But the ball must travel forward at least 10 yd. (9.14 m), and be touched by a member of the receiving team before an onside recovery is possible.

Teams and positions

Both sides field 11 men. The team with possession of the ball, the *offense*, may line up behind the ball in a variety of ways, or *formations*, but with certain constraints: The *center* hunkers over the ball; on either side of him are the *guards* and *tackles*. Taken together these five players form the *offensive line*.

Just behind the center is the *quarterback*; on his signal the center will put the ball in play, 'hiking' (snapping) it back and into the quarterback's hands. The other five offensive positions are assigned according to the plan of a particular play. One, two, three, or even four players may range themselves on or near the *line of scrimmage* at various distances from the rest of the team. A player taking up station close to a tackle becomes a *tight end*; at a further distance, a *split end*; and out on the wings, a *wide receiver*. These are players who will generally run a *pattern* downfield and, if everything works well, catch a pass thrown by the quarterback.

The remaining offensive players are *backs*, in practice usually no more than two of them, who take up position behind or to one side of the quarterback. The quarterback may hand the ball off to one of them, in a running play, or they may be required to block and protect the quarterback as he searches for an open pass receiver elsewhere on the field. Most commonly these are *fullback* and *halfback* positions,

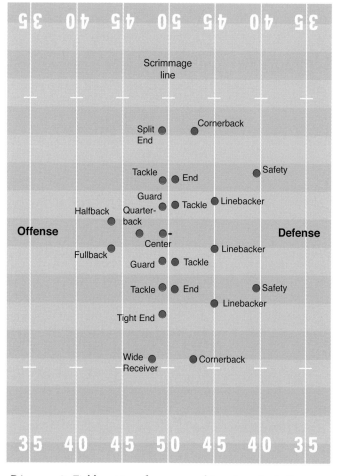

Diagram 9: Field positions for a game of American football

though other terms (such as *tailback*, *wingback*) are often used in describing nuanced formations. In today's game, with its emphasis on passing, the generalist term *running back* is often employed in the professional game. Basic backfield formations include:

- **I formation:** Two backs, in line behind the quarterback
- **Shotgun formation:** Quarterback several yards behind the line, in position to pass immediately on receiving the snap; almost always indicates a pass play
- **T formation:** Three backs, spread at the same depth behind the quarterback
- **Wishbone formation:** Two backs, behind and to either side of the quarterback.

On the *defensive* side—though many variations are possible—usually four players line up directly in front of the offense; these are the *defensive tackles* and *ends*, often referred to as the *front four*. Behind them are three *linebackers* (right, middle, and left). Two *cornerbacks* oppose offensive pass receivers, wherever these may have positioned themselves along the line of scrimmage. The remaining two defenders are safeties, the *free safety* and the *strong safety*, who range with the play, covering potential pass receivers. Collectively, the positions behind the front line are often referred to as the *defensive secondary*.

Substitutions are unlimited. Players come and go between plays as the coach deems best. Whole substitute squads may take the field for special defensive or offensive tasks, such as a kickoff, field goal attempt, or an unusual play.

Rules

The game has developed a rather large set of rules governing play and the time clock. The following are the most important.

- **Blocking:** Offensive linemen must keep their hands in front of them when blocking; defensive players have a little more freedom. No player is allowed to hold (especially by the face mask), intentionally trip, block from behind (*clipping*), or execute certain other physically

perilous plays. Pass receivers may be jostled within 5 yards of the line of scrimmage, but cannot be interfered with further downfield.

- **Eligibility:** Offensive linemen may not receive the ball; they are not 'eligible' to run a play or catch a pass. Neither may they proceed up the field more than a few yards ahead of the ball—it could unfairly complicate the defense's job of trying to cover potential pass receivers. (Any player may recover a fumbled ball and—in the pro leagues—advance it, if the play has not yet been *whistled dead*.)

Variations

Getting together to play a full-scale game of football would require a daunting amount of equipment and a special field, not to mention all the game officials. Two more convenient variations of the game are often seen in informal settings.

- **Touch football:** In this version, two hands brought into contact with a ball carrier are considered a tackle. Tackling itself is not allowed, and neither are blocks to the head or other techniques that might be dangerous in the absence of protective helmets and pads. The regular rules—as many as seem enforceable—are adopted by agreement before play begins.

- **Flag football:** This is perhaps slightly superior to touch, in that tackling is accomplished by snatching a kerchief or cloth 'flag' dangling from a ball carrier's back pocket. In this way there can be no argument about whether a two-hand touch has been made, and eligible players are easily identified by the flags in their pockets.

Above: *An American football stadium; this is the Louisiana Superdome, home of the New Orleans Saints.*

- **Formations:** The offensive team must station seven players on the line of scrimmage, and the two at either end are *eligible*. However, stationing an offensive lineman (who must wear a uniform numbered from 50 to 79) at one end does not make him eligible; the rule requires a player to be eligible by 'number and position.' Thus, five of the team members are always ineligible; the remainder are eligible unless, mistakenly, there are too many on the line of scrimmage—which will draw a penalty for an illegal formation. Because modern tactics routinely employ more pass receivers at the line than the two end positions, these other receivers take up a presnap stance 1 yd. (0.91 m) short of the line of scrimmage, upright and ready to run a pattern downfield.

- **Motion:** From the time linemen set themselves, before a play, in a *three-point crouch,* they may not move until the

ball is snapped. For the offense one eligible player at a time may be *in motion,* shifting position while the quarterback is calling out the snap count or last-minute play changes (an *audible*). Comparatively unrestricted motion is allowed the defensive secondary. Linebackers often *stunt,* changing position so as to threaten a tackle or to startle an offensive lineman into committing a motion infraction.

- **Pass interference:** From the time a pass is thrown, a pass receiver and a defender are to have equal, unobstructed opportunity to catch it—no shoving or restraint is allowed. If a defender interferes, the pass (if deemed potentially catchable) is ruled completed at the point where the foul was committed; on the offensive side, interference brings a 15 yd. (13.7 m) penalty marked from the original line of scrimmage.

- **Passing:** A forward pass must be thrown from behind the line of scrimmage; a sideways, underhand toss, called a *lateral*, may be thrown from anywhere. Without a receiver in prospect the quarterback may not throw the ball merely to avoid being tackled or to stop the clock; this is intentional grounding.

- **Penalties:** Officials throw a cloth, called a *flag*, at the spot where an infraction has occurred. Penalties assessed may be 5 yd. (4.57 m), 10 yd. (9.14 m) or 15 yd. (13.72 m)—depending on which rule has been broken—and distance is stepped off against the offending team. Some infractions require a loss of down, if the offense is at fault, as well as loss of yardage; similarly, against the defense, an automatic first down may be included as a part of some penalties. In situations, not uncommon, where a penalty would give to the guilty side a more advantageous outcome than the completed, illegal play, the other team has an option to decline the penalty. After a poor third-down play, for example, the defense would certainly decline any penalty that gave the offense a replay of the down, and thus another chance to make the necessary yardage for a first down.

- **Tackling:** Only a player in possession of the ball may be tackled, and once brought to the ground may not be piled on by late tacklers.

- **Time clock:** Football is ruled by the clock. Although only four 15-minute quarters elapse in a regulation game, that can easily amount to two and a half hours of real, spectator time. The game clock is stopped during measurements (when first-down yardage is in doubt); during injury time-outs; after a score; when the ball is run out-of-bounds; while the ball is being retrieved after an incomplete pass; at the two-minute warning point before a half expires; while the teams change ends between quarters (and during the 15-minute halftime, of course); and when a team uses a one-minute time-out— each team is allowed three of these per half. Regulations differ somewhat between the collegiate and professional leagues. In addition, every play must commence within 25 seconds (the 'play clock') of the referee's signal that the ball is spotted and ready. Otherwise, once again, the play clock is stopped, and the offense is penalized 5 yd. (4.5 m).

A few typical plays

The core of football is the planning and execution of specific plays. They are thought up by coaches, set out in diagrams, tried out in practices and, if adopted, installed in a team's playbook. Each player-position has an exact role in every play.

Offensive plays fall into two general categories, *pass* and *run* (plus option plays, which provide during the play itself possibilities for either line of attack). Running plays dominated the game in its early days, but passing has become a most popular part of the modern game. There is a need, however, to balance the two kinds of offense, for if only passes were thrown, the opponents would pull players back from the line of scrimmage—no longer worried about blocking a run—and

Above: A large set of rules govern the game of American football.

intensify their pass defense. Teams try to disguise their intentions as well, running very different plays from similar starting formations. Quarterbacks often fake handoffs or passes. A few of the more commonly seen types of play (known by name to most fans) include:

- **Blitz:** This is a defensive play (the defense has play formations, too, better to counter anticipated offensive running or pass plays). Expecting a pass, the defense rushes an extra man, usually a linebacker or safety, at the quarterback. As there may be no offensive player available to block the extra rusher, the probability is higher of sacking the quarterback, tackling him for a loss of yardage before he can throw the ball. A blitz, however, weakens the defense's effectiveness against the run, and thus must be used with good game sense and judgment.

- **Draw play:** In this play, the momentum of the charging defenders takes the play backward. The offensive line seems beaten, giving ground and collapsing into a tight knot around the quarterback, but in reality deflecting defenders to the side. A back then emerges from the tangle, often with 10 to 14 yd. (9.14 to 12.7 m) of clear field in front of him.

- **Reverse:** This has many variations. Basically the quarterback hands off to a running back who appears to be aiming at going around one end of the line—a routine play called an *end around,* or *sweep*—but who hands off in turn to a back crossing toward the other end. It may become a double reverse, with an additional crisscrossing handoff; or after one reverse the ball carrier, still behind the line of scrimmage, may stop dead and throw a pass up the field. (The thinking here is that much of the defense will have committed itself to stopping the run, and pass coverage may be minimal or confused—though professional teams are seldom dazzled by this sleight of hand.)

- **Screen pass:** This pass develops rather slowly. Several linemen break toward the sidelines and then turn

downfield, just as a pass is thrown to a back who has arrived behind them. The linemen then block ahead for the ball-carrying back.

Among the basic passing plays are *crossing, sideline, slant,* and *deep* patterns—whose names speak for themselves. In a *post pattern,* the receiver's route takes him straight upfield for 10 to 15 yd. (9 to 14 m), where he turns in at a 45-degree angle, heading more or less toward a goalpost. A pass into *the flat* is one thrown into the area behind the active defensive rushers but in front of the defensive secondary. A very quick throw, short and just over the rushers' heads, is a *dump pass*—often called as an audible when the quarterback suspects a blitz is coming.

FRISBEE®

A variety of games can be played with the Frisbee, a plastic disc approximately 12 in. (30 cm) in diameter, whose rim curves down and slightly inward. When thrown so as to set it spinning, like a flying saucer, it can soar for long distances with very little change in orientation. Although the original informal, noncompetitive rounds of catch played with the Frisbee have evolved into games with rules and winners, a tradition of gentility and sportsmanship remains important.

Variations

Double Disc Court

This game is played by two teams of two players, each team standing within its own 42 ft. (14 m) square court. One player from each team simultaneously throws a Frisbee from inside his own court into the opposing court, 51 ft. (17 m) away. Players attempt to catch and return the Frisbees, and play continues until a Frisbee is dead on the ground or one team scores a point, at which time new simultaneous serves are made. Points are scored by having a Frisbee come to rest within the opponent's court without having gone out of bounds (1 point), or by causing both discs to be touched by one or both opponents at the same time (2 points). A team also scores a point when an opponent throws a disc out-of-bounds. The first team to score at least 15 points while being 2 points ahead wins.

Guts

Two teams of one to five players face each other in lines 42 ft. (13 m) apart. The aim of the game is to score points by throwing the Frisbee in such a way that at least one member of the opposing team can reach it, but can't actually catch it cleanly. A good throw without a catch scores a point for the throwing team, and a bad throw scores a point for the receiving team. Twenty-one points wins the game.

Ultimate Frisbee

This game is played by two teams of seven on a 70 x 40 yd. (64 x 36 m) rectangular playing field with two end zones measuring 25 x 40 yd. (23 x 36 m). A point is scored when a player catches the Frisbee within the opponent's end zone. The Frisbee is advanced only by throwing it from one team member to the other; a player may not run the Frisbee downfield. Defenders try to disrupt or intercept throws, but intentional contact is not allowed. The Frisbee changes hands when it hits the ground, when a throw is intercepted, or when

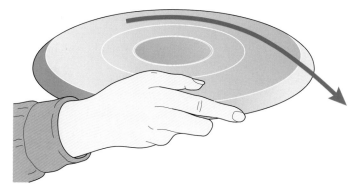

Diagram 10: Throwing a Frisbee

it is caught out-of-bounds. To win, a team must score at least 21 points with a lead of at least 2, or 25 points. A 10-minute halftime occurs the first time either team reaches 11 goals.

Other Frisbee sports

Additional popular Frisbee games and contests include:

- Individual competitions involving distance, accuracy, time aloft
- Creative movement, to music
- Discathons, in which Frisbees must be thrown in specific, obstacle-strewn flight paths around a course
- Golf tournaments, where the disc is thrown around the course
- Frisbee-catching contests for dogs.

HORSESHOE PITCHING

NUMBER OF PLAYERS: Two, or four playing as pairs

EQUIPMENT: Set of specially made horseshoes

DIFFICULTY: Needs practice

DURATION: Half an hour

A game similar to Quoits, which possibly originated in France, horseshoe pitching is a uniquely American pastime, little-known in other parts of the world. Participants toss or fling horseshoes toward metal stakes with the aim of landing a shoe to enclose the target, or at least coming to rest nearby.

Setup

Horseshoe pitching uses equipment made for the purpose, and not shoes made for horses. Regulation horseshoes are up to 7 in. (18 cm) wide and 7.6 in. (19 cm) in length, with an opening of up to 3 in. (8 cm). They can weigh as much as 2 lbs. 10 oz. (1.2 kg).

The *pitch* (playing area) is marked at either end with a 6 ft. (1.8 m) square *pitcher's box*. Within each is a pit about 3 x 6 ft.

(1 x 1.8 m) in size, filled with a shock-absorbing material such as sand. There is a stake in the middle of each pit, protruding about 15 in. (38 cm) out of the ground and inclined about 3 in. (7.5 cm) toward the other stake. Stakes are 40 ft. (12 m) apart. Players pitch from either side of one pit toward the stake in the opposite pit. The foul line for stronger players—the nearer endline of the pitcher's box—lies 37 ft. (11 m) from the target stake. For those needing a shorter throwing distance, a 27 ft. (8 m) foul line can be marked off.

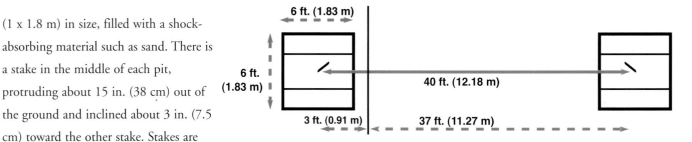

Diagram 11: A horseshoe pitch

Playing the Game

Players take turns, each time throwing two horseshoes toward the same pit, (an *inning*). To throw, grip the horseshoe in the center between thumb and outstretched fingers. All throws are taken from behind the foul line, with at least one foot on the ground. The object is to get the shoe to land around the stake (a *ringer*), or as close to it as possible. For a ringer, which scores 3 points, the horseshoe must encircle the stake so that a straight edge does not touch the stake when held against the ends of the horseshoe. If a shoe lands within 6 in. (15 cm) of the stake it is a *shoe in count*, scoring 1 point.

Sometimes a player will throw a *leaner*, a shoe that ends up leaning against the stake. Since it is within 6 in. (15 cm) of the stake, a leaner is in count and yields 1 point. A horseshoe that bounces off another surface, such as a fence or a backboard, cannot score.

In singles play, after each one has had a turn, the players walk to the opposite pit, agree on their scores, and take their next turns pitching the shoes back to the pit from which they started. The player who originally went first takes the second turn. Play is the same for teams, except that participants stay at one pit for the entire game. Scores are marked by their teammates in the opposite pit, who then take their turns, throwing the shoes back toward the first pit. Of course,

players must take care to stay well clear of the stakes when horseshoes are flying.

Scoring

There are two distinct methods of scoring horseshoes: *Cancellation* scoring and *count-all scoring*. In the first method, one player's ringer cancels out that of the other, and only one player can score in a round. Thus, if both players score the same number of ringers, neither gets points for them. If a player scores a ringer and his opponent does not, he gets both the points for the ringer and a point for any other shoe in count, but the other player scores nothing, even if he also has a shoe in count. If neither scores a ringer, the player with the closest shoe in count scores one point and the other player scores nothing. In count-all scoring, all scores by all players are counted.

Diagram 12: An example of cancellation scoring—here, the ringer scores 3 points, and the point for the leaner goes to the person who threw the ringer.

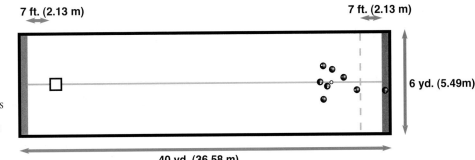

Winning the Game

The winner may be either the first player to reach an agreed number of points, usually 40, or the player who is ahead after an agreed number of innings. Players agree on the scoring and winning options they will use prior to play.

7 ft. (2.13 m)　　　　**7 ft. (2.13 m)**

6 yd. (5.49m)

40 yd. (36.58 m)

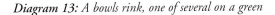

Diagram 13: A bowls rink, one of several on a green

LAWN BOWLS

NUMBER OF PLAYERS: Can be played singly, in pairs, triples, or teams

EQUIPMENT: Set of bowls, a jack, a mat

DIFFICULTY: Easy to play a basic game

DURATION: About 15 minutes

A game with a history stretching back thousands of years, lawn bowls features players bowling across grass. They try to position their balls, called bowls, *as close as possible to a smaller ball, the* jack, *while keeping their opponents' bowls away from it.*

Setup

A set of bowls comprises four matching rubber, plastic, or wooden balls about 5 in. (12.7 cm) in diameter that can weigh up to 3.5 lbs. (1.6 kg). Bowls are

Above: Lawn bowls players (usually dressed in white) must bowl with extreme accuracy.

constructed to be slightly asymmetrical, so that they *curve* or *draw* as they slow down, a matter that must be considered when taking aim. The jack is a white or yellow plastic ball, 2 in. (5 cm) in diameter and weighing 8 to 10 oz. (249 to 311 g). Players bowl from a rectangular mat measuring 35.6 in. (90 cm) x 14 in. (36 cm).

The game is played on a *lane*, or *rink*, that is 40 to 43 yd. (37 to 40 m) long and 6 to 6.3 yd. (5.5 to 5.8 m) wide. A *green* consists of several rinks, parallel to one another; the green is bounded at its ends by a ditch and slightly raised bank.

Playing the Game

The first step in a game is to bowl, or *deliver*, the jack. (Like a bowl, the jack is held in the palm of the hand and delivered underhand after a slight backward swing.) The first player (chosen by a coin flip) positions the mat on the central line of the rink with its back edge 7 ft. (2 m) from the *rear ditch*. (At the beginning of the first series of turns, the mat may be placed farther back, though not farther up.)

The jack must travel at least 70 ft. (21 m) from the mat and stay inbounds. When it comes to a stop, it is placed on the central line of the rink at the length at which it stopped. If the jack stops within 7 ft. (2 m) of the *front ditch* (at the far end), it is centered at 7 ft. (2 m). If the jack is delivered foul, the opponent redelivers it, although the first player still gets to go first.

Strategy

In singles, players take turns bowling, one shot at a time, until each has delivered all four of his bowls. This series of shots is called an *end*. Strategically, a particular shot may have one of several purposes:

- To get as close as possible to the jack
- To move the jack
- To move the opponent's bowl
- To block an opponent's bowl.

Delivered bowls are either *live* or *dead*. A dead bowl cannot participate in scoring. A bowl that travels less than 46 ft. (14 m) is dead. Also dead is a bowl that is off the rink—and it is permissible to hit an opponent's bowl off the rink. An exception to the dead bowl rule occurs if an otherwise dead bowl is the *toucher*, or the first bowl in an end that touches the jack. A toucher can be returned to play. If the jack is hit off the rink, the end must start over. In team play, turn-taking is slightly different:

- **Pairs Bowls (two per team):** Two opposing players bowl at one end, and the other two players then bowl back. Game is usually to 21 ends.
- **Triples Bowls (three per team):** Each player delivers two or three bowls in a turn. Game is usually to 18 ends.

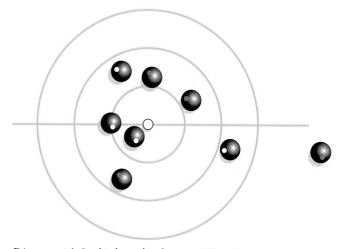

Diagram 14: In this lawn bowls game, White has won 2 points and Red none.

- **Fours Bowls (four players per team):** Each player delivers two bowls per turn. Game is usually to 21 ends.

Scoring

Only one player scores after each end: the player whose bowl is closest to the jack. This player gets a point for each bowl that is closer to the jack than any of the opponent's bowls (see diagram 14). The winner of an end delivers the jack for the next end, and also places the mat. The game continues until either 21 points or an agreed number of ends is reached.

ROUNDERS

NUMBER OF PLAYERS: Variable (from seven to ten per side works well)

EQUIPMENT: Ball, bat, field markers, such as stakes or poles

DIFFICULTY: Easy

DURATION: Variable, but usually two innings

A direct ancestor of modern baseball, rounders dates back at least to the 16th century. Nothing about the game, then or now, is really standardized, except that a batter, called the striker, attempts to hit a ball and then advance around a series of stations, or sanctuaries, until a full scoring circuit is made. Teams may be of any size, though fewer than seven may have difficulty fielding effectively, and more than ten make for a long wait between turns at bat. Where rules exist, it is sometimes stipulated that no more than nine on a team can be on the field at one time.

Setup

The playing area consists of a *castle*, where the striker stands, and four sanctuaries, 30 to 45 ft. (10 to 15 m) apart, forming a rough pentagon. Each sanctuary is a 4 to 5 ft. (1.2 to 1.5 m) high pole or stake, driven into the ground. The castle area must be large enough to accommodate the whole team, as they all stand inside it while waiting to hit or after scoring.

Within the castle, serving rather as home plate, is a 6 to 10 in. (15 to 25 cm) marker called the *castle rock.* (In a later, popular version called townball—also stickball—the castle had become the fort and was no longer an enclosure but a back boundary line drawn through the batting area.)

An acceptable ball is approximately spherical, often of leather, stuffed with whatever lends the desired play quality. A tennis ball would be suitable. Any kind of stick can serve as a bat.

Playing the Game

A striker may swing at pitches until he hits the ball—all hits outside of the castle are fair. Indeed, the striker can instruct

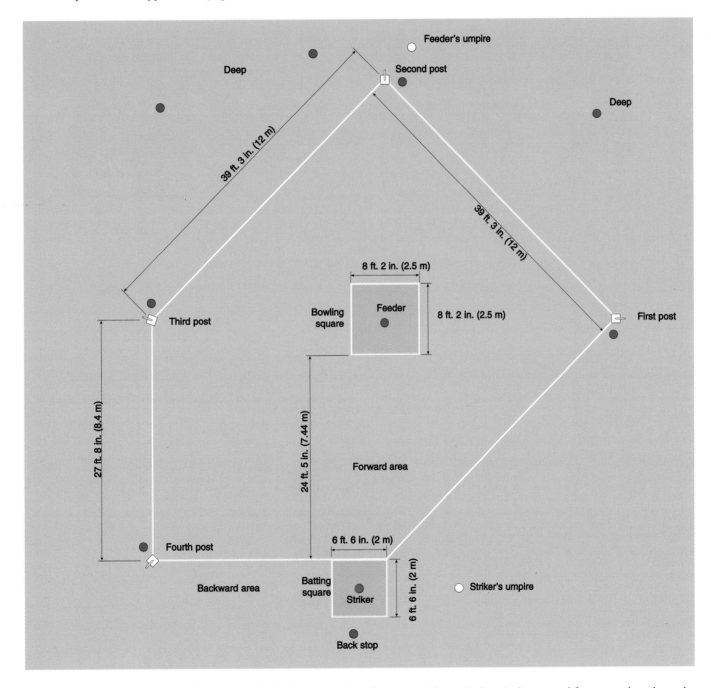

Diagram 15: A modern, regulation rounders pitch; the league game has done away with certain historical terms and features, such as the castle.

the pitcher, called the *feeder*, to serve up the ball in a certain way. After hitting, the striker runs counterclockwise toward the first sanctuary. He does not have to touch any sanctuary, but his path must take him to the outside of their array.

He can choose to grab a sanctuary if being put out seems otherwise imminent; he is safe while holding onto a sanctuary. Once a particular sanctuary is used, there can be no return to it in any subsequent running attempt. Note that any number of runners may linger at the same sanctuary at the same time. And at the beginning of each play, until the ball is hit, all runners must be holding onto a sanctuary. (In townball only one runner at a time may use the same sanctuary—called a *hideout* in this variant.)

A striker is out when the ball is caught on the fly or after one bounce. A runner is out when hit, or *plugged*, by any member of the fielding team; that is, when the fielder hits him with a thrown ball and the runner is outside of a sanctuary.

A team's innings continue until all are out. However, if all not-out players have reached sanctuary, leaving the castle empty, a fielder may then plug the castle rock, whereupon the side is out. Scoring in one run, the equivalent of a homer, is called a *rounder*. In the rare event that the last not-out striker makes two rounders in a row, his entire team is allowed back in.

Winning the Game

The game ends after any agreed upon number of innings; the team with the most runs, the highest tally, wins.

SKITTLES

NUMBER OF PLAYERS: Two teams of eight or more

EQUIPMENT: Skittles and skittle alley

DIFFICULTY: Takes practice to play well

DURATION: About 2 hours

A traditional British pub game, similar in principle to the American pastime of bowling, skittles involves rolling or throwing a ball toward an array of nine wooden pins, or skittles, and knocking down as many as possible. There are no standardized national or international rules, and several regional variations exist.

Setup

Typically, skittles are set upright in a diamond-shaped array at one end of a wooden alley about 6 ft. (1.8 m) wide and 24 ft. (7 m) long. The distance between pins is approximately 20 in. (50 cm) from center to center. The pins are about 10 in. (25 cm) high, and about 4 in. (10 cm) in diameter in the middle, tapering to 2 in. (5 cm) at the ends. Sometimes one of the pins, called the kingpin, is slightly larger than the others. If used, it is placed in the middle or at the front. Balls are wooden, from 3–7 in. (7.5–18 cm) in diameter. A tabletop form of the game uses smaller versions of this equipment.

Playing the Game

Two teams with eight or so members play a series of *legs*, usually five. In a leg each player is allowed one turn of three balls. The player throws the ball underhand down the alley from behind the throwing line so that it rolls toward the pins. After each throw any pins knocked down are removed mechanically. If, after the first or second throw, all the pins are knocked down, the entire array is reset for the next throw. Knocking down all the pins on the first throw is called a *strike*, or *flopper*. Knocking down all the pins on the second throw is called a *spare*. Play alternates between teams until each player has had a turn, completing a leg.

Scoring

Players score for each pin knocked over during a leg. The total pin score numbers for all members of the team are added up, and the team with the most wins that leg receives 1 point. (For tied leg scores, half a point is awarded to each team.) After all legs have been completed, scores for all legs are counted for each team and 2 points awarded for the highest team total.

Each team's points are then added up to determine a winner. If a kingpin is used, each player must knock over this pin before scoring any points, so that it would be possible to knock over all the other pins and still score zero for the turn.

Other scoring methods are possible, and in use, based on pin scores alone or on number of legs won.

Variation
Long Alley Skittles

As the name suggests, this game uses a 33 to 36 ft. (10 to 11 m) alley divided into a front area, which is essentially unused, and a back area that begins several feet in front of the skittles. Instead of a ball, a lozenge-shaped projectile called the *cheese* is thrown. It must not touch in the front area, and must bounce once in the back area of the alley before hitting the pins. Otherwise, pins knocked down will not count. Rather than being removed, fallen pins remain where they are during subsequent throws, although pins that topple without scoring are reset. A variation of Long Alley Skittles uses balls instead of cheeses, and employs a strip of metal called the *tin* to mark the line beyond which the ball must bounce. The noise of ball on metal provides indisputable evidence when it hits too soon.

SOCCER (FOOTBALL)

NUMBER OF PLAYERS: Two teams of 11

EQUIPMENT: Football, 2 goalposts

DIFFICULTY: Depends on the level of the players

DURATION: 90 minutes

Soccer, or football as it is known to much of the world, is the most international of all major sports and counts easily the greatest number of participants around the world. The game's rules are elegantly spare; its equipment—essentially a ball and goalposts—could not be simpler.

Setup

An official soccer field forms a rectangle, at least 100 yd. (90 m) long and 50 yd. (45 m) wide, with an allowable further 30 yd. (30 m) of length and 50 yd. (45 m) of width. (International matches are played on fields with narrower variation, in the middling range of the ordinary figures.) Boundaries at the field sides are called *touch lines* or *sidelines*; those at the rectangle's ends are *goal lines.* In addition, a line divides the field into two halves. This line has a 10 yd. (9.15 m) radius circle, the mid-circle, marked out from its middle point.

Two goalposts and a crossbar connecting them are placed at each end, centered, 8 yd. (7.32 m) apart, with clearance 8 ft. (2.44 m) from the ground to the crossbar's bottom edge. Marked out in front of each goal are two more rectangles: the *goal area* and the *penalty area.* The smaller of these, the goal area, is 20 yd. (18.32 m) wide by 6 yd. (5.5 m) deep. Enclosing the goal area, the penalty area's larger rectangle 44 yd. x 18 yd. (40.32 m x 16.5 m) is capped by an arc of 10 yd. (9.15 m) radius. The arc's center is a point, the *penalty mark,* 12 yd. (11 m) in front of the goal. In each corner of the field are a short flag post and a quarter-circle corner arc of 1 yd. (0.91 m) radius.

Soccer is also often played, informally, on available fields of any size, with roughly improvised boundaries and goals marked out with anything on hand, often clothing.

Right: Soccer is a popular sport for women in the United States.

Playing the Game

The object is to send the ball into the other team's goal while, naturally, preventing the opponents from achieving the same end. Generally the ball is moved along with the feet, though it may be trapped, redirected, or rebounded with any part of the body except for the hands and arms.

Each team comprises 11 members, of whom one is the *goalkeeper*, with special responsibilities and the ability to control the ball with his hands. The other players have complete freedom of the field. With only one exception (*offside*, explained on page 242), they may range anywhere in the course of play.

The game starts after a coin toss to determine possession; the winning team puts the ball into play from the center mark for the *kickoff* (usually just a short pass to a teammate). Play is continuous thereafter, except when interrupted by a score, foul, or ball sent out-of-bounds. A game is divided into two halves, each of 45 minutes, with a 15-minute break between them—teams switch ends for the second half.

If the ball goes out across a touchline, *into touch*, (in the U.S., the term *out-of-bounds* is used), the team that last made contact with the ball (even inadvertently) loses possession. A member of the other team throws it back in from the out-of-bounds point. Should the ball cross the goal line, other than inside the goal itself, it comes back into play by a corner kick if the attackers are given possession, or is sent upfield by a goal kick if the defenders have possession. After a score the game restarts with a kickoff from the center mark.

Following an infraction a *free kick* or *penalty kick* may be awarded to the nonoffending team. Free kicks may be *direct* or *indirect*, as explained further on.

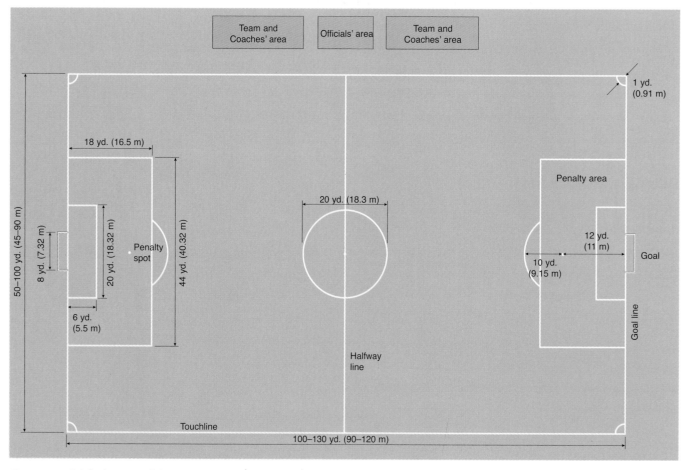

Diagram 16: The layout and dimensions of an official soccer field.

Players

Fielders—ten of the team's 11—have a loose positional arrangement. *Fullbacks* tend to remain at the rear of play and, on defense, are nearest the goalkeeper. A *sweeper* is a fullback in central position behind the other fielders; a fullback in front of the sweeper is a *stopper. Midfielders,* and ahead of them *forwards*, complete the array. Fielders who play principally out to the sides may be termed *wings*; those whose chief team role is to get into position to make a goal are usually called *strikers.*

The player positioning adopted by a team is called a *formation.* For example, electing to keep three players at the rear (fullbacks), five in mid-position, and two forward makes up a 3-5-2 formation. In a 4-4-2 formation there is one more fullback and one less midfielder. Formations evolve, however, in the course of play. Fielders constantly pass among themselves—out to the wings, back to the middle, sometimes to the rear—trying to keep the ball moving ahead and the opponents off balance. As one fielder is drawn away by opportunity, a rehearsed play, or defensive need, another generally fills in at that part of the field. The team, thus, is said to maintain its shape.

The goalkeeper, the very last line of defense, may control the ball with his hands within his own penalty area, but not outside those bounds. After a save, the 'goalie' usually chooses either to throw the ball toward a particular fielder or kick it well upfield.

Above: A goalkeeper narrowly misses a save during a soccer game.

Free kicks and penalty kicks

A direct free kick is awarded for such infractions as tripping, charging, kicking, pushing, holding, or jumping at an opponent; fouls similarly treated include illegal tackling (in trying to take possession, contacting an opponent before the ball) and deliberately handling the ball. Misconduct such as trying to strike or spit at an opponent also results in a direct free kick (and often the offender is sent off the field, as well).

An indirect free kick will follow an offside foul, and certain goalkeeper fouls, such as holding the ball for more than six seconds or handling it again before it has touched another player. But some more general misdemeanors will incur the penalty of a free kick for the opposing side, including dangerous play or impeding the progress of an opponent— these determinations are very much within the discretion of the referee.

When an infraction occurs, the referee positions the ball at the point of the foul. A direct free kick may enter the goal and score; an indirect free kick must touch another player before scoring is possible—and in neither case may the kicker contact the ball again until it has touched another player. In the event a direct free kick is taken within scoring range, the defending team generally puts its players into a tight obstructive line, called a *wall*, between the kicker and goal. Opponents in all cases must station themselves at least 30 ft. (10 m) from the ball until play restarts.

A penalty kick arises from the same fouls as a direct free kick but committed within the penalty area. The ball is spotted on the penalty mark and no players intervene between the kicker and goalkeeper. This is an especially perilous situation for the defending team, as scoring chances are high.

Offside

An attacking player, while in the defenders' half of the field, must keep two opponents (usually the goalkeeper plus the nearest fullback) between himself and the goal, unless the ball has preceded him into such a position. Merely occupying an offside position—with fewer than two opponents to the front—does not constitute an offense; it becomes an infraction when a player takes part in play or gains advantage while offside. The offense results in an indirect free kick for the defending team. No offside foul is committed if a player receives the ball from a corner kick, goal kick, or throw-in, described below.

Out of play and scoring

The ball is out, across a touchline (sideline in the U.S.) or goal line, only when its whole circumference has crossed beyond a boundary line; it may, for example, rest just beyond the line, but is not out if some part of it is still within bounds. Likewise, in scoring, the ball must travel completely across the line.

Corner kicks; goal kicks; throw-ins

A *corner kick*—by the attacking team after the ball crosses the

goal line off a defender—is one of soccer's more exciting plays. From the corner arc, the kicker attempts to send the ball curving inwardly toward the goal and into a mass of attackers and defenders crowding the goal area. A lancing *header*—when the player directs the ball with his head—or short kick into the goal may come from any angle, making the goalkeeper's task that much harder.

When the ball has gone out over the goal line off an attacker, a defender (usually the goalkeeper) places the ball anywhere within the goal area and kicks it back into play. This is known as a *goal kick*.

Diagram 17: Player positions in soccer

A *throw-in*, bringing the ball back into play across a touch line, is accomplished by throwing with both arms from over the head while facing the field of play; both feet must be partially on or behind the touchline.

Substitutions

When substituting, the referee must be informed beforehand. The substitute enters the field at the half line during a time-out.

Resolving ties

Soccer matches last 90 minutes, plus any time added on by the referees to make up for time lost in stoppages due to injuries, substitutions, wasted time, and other causes. If a match is tied after all official time has elapsed, rules allow a decision to be reached by adding up to two short periods to the game, in which the first team to score—the golden goal—wins.

If, at the end of extra periods, the game is still tied, the outcome is determined by kicks from the penalty mark 12 yd. (11 m) from the goal mouth. In this procedure players of each team take kicks at the goal, opposed only by the goalkeeper. The first team to kick makes five attempts, each by a different player; the second team does the same. Kicks continue, by groups of ten, with kickers rotating through the entire on-field team in the same order, until one team has finally outscored the other.

Yellow card, red card: Serious offenses

A player may be *cautioned*, shown the *yellow card,* for unsporting behavior, persistent rules violations, delaying restart of the game, or not maintaining the required distance from a free kick or corner kick. Entering or leaving the field without the referee's permission is a cautionable offense. Open disapproval of a referee's actions will almost certainly bring out the yellow card, as well.

Once cautioned, a second yellow card offense results in being shown the *red card* and sent off the field and out of the match. But a player may be sent off without a caution for shocking misconduct, including serious foul play, violence, abusive language, or spitting at any person. Illegal interference to prevent a clear and likely score (for example, deliberately handling the ball to block a certain goal) may also result in being sent off.

SOFTBALL

NUMBER OF PLAYERS: Usually ten per team

EQUIPMENT: Ball, bat, gloves

DIFFICULTY: Easier than baseball

DURATION: 60 to 90 minutes

Baseball is a game of high velocity, played with a very hard ball; a less intimidating version, softball, is often the recreational or schoolyard choice. The ball is somewhat softer, as its names implies, but also larger (at about 12 in. [30 cm] in circumference) and less dense. It loses speed quickly when batted or thrown.

Playing the Game

The basic rules and layout for softball remain the same as for baseball (see page 211), though the diamond is generally smaller: 60 ft. (18.29 m) between bases, with the pitcher 43 to 46 ft. (13.11 to 14.02 m) from home plate. The ball is always pitched underhand, but there are two distinct forms of the game:

- **Slow pitch:** The pitcher floats the ball in a high arc to the plate. Everyone has an excellent chance of hitting; the action really is in the fielding and running.
- **Fast pitch:** The ball arrives at high speed, often delivered with a windmilling motion. Batting can be as challenging as in hardball (baseball).

Traditionally, softball teams use a tenth player—between first and second base—but local leagues make their own rules

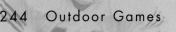

concerning team size. There are differences in equipment, too. Aluminum bats are nearly universal in softball, and softball gloves, with larger pockets, can be used.

A softball game may run a full nine innings, or it may, by agreement, end in fewer. Time limits are often used, as well. One frequently adopted rule awards the game to a team that has built a daunting lead—say, 10 or 15 runs—within a specified number of innings.

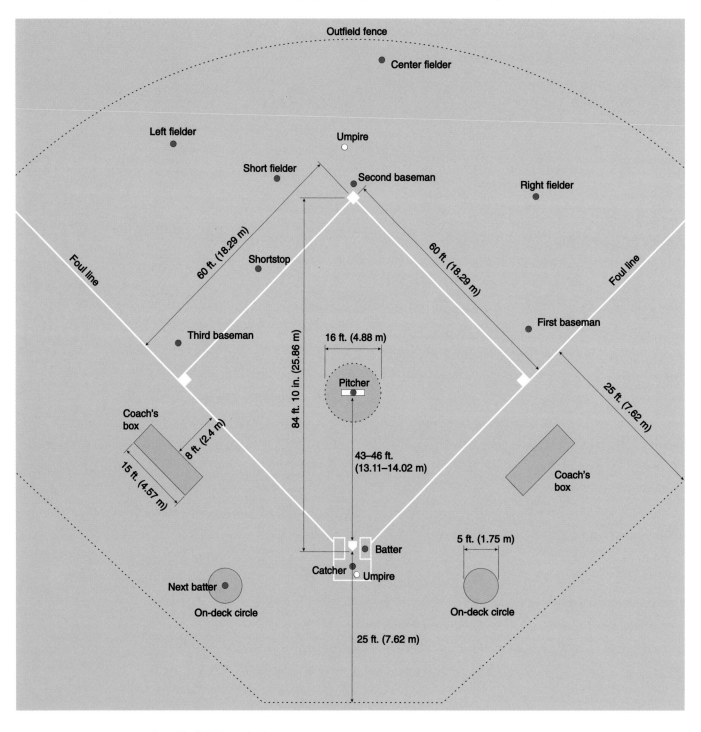

Diagram 18: Dimensions of a softball field, with player positions

VOLLEYBALL

NUMBER OF PLAYERS: Between two and six

EQUIPMENT: Volleyball and net

DIFFICULTY: Depends on the level of the players

DURATION: An average match lasts 1½ hours

Volleyball is essentially a game of rebound and reaction, with the object of keeping the ball aloft. The game has changed dramatically from the indoor recreation that was designed, in 1895, to keep women active in Mount Holyoke, Massachusetts. It has been an Olympic sport since its inclusion in 1964 at the Tokyo Games. Widely enjoyed versions (for as few as two players) are now played on beaches, lawns, indoor and outdoor courts, and by men's, women's, and mixed teams, both professional and amateur.

Setup

The standard indoor court measures 59 ft. x 29 ft. 6 in. (18 x 9 m), divided in half at the middle line, providing two team courts measuring 29 ft. 6 in. x 29 ft. 6 in. (9 m x 9 m). Each side of the court is marked into two unequal zones by an *attack line* 9 ft 10 in. (3 m) from the net, dividing it into a frontcourt and backcourt. A *free zone* outside the court is also recommended, allowing players to follow the ball for continuation of play. As balls in play often soar high above the court, it is best that the area above the court be free of obstruction to a height of at least 23 ft. (7 m).

The net is 39 in. (1 m) wide and 29 ft. (9 m) long, stretched horizontally over the central line; top and bottom are fastened tightly to the posts at each end. The top of the net is set at a height of almost 8 ft. (2.4 m) for men and just below 7 ft. 5 in. (2.2 m) for women; it may vary, however, for mixed teams and by age groups.

The ball

The ball is spherical and should be very elastic; it is made of 12 or more pieces of uniform flexible leather, or leatherlike material, with a rubber interior bladder. Size ranges between 25½ in. (65 cm) and 27 in. (69 cm) in circumference, weighing 9 oz. (250 g) to 10 oz. (280 g), with an interior pressure of around 4 lb. (2 kg) per square inch. Depending on how the ball is hit relative to its center of gravity, it will carry *top*, *side*, or *underspin*, which will affect its flight path.

Playing the Game

The object in volleyball is to keep the ball aloft. Should it drop onto the court, a point is won, or service passes from one team to the other—depending upon whose court the ball has dropped into, and whether it is in or out-of-bounds. The tricky part is that, while in play, the ball may not be thrown, held, cradled, or arrested in any way; it may be batted, struck, or deflected with any part of the arms and hands, but cannot be legally handled in any other way. In the course of playing the ball as it comes over the net a team is allowed three *contacts* with the ball, or three *hits*, but no player may contact it twice in a row. (A block, discussed below, does not count as a contact.)

The ball is *served* into play from behind the backcourt boundary so that, if unimpeded by the other team, it would land inbounds in the opponents' court. If it is served long or wide, or into the net, the ball and service are lost to the other team. A good serve, though, must be controlled and returned, and that often happens in a three-stage response.

First, a player in the serve's vicinity receives, trying to take velocity off the ball and put it up so that the next player, a *setter*, can get to it easily. Next, the setter attempts to direct the ball, now with more accuracy and control, to a point near the net where, finally, an *attacker* will drive it back over the net. The other team must then try, in no more than three contacts, to do the same.

Of course in actual play, tactics must often be improvised. The ball may be difficult to handle, so that the receiver is lucky just to keep it in the air; no proper set is possible and

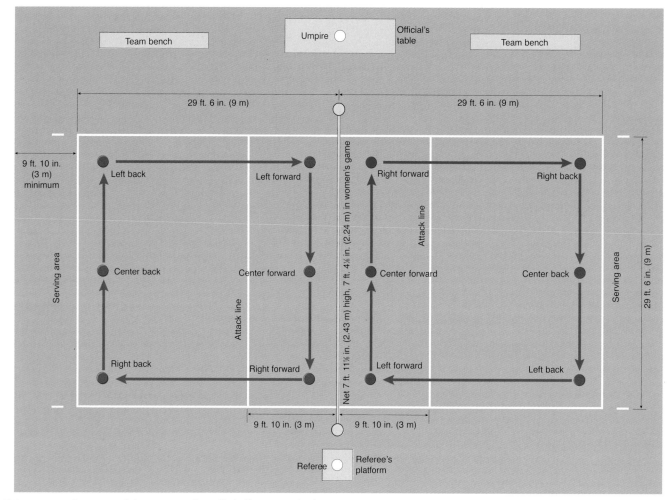

Diagram 19: Layout and dimensions of a volleyball court with player positions

players scramble simply to get it back over the net. Or the ball might be blocked right at the net—often an effective play—and further handling is unnecessary. Good strategy mixes surprise, misdirection, and power to force errors upon the opposition.

Scoring

Points are scored only by the team with *service*; service passes to the opposition when an error is committed by the serving team *(side out)*, but no point is awarded. With the service, a point is gained when the nonserving team allows the ball to drop into its court or causes it to land out-of-bounds. Points are scored, too, if the ball is caught or thrown, if more than three hits occur, or if a player uses any

structure, object, or teammate in order to reach the ball.

With 15 points, and ahead by 2, a team wins. Recently, rally scoring to 30 points has been admitted to the game (every error results in a point, not just when serving, and the first team to 30 wins). Typically, volleyball is played as a match: best two out of three, or three out of five games.

Players

The six members of a team position themselves on the court in two ranks: three in the frontcourt, three in the backcourt. The right-most backcourt player serves, if the team has the service, and remains server until the team commits an error, whereupon service passes over to the opponents. When they have next won the serve, players all rotate one place clockwise (counterclockwise in the U.K.), so that a new player is in the serving position.

After the ball is served, players are not restricted in any way to an area of their court. However, a recent change in the game of volleyball allows one player to be designated a *libero*. The libero is restricted to playing back row and cannot attack the ball from anywhere on the court if the ball is above the height of the net. The libero can replace any player in the backcourt position but is not allowed to serve or block.

Serve

The server may stand anywhere outside the team's court at the end line. An error is committed if the server steps on the end line before the ball is contacted. One of the recent changes in volleyball allows a ball that hits the net and continues into the other court to be a legal serve. There are many types of serve, but the ball must always be hit with one hand or any part of one arm. Styles include *underhand, overhand, sidearm,* and *jump* serves.

Attack

The *spike* is the most powerful and exciting method of attack. It is a hard downward slam over the net at a sharp angle. For the spike to work effectively, the spiker must also be able to vary the attack with other shots and use as much deception as possible, so that the opposing team cannot predict what style of hit will be used. Other kinds of hit include *off-speed shots, tips, shoves,* and *wipe-offs* (deliberately into a blocker's hands so as to make the ball fly out-of-bounds).

Defending

While one team is attacking, the other team is mounting a defense. There are two parts: *blocking* and *floor defense.* In blocking, the ball is intercepted before, during, or immediately after it crosses the net. The blockers line up across from the attacker and, at precisely the right moment, jump and reach over the net to stop or change the ball's flight. Their presence shields a portion of their own court and may also have the advantageous effect of intimidating the attacker.

Sometimes in the course of attacking and blocking, players of opposing teams may cause the ball to rest on top of the net by simultaneous contact. This is called a *joust* and not a fault; the ball continues in play or is replayed, depending on the referee's decision. Needless to say, to block effectively, a player must have a good sense of timing and try with some success to anticipate the intentions of an attacker.

As the block forms up at the net, the remainder of the team is distributed around the court, charged with the responsibility of keeping the ball off the floor and transforming the action back to offense. Their positioning depends on many factors, including strategy, location of the block, and their own agility and skill. Most unblocked balls are received with the forearm pass from a low body position, often called *digging.* In the quick movements of defense two or more teammates may touch the ball simultaneously, which is deemed a single contact.

Some basic techniques

- **Setting:** The set is usually the second contact with the ball; it will determine timing and location of the attack. A set is often executed above the head with the fingertips of both hands. However, it can also be done with the fingertips of one hand, or with a forearm pass. Contact should occur in a smooth, gentle action, the ball coming into the hands without being caught.

- **Passing:** The forearm pass is most useful for balls arriving below chest level: Hands together, palms upward, contact is made several inches above the wrists with the soft inside part of the forearms. The ball can also be directed with an overhead finger pass, similar to a set, or through contact with one arm in a clean continuous motion. It is important to remember that the ball cannot be caught or thrown.

Index

Page numbers in *italics* refer to diagrams or illustrations; see also specialized indexes on pages 253–256

A

Aces in the Pot 20
Agnes 105–6, *106*
All Fives (Muggins) *28*, 29–30
Alphabet Race 183
  see also Scrabble
Alquerque *62*, *62*, 63
Alsace 87
American Football *see* Football
  (American)
American Hearts 93
Anagrams 183–4
Analogies 194
Apple Ducking 132–3
Apples to Apples® 14
Arabic civilizations 63
Association 159
Astroturf® 213
Australia 88

B

Babe Ruth *216*
Back-to-Back Race 150
Backgammon 38–40
bearing off *39*, 39
  starting position *38*
Badminton *210*, 210–11
  court *210*
  playing the game 211
  scoring 210–11
  setup 210–11
Balloon Race 150, *150*
Baseball 211–17, *214*
  batting 215
  field *212*
  history 216
  home plate *213*
  pitching *215*, 215–16

playing the game 213
setup 211–13
state of the game 213
strategy 216–17
see also Rounders; Softball
Battleship *184*, 184–5
Beetle 140
Beggar my Neighbor 110, *110*
Bergen *30*, 30–1
Billiards, Carom *169*, 169–70
Binokel 94
Black Lady 93
Black Maria *92*, 93
Blackjack (Twenty-One) 119–22
  playing the game 119–22
  setup 119
  special player options 121–2
  strategy 122
Blind Hughie *31*, 31
Blindman's Bluff 132
Block Dominoes 26, 27
Blow Ball 140
Bobbing for Apples (Apple Ducking)
  132–3
Bonaparte, Napoleon 100
Botticelli 159–60
Bowls *see* Lawn Bowls
  The Box 159–60
Boxes 185, *185*
  see also Sprouts
Breton, André 187
Bridge *see* Contract Bridge
Bridge the Word 185–6
Bulldog 202–3
Buzz and Buzz-Fizz 154

C

Canadian Checkers 49–50, *50*
Canasta 74–6
  melds and canastas *74*
  playing the game 74–5
  scoring 75–6

winning the game 76
Canoga 22
Card games 73, 87, 100
Carom Billiards *169*, 169–70
Cartwright, Alexander 211
Casino 76–8
  builds *77*, 77
  capturing *76*, 76–7
  playing the game 76–7
  scoring 78
  sweeps *76*, 77
Castro, Fidel 15
Cat and Mouse 201
Categories 186, *186*
Cat's Cradle 170–1, *171*
Central America 211
Century Game 186–7
Charades 142
Cheat (I Doubt It) 110–11
Checkers (Draughts) 46–50
  eleven-man ballot 47
  endgame *46*
  go-as-you-please (GAYP) 47
  greatest player 49, *49*
  sacrifice play *46*
  starting position *46*
Chess 50–8
  capturing 53
  castling 53
  checkmate *54*, 54
  the *fork* *55*, 56
  history of 63
  moves *52*, 53, *53*
  notation 57
  pieces *51*, 51–2
  the *pin* *55*, 56
  playing the game 51–2
  scoring 52
  setup 50–1
  the *skewer* *55*, 56
  special moves 53
  starting position *51*

strategy 55–6
tactics and combinations 55–6
variations 56–8
Chicago Poker 127
Children's Parties 135
China 32, 33, 63
Chinese Checkers *43*, 43–4
Chinese chess *see* Xiangqi
Chinese Jump Rope 205
Chinese Table Tennis 179
Chinook computer program *49*
Chutes and Ladders® (Snakes and
	Ladders) *40*, 40
Clapping Games 201
Clock Patience 101, *101*
Clue® (Cluedo®) 14–15
Coffee Pot 194
Computer Solitaire 105
Concentration (Pelmanism) *111*,
	111–12
Consequences 187–8
Contract Bridge 78–83
	bidding 79, 80–2
	evolution of 81
	finessing *80*, 80
	rank of suits *78*
	responses 81–2
	scoring 78–9, 82–3
	setup 78
	slams 82, 83
	strategy 79–80
Cooperstown 211
Cows and Leopards *41*, 41–2
Crazy Eights 84
Cribbage 84–6
	board *84*, 85
	playing the game 84–5
	scoring 85–6
	three or four players 86
Cricket 217–23
	batsman *217*
	bowling 222–3
	fielding *218*, 220–2, *222*
	getting out 220
	special terms 220

pitch dimensions *219*
playing the game 218–19
scoring 219–20
setup 218
Crooky 224
Croquet 223–6, *224*
	court *223*
	playing the game 223–5
	setup 223
	six-wicket court *225*
	variations 225–6
Cross Dominoes *27*
Crossword 188, *188*
Cuba 15
Cyprus 27, *27*

D
Darrow, Charles 15
Darts *171*, 171–2
Dead Lions 133
Deep Blue computer program 54
Definitions 160
Dice Games 20
Dictionary Game 194–5
Dinner Party Murder Mystery 154–5
Do You Love Your Neighbor? 147
Dodge Ball 201–2
	Free zone dodge ball *201*
	Train dodge ball *202*
Dominoes *24*, *25*, 25–9
	history of 32
	playing the game 25
	scoring 25–6
	setup 25
	strategy 26
	variations 26–9
Donkey 112
Double Cross Dominoes 27, *27*
Double Dutch Jump Rope 205–6
Double Nine Cross Dominoes 27, *28*
Doubleday, Abner 211
Draughts *see* Checkers
Draw Poker 126
Drop Dead 20
Dumb Crambo 140–1

E
Earl of Coventry 116
Earth, Water, Air 160
Egg and Spoon Race *150*, 150–1
Egypt 63, 207
Euchre 86–8
	dealing 87
	playing the game 87–8
	scoring 88, *88*
Exchange Tag 202–3

F
Farmer in the Dell 133–4
Feather 147
Fingers 165
Fischer, Bobby 57
Five Card Stud Poker 127, *128*
Five Hundred 88–90
	playing the game 89
	scoring 89–90
	setup 88–9
	variations 90
Five of a Kind 161
Five Stones *172*, 172–3
	see also Jacks
Five Up 31–3, *32*
Follow the Leader (outdoor game) 203
Follow the Leader (parlor game) 147
Foosball® (Table Football) *173*, 173–5
	playing the game 174
	roots of the game 174
	setup 173
Football *see* Soccer (Football)
Football (American) *226*, 226–32
	field *227*
	playing the game 227–32
	rules 229–31
	setup 226
	teams and positions 228–9
	typical plays 231–2
	variations 229
Forbidden Words 195
The Four Corners *102*, 102–3
Four Field Kono 62
	starting position *62*

Fox and Geese 40–2, *41*
Fox and Geese Solitaire 42
Fox and Rabbit 203
France 63, 76, 106, 120
Free Cell 105
Frisbee® 232–3, *233*

G
The Game 141–2
  signals *141, 142*
  see also Pictures
game theory 16
General 23
German Checkers 48
Germany 174
Ghosts 195–6
Gin Rummy 90–2
  playing the game 91
  scoring 91, *91*
  sequence *91*
  set *91*
  setup 91
  variations 91–2
Go 62–6
  atari *64*, 65, *65*
  board and stones *63*
  capturing territory *63*
  dead or alive *64*, 65
  Ko *65*, 66
  legal and illegal moves *64*, *65*, *66*
  liberties *63*, 65
  playing the game 63–4
  winning the game 64
Go Boom 112–13, *113*
Go Fish *113*, 113
Good Morning, Madam 155, *156*
Grandfather's Clock *103*, 103–4, *104*
Guess the Smell 134
Guggenheim (Scattergories®) 188,
  188–9

H
Halma *42*, 42–4
Hangman 165
Hare and Hounds 203

Hasegawa, Goro 69
Headlines 189
Hearts 92–3
Hearts Due 21
Hein, Piet 67
Help Your Neighbor 21
Hex *66*, 66–7
Hide and Seek 203–4
Hollywood 91–2
Homeward Bound 44
Hop 69
Hop Ching Checkers 43
Hopscotch 204, *204*
Horseshoe *67*, 67–8
Horseshoe Pitching 233–5
  pitch *234*
  playing the game 234
  scoring 234, *234*
  setup 233–4
Hot and Cold 147
How Many Words? 161

I
I Doubt It 110–11
I Have Never 156
I Love My Love 196
I Packed My Bag 197
I Spy 161
In the Manner of the Word 142–3
Indian Poker 127
International Checkers 49
Inuit 170
Italian Checkers 47–8

J
Jacks 175–6
Japan 69, 211
Japanese Chess 58–9
Jokers 87
Juggling 206–7
Jump Rope (Skipping) *204*, 204–6
  tricks and rhymes 206

K
Kasparov, Gary 54

Klondike 104–6
  layout *104, 105*
  playing the game 104–5
  setup 104
  strategy 105
  variations 105–6
Kramnik, Vladimir 54
Kriegspiel 56

L
La Belle Lucie 106
Lamb, Charles 170
Lawn Bowls 235–6
  playing the game 235–6
  rink *235*
  scoring *236*
  setup 235
  strategy 236
Leapfrog 207, *207*
Legs 189–90
License Plates 161–2
Lookabout 148
Losing Checkers 47
Lotto 190
Lovely Lucy 106–7
  layout *106, 107*
Low-Hole Card Wild Poker 127
Ludo 44, *44*

M
Magie, Elizabeth 15
Mah-Jongg 33–6
  flowers and seasons 36
  opening the wall *35*
  tiles *34*
Maltese Cross Dominoes *28*, 28
Mancala Games 63
Marbles 176–7
  Ring Taw *177*
  shooting the ring *176*
Maris, Roger 216
Matador *28*, 28–9
Matchbox Race 134
Michigan (Newmarket) 122–3
Microsoft Solitaire 105

Middle Ages 76, 207
Mill (Nine Men's Morris) 63, *68*, 68–9
Monopoly® 15–16
Monte Carlo 107–8, *108*
Mother Goose rhymes 137
Mount Holyoke, Massachusetts 245
Muggins *see* All Fives
Mummies 148
Murder in the Dark 143
Murder Mystery 154–5
Musical Chairs 134–5
My Ship Sails 114

N

Navajo 170
Newmarket 122–3
Nine Men's Morris 63, *68*, 68–9
Ninety-One 108, *108*
No Peek Poker 127
Nok Hockey® 177
Noughts and Crosses 165
Nursery Rhymes 137

O

Old Maid 114
Olympic Sports 245
Oranges and Lemons 135–6
Othello® (Reversi®) *69*, 69–70
Outlines 165
Owari 63, *70*, 70–1, *71*

P

Pachesi (*also* Patchesi, Parcheesi) 44
Pall Mall 224
Parlor Games 148
Pascal, Blaise 16
Pass the Balloon 136
Pass the Package 136
Pass the Slipper 148
Patience 100–8
Pelmanism *111*, 111–12
Pickup Sticks 177–8
Pictionary® 143–4
Pictures *190*, 190–1
  see also The Game

Pig 21–2
Pig (card game) 112
Piggyback Race 151
Ping-Pong® *see* Table Tennis
Pinochle 93–7
  melding rules 96, *96*
  melds and scoring *94*, 95–6
  playing the game 94–5
  scoring *94*
  three of four players 96–7
Poetry Game 191
Poker *123*, 123–9
  betting 125–6
  hands *124*, *125*, *128*
  playing the game 126
  setup 124
  strategy 129
  terminology 129
  variations 126–9
Polish Checkers 49, *50*
Pontoon 120
  see also Blackjack
Pool Checkers 48
Potato Race 151
Pouilleux, Le 114
J. Pressman & Co. 43
probability 16
Progressive Chess 56

Q

Quebec 49
Quizzes 191
Quoits 233

R

Random Chess *57*, 57–8
Relay Races 151–2
Reversi® *see* Othello®
Ring-Around-the-Rosy (Ring-a-Ring-a-Roses) 136–7
Risk® 16–17
Rock, Paper, Scissors 165
Roll Your Own Poker 127
Rolling Stone 114–15
Roman Dice 20

Round Dozen 22
Rounders 236–8
  pitch *237*
  playing the game 237–8
  setup 236–7
  see also Baseball; Softball
Rubik's Cube® 162
Russian Checkers (Shaski) 48–9

S

Sack Race 152, *152*
Sardines 144
Scattergories® *188*, 188–9
Scissors, Paper, Stone 165
Scopa 97, *97*
Scrabble® 17–18
  see also Alphabet Race
Secret Mission Risk 17
Seven-Card Stud Poker 127–8
  strategy 129
Sevens 207–8
Seventeen Geese 41
Shamrocks 107
Shogi (Japanese Chess) 58–9
  pieces *58*
  starting position *58*
Short Stories 191–2
Shut the Box *22*, 22
Simon Says 137
Skipping *204*, 204–6
  tricks and rhymes 206
Skittles 238–9
Slapjack 115
Slobberhannes 98
Snakes and Ladders *see* Chutes and Ladders®
Snap 115–16
Snip Snap Snorem 116
Soccer (Football) *239*, 239–43
  field *240*
  free kicks and penalties 242–3
  goalkeeper *242*
  players 241, *242*
  playing the game 240
  setup 239

Softball 243–4
  field *234*
  see also Baseball; Rounders
Solitaire 100–8
Soma Cube 67
South America 74, 211
Spain 90
Spanish Checkers 48
Speed *116*, 116–17, 116–17
Spelling Round 197
Spit (Speed) *116*, 116–17
Spoof 165
Spot Hearts *93*, 93
Sprouts 192
  see also Boxes
Squeak, Piggy, Squeak! 137–8
Sri Lanka 41
Stairway 192
Statues 138
Stewart, Ian 16
String weaving *170*
Stud Poker 127–8

T
Table Football *see* Foosball (Table
  Football)
Table Tennis (Ping Pong®) 178–9
  pencil grip *178*
  table *178*
Taboo 198
Tag 202–3
Telephone 138
Texas Hold 'Em Poker 129
Three-Legged Race 152
Tic-Tac-Toe (Noughts and Crosses)
  166
Tiddlywinks 179–81
  scoring 181
  setup 179–80
  shots *181*
  starting position *180*
  words 180
Tinsley, Marion *49*
Transformation 192
Treasure Hunt 208

Trefoil 107
Trivial Pursuit® 18
Trumps 81
Tug of War 208
Turkish Checkers 50, *50*
Twenty-One *see* Blackjack
Twenty Questions 163
Twister® 144–5

U
United Kingdom 148, *224*
United States 148, 211, 233
U.S. Table Soccer Association 174
U.S. Playing Card Company 88

V
Victorian pastimes 148, *224*
Vingt-et-Un 120
Volleyball 245–7
  court *246*
  playing the game 245–6
  scoring 246
  setup 245

W
War 117
Watch Solitaire 101
Waterman, Lewis 69
What's on the Tray? 138
Wheelbarrow Race 152
Whist 81, 98–9
  English rules *98*, 99
  establishing a suit 99, *99*
  leading 99
  scoring 99
Who Am I? 198
Winking 145
Wolf and Goats *41*, 42

X
Xiangqi (Chinese Chess) 59–60
  pieces *60*
  starting position *60*

Y
Yacht 22–3
Yahtzee 22–3

Games for One Person

Cat's Cradle 170–1
Clock Patience 101
The Four Corners 102–3
Grandfather's Clock 103–4
Jacks 175–6

Juggling 206–7
Jump Rope (Skipping) 204–5
Klondike 104–6
Lovely Lucy 106–7
Monte Carlo 107–8

Ninety-One 108
Rubik's Cube® 162
Sevens 207–8
Skipping 204–5

Games for Two People

Aces in the Pot 20
All Fives (Muggins) 29–30
Alphabet Race 183
Alquerque 62
Anagrams 183–4
Backgammon 38–40
Badminton 210–11
Battleship 184–5
Beggar my Neighbor 110
Bergen 30–1
Blackjack (Twenty-One) 119–22
Blind Hughie 31
Boxes 185
Carom Billiards 169–70
Casino 76–8
Century Game 186–7
Cheat (I Doubt It) 110–11
Checkers (Draughts) 46–50
Chess 50–8
Chinese Checkers 43–4
Chinese Chess (Xiangqi) 59–60
Chutes and Ladders® (Snakes and
   Ladders) 40
Clapping Games 201
Concentration (Pelmanism) 111–12
Consequences 187–8
Crazy Eights 84
Cribbage 84–6
Croquet 223–6
Crossword 188

Darts 171–2
Dominoes 25–9
Draughts (Checkers) 46–50
Drop Dead 20
Earl of Coventry (Snip Snap Snorem)
   116
Fingers 165
Five Hundred 88–90
Fivestones 172–3
Foosball® (Table football) 173–5
Forbidden Words 195
Four Field Kono 62
Fox and Geese 40–2
Gin Rummy 90–2
Go 62–6
Go Boom 112–13
Go Fish 113
Guggenheim (Scattergories®) 188–9
Halma 42–4
Hangman 165
Hearts Due 21
Help your Neighbor 21
Hex 66–7
Horseshoe 67–8
Horseshoe Pitching 233–4
I Packed My Bag 197
Jacks 175–6
Japanese Chess 58–9
Lawn Bowls 235–6
Leapfrog 207

Ludo 44
Mah-Jongg 33–6
Marbles 176–7
Mill (Nine Men's Morris) 68–9
Monopoly® 15–16
Muggins (All Fives) 29–30
Nine Men's Morris (Mill) 68–9
Nok Hockey® 177
Noughts and Crosses 166
Othello® (Reversi®) 69–70
Outlines 165
Owari 70–1
Pelmanism (Concentration)
   111–12
Pickup Sticks 177–8
Pig 21–2
Ping-Pong® (Table Tennis) 178–9
Pinochle 93–7
Reversi® (Othello®) 69–70
Risk® 16–17
Rock, Paper, Scissors 166
Scattergories® (Guggenheim) 188–9
Scissors, Paper, Stone 166
Scopa 97
Scrabble® 17–18
Shogi (Japanese Chess) 58–9
Shut the Box 22
Slapjack 115
Snakes and Ladders 40
Snap 115–16

Games for Two People (continued)

Snip Snap Snorem (Earl of Coventry) 116

Spit (Speed) 116–17

Spoof 166

Sprouts 192

Stairway 192

Table Football 173–5

Table Tennis (Ping-Pong®) 178–9

Tic-Tac-Toe 166

Tiddlywinks 179–81

Trivial Pursuit® 18

Twenty-One (Blackjack) 119–22

War 117

Xiangqi (Chinese Chess) 59–60

Yacht 22–3

Games for Eight or More

Analogies 194

Apples to Apples® 14

Association 159

Back-to-Back Race 150

Balloon Race 150

Baseball 211–17

Beetle 140

Botticelli 159–60

Bulldog 202–3

Buzz & Buzz-Fizz 154

Coffee Pot 194

Cricket 217–23

Definitions 160

Dinner Party Murder Mystery 154–5

Do You Love Your Neighbor? 147

Dodge Ball 201–2

Dumb Crambo 140–1

Earl of Coventry (Snip Snap Snorem) 116

Earth, Water, Air 160

Egg and Spoon Race 150–1

Exchange Tag 202–3

Farmer in the Dell 133–4

Feather 147

Follow the Leader 203

Follow the Leader (parlor game) 147

Football (American) 226–32

Football (Soccer) 239–43

Frisbee® 232–3

The Game 141–2

Ghosts 195–6

Go Boom 112–13

Good Morning, Madam 155

Hare and Hounds 203

Headlines 189

Hide and Seek 203–4

Hopscotch 204

Hot and Cold 147

I Have Never 156

I Love My Love 196

Lawn Bowls 235–6

Legs 189–90

Likes and Dislikes 156

Lookabout 148

Lotto 190–1

Matchbox Race 134

Michigan (Newmarket) 122–3

Mummies 148

Murder in the Dark 143

Musical Chairs 134–5

Newmarket 122–3

Oranges and Lemons 135–6

Pass the Balloon 136

Pass the Package 136

Pass the Slipper 148

Pictures 190–1

Piggyback Race 151

Poetry Game 191

Potato Race 151

Quizzes 191

Relay Races 151–2

Ring-Around-the-Rosy (Ring-a-Ring-a-Roses) 136–7

Rounders 236–8

Sack Race 152

Sardines 144

Short Stories 191–2

Simon Says 137

Skittles 238–9

Snip Snap Snorem (Earl of Coventry) 116

Soccer (Football) 239–43

Softball 243–4

Spelling Round 197–8

Statues 138

Taboo 198

Tag 202–3

Telephone 138

Three-Legged Race 152

Treasure Hunt 208

Tug of War 208

Twenty Questions 163

What's on the Tray? 138

Wheelbarrow Race 152

Who Am I? 198

Winking 145

Yacht 22–3

Games for Children

Aces in the Pot 20
Alphabet Race 183
Back-to-Back Race 150
Balloon Race 150
Battleship 184–5
Beetle 140
Beggar my Neighbor 110
Bergen 30–1
Billiards, Carom 169–70
Blind Hughie 31
Blindman's Bluff 132
Blow Ball 140
Bobbing for Apples 132–3
Boxes 185
Bridge the Word 185–6
Bulldog 202–3
Buzz & Buzz-Fizz 154
Carom Billiards 169–70
Cat and Mouse 201
Categories 186
Cat's Cradle 170–1
Century Game 186–7

Charades 142
Cheat (I Doubt It) 110–11
Chutes and Ladders® (Snakes and
   Ladders) 40
Clapping Games 201
Clock Patience 101
Clue® (Cluedo®) 14–15
Concentration (Pelmanism) 111–12
Consequences 187–8
Crazy Eights 84
Crossword 188
Dead Lions 133
Do You Love Your Neighbor? 147
Dodge Ball 201–2
Dominoes 25–9
Donkey 112
Draughts 46–50
Drop Dead 20
Dumb Crambo 140–1
Earl of Coventry 116
Earth, Water, Air 160
Egg and Spoon Race 150–1
Exchange Tag 202–3
Farmer in the Dell 133–4
Feather 147
Fingers 165
Five of a Kind 161
Five Stones 172–3
Follow the Leader 203
Follow the Leader (parlor game) 147
Foosball® (Table Football) 173–5
Forbidden Words 195
Fox and Rabbit 203
Frisbee® 232–3
The Game 141–2
Go Boom 112–13
Go Fish 113
Good Morning, Madam 155
Grandfather's Clock 103–4
Guess the Smell 134
Guggenheim (Scattergories®) 188–9
Hangman 165

Hare and Hounds 203
Hearts Due 21
Help Your Neighbor 21
Hide and Seek 203–4
Hopscotch 204
Hot and Cold 147
How Many Words? 161
I Doubt It 110–11
I Packed My Bag 197
I Spy 161
Jacks 175–6
Jump Rope (Skipping) 204–5
Leapfrog 207
License Plates 161–2
Lookabout 148
Lotto 190–1
Ludo 44
In the Manner of the Word 142–3
Marbles 176–7
Matchbox Race 134
Monopoly® 15–16
Monte Carlo 107–8
Mummies 148
Murder in the Dark 143
Musical Chairs 134–5
My Ship Sails 114
Nok Hockey® 177
Noughts and Crosses 166
Old Maid 114
Oranges and Lemons 135–6
Outlines 165
Pass the Balloon 136
Pass the Package 136
Pass the Slipper 148
Pelmanism (Concentration) 111–12
Pickup Sticks 177–8
Pictionary® 143–4
Pig 21–2
Piggyback Race 151
Ping-Pong® (Table Tennis) 178–9
Poetry Game 191
Potato Race 151

Games for Children (continued)

Quizzes 191
Relay Races 151–2
Ring-Around-the-Rosy (Ring-a-Ring-a-
    Roses) 136–7
Rock, Paper, Scissors 166
Rolling Stone 114–15
Rounders 236–8
Sack Race 152
Sardines 144
Scattergories® 188–9
Scissors, Paper, Stone 166
Scopa 97
Scrabble® 17–18
Sevens 207–8
Short Stories 191–2
Shut the Box 22
Simon Says 137

Skipping 204–5
Skittles 238–9
Slapjack 115
Slobberhannes 98
Snakes and Ladders 40
Snap 115–16
Snip Snap Snorem (Earl of Coventry)
    116
Speed 116–17
Spelling Round 197–8
Spoof 166
Sprouts 192
Squeak, Piggy, Squeak! 137–8
Stairway 192
Statues 138
Table Football 173–5
Table Tennis (Ping-Pong®) 178–9

Taboo 198
Tag 202–3
Telephone 138
Three-Legged Race 152
Tic-Tac-Toe 166
Tiddlywinks 179–81
Treasure Hunt 208
Tug of War 208
Twister® 144–5
War 117
What's on the Tray? 138
Wheelbarrow Race 152
Who Am I? 198
Winking 145
Yacht 22–3

Picture Credits

Key: l = left, r = right, b = bottom,
t = top.

Amber Books Ltd: 22r, 25, 27, 28, 29,
30, 31, 32r, 34, 35, 38, 39, 40, 41, 42,
43, 44, 46, 48, 50, 51, 52, 53, 54, 55,
57, 58, 60, 62, 63, 64, 65, 66, 67, 68,
69, 70, 74, 76, 77, 78, 80, 86, 87, 88,
91, 92, 93, 94, 96, 97, 98, 99, 101,
102, 103, 104, 105, 106, 107, 108,
110l, 115, 116, 119, 124, 125, 128t,
141, 142, 169, 171b, 172, 173t, 176,
177l, 178, 180, 181b, 184, 185l, 187,
190b, 190, 201b, 202, 204r, 210b,
214, 223, 225, 234 (both), 235t, 236

Black Hat: 8, 14 (both), 15, 16, 17,
18, 20, 21, 22l, 110r, 111, 113, 114
(all), 117, 140 (both), 143 (both), 145,

147 (both), 155r, 159, 160, 161l, 163
(both), 165, 166, 177r, 185r, 189,
190tr, 192, 194, 196, 197, 198, 201t,
203, 204l, 208t

Corbis: 9, 10, 11, 23, 26, 56, 95, 121,
123, 150r, 156, 170, 216, 221, 230,
231, 235b, 239, 241

© Dorling Kindersley: 71, 83, 150l,
207, 208b

Getty Images: 128b, 152, 173b, 210t,
215, 226

Mary Evans Picture Library: 32l, 148,
205, 224

Mike Moran: 13, 19, 24, 37, 45, 61,

73, 100, 109, 118, 139, 144, 146, 149,
151, 153, 155l, 158, 161r, 164, 168,
181t, 182, 193, 200, 209

Peter Harper: 171t, 212, 213, 218,
219, 227, 228, 233, 237, 240, 242,
244, 246

POPPERFOTO/Reuters: 217, 222

**Courtesy of the Department of
Computing Science, University of
Alberta:** 49 (Thanks to Rob Lake, Paul
Lu, Stephanie and Jonathan Schaeffer)

Part opener photograph by Christine
Bronico